BAR INTERNATIONAL SERIES 3080 | 2022

Past Imperfect

The contested early history of the Mapungubwe Archive, South Africa

Sian Tiley-Nel

BAR PUBLISHING

Published in 2022 by
BAR Publishing, Oxford

BAR International Series 3080

African Archaeology, volume 96
Past Imperfect

ISBN 978 1 4073 5963 2   paperback
ISBN 978 1 4073 5964 9   e-format

DOI https://doi.org/10.30861/9781407359632

A catalogue record for this book is available from the British Library

COVER IMAGE *The Transvaal University College (TUC), later known as the University of Pretoria (UP). The building was declared a national monument in 1968. Today it houses in the entrance the Mapungubwe Archive. Image copyright University of Pretoria Archives.*

BAR
PUBLISHING

BAR titles are available from:

BAR Publishing
122 Banbury Rd, Oxford, OX2 7BP, UK
EMAIL   info@barpublishing.com
PHONE   +44 (0)1865 310431
FAX   +44 (0)1865 316916
www.barpublishing.com

AFRICAN ARCHAEOLOGY

Series editors: Kevin MacDonald (UCL) and Paul Lane (Cambridge)

Past decades have witnessed a revolution in the archaeological narratives of early African agriculture, technology, urbanism and socio-political complexity. Indeed, the archaeology of Africa continues to expand significantly, with three major international journals working to capacity to publish recent findings. However, given the vastness of the continent and the time depth of its past, field research remains relatively scattered. Each new data point therefore adds significantly to the bigger picture. This series (formerly known as the *Cambridge Monographs in African Archaeology* series) focuses on new contributions to the Holocene archaeology of Africa, particularly primary information on important excavation projects and artefactual assemblage analyses which are beyond the scope of journal publication. In particular, we seek works relevant to the archaeology of food production, metallurgy, complex societies, historical archaeology and material culture studies.

African Archaeology is a continuation of *Cambridge Monographs in African Archaeology*, conceived by John Alexander and Anthony Hands (founder of BAR), more recently edited by Laurence Smith, Timothy Insoll, Brian Stewart and Stephanie Wynne-Jones. The first title was published in the BAR international series in 1980. Since then, 90 titles have been published in the BAR series and have contributed to the advancement of the subject in the region and around the world.

If you wish to publish in this series, please contact editor@barpublishing.com

For more information on *African Archaeology* go to the BAR Publishing website: www.barpublishing.com/sub-series

Editorial advisory board

David Edwards, Leicester, UK

Amanda Esterhuysen, Witwatersrand, RSA

Francois-Xavier Fauvelle, Toulouse, France

Per Ditlef Fredriksen, Oslo, Norway

Adria Laviolette, Virginia, USA

Alexandre Livingstone Smith, Tervuren, Belgium

Cameron Monroe, California, USA

Catherine Namono, Witwatersrand, RSA

Akin Ogundiran, Charlotte, USA

Innocent Pikirayi, Pretoria, RSA

Ibrahima Thiaw, Dakar, Senegal

Titles in the Series

No 48 **Échanges et contacts le long du Nil et de la Mer Rouge dans l'époque protohistorique (IIIe et IIe millénaires avant J.-C.)** *Une synthèse préliminaire* by Andrea Manzo, BAR S782, 1999, ISBN 9781841710020

No 49 **Ethno-Archaeology in Jenné, Mali** *Craft and status among smiths, potters and masons* by Adria LaViolette, BAR S838, 2000, ISBN 9781841710433

No 50 **Hunter-Gatherers and Farmers** *An enduring Frontier in the Caledon Valley, South Africa* by Carolyn R. Thorp, BAR S860, 2000, ISBN 9781841710617

No 51 **The Kintampo Complex** *The Late Holocene on the Gambaga Escarpment, Northern Ghana* by Joanna Casey, BAR S906, 2000, ISBN 9781841712024

No 52 **The Middle and Later Stone Ages in the Mukogodo Hills of Central Kenya** *A Comparative Analysis of Lithic Artefacts from Shurmai (GnJm1) and Kakwa Lelash (GnJm2) Rockshelters* by G-Young Gang, BAR S964, 2001, ISBN 9781841712512

No 53 **Darfur (Sudan) In the Age of Stone Architecture c. 1000 – 1750 AD** *Problems in historical reconstruction* by Andrew James McGregor, BAR S1006, 2001, ISBN 9781841712857

No 54 **Holocene Foragers, Fishers and Herders of Western Kenya** by Karega-Mũnene, BAR S1037, 2002, ISBN 9781841714172

No 55 **Archaeology and History in Ìlàrè District (Central Yorubaland, Nigeria) 1200–1900 A.D.** by Akinwumi O. Ogundiran, BAR S1090, 2002, ISBN 9781841714684

No 56 **Ethnoarchaeology in the Zinder Region, Republic of Niger** *The site of Kufan Kanawa* by Anne Haour, BAR S1133, 2003, ISBN 9781841715063

No 57 **Le Capsien typique et le Capsien supérieur** *Évolution ou contemporanéité. Les données technologiques* by Noura Rahmani, BAR S1187, 2003, ISBN 9781841715537

No 58 **Fortifications et urbanisation en Afrique orientale** by Stéphane Pradines, BAR S1216, 2004, ISBN 9781841715766

No 59 **Archaeology and Geoarchaeology of the Mukogodo Hills and Ewaso Ng'iro Plains, Central Kenya** by Frederic Pearl, BAR S1247, 2004, ISBN 9781841716077

No 50 **Islamic Archaeology in the Sudan** by Intisar Soghayroun Elzein, BAR S1289, 2004, ISBN 9781841716398

No 51 **An Ethnoarchaeological Study of Iron-Smelting Practices among the Pangwa and Fipa in Tanzania** by Randi Barndon, BAR S1308, 2004, ISBN 9781841716572

No 52 **Archaeology and History in North-Western Benin** by Lucas Pieter Petit, BAR S1398, 2005, ISBN 9781841718378

No 53 **Traditions céramiques, Identités et Peuplement en Sénégambie** *Ethnographie comparée et essai de reconstitution historique* by Moustapha Sall, BAR S1407, 2005, ISBN 9781841718507

No 54 **Changing Settlement Patterns in the Aksum-Yeha Region of Ethiopia: 700 BC – AD 850** by Joseph W. Michels, BAR S1446, 2005, ISBN 9781841718828

No 65 **Safeguarding Africa's Archaeological Past** *Selected papers from a workshop held at the School of Oriental and African Studies, University of London, 2001* Edited by Niall Finneran, BAR S1454, 2006, ISBN 9781841718927

No 66 **Excavations at Kasteelberg and the Origins of the Khoekhoen in the Western Cape, South Africa** by Andrew B. Smith, BAR S1537, 2006, ISBN 9781841719696

No 67 **Archéologie du Diamaré au Cameroun Septentrional** *Milieux et peuplements entre Mandara, Logone, Bénoué et Tchad pendant les deux derniers millénaires* by Alain Marliac, BAR S1549, 2006, ISBN 9781841719788

No 68 **Chasse et élevage dans la Corne de l'Afrique entre le Néolithique et les temps historiques** by Joséphine Lesur, BAR S1602, 2007, ISBN 9781407300191

No 69 **The Emergence of Social and Political Complexity in the Shashi-Limpopo Valley of Southern Africa, AD 900 to 1300** *Ethnicity, class and polity* by John Anthony Calabrese, BAR S1617, 2007, ISBN 9781407300290

No 70 **Archaeofaunal remains from the past 4000 years in Sahelian West Africa** *Domestic livestock, subsistence strategies and environmental changes* by Veerle Linseele, BAR S1658, 2007, ISBN 9781407300948

No 71 **Il Sahara centro-orientale Dalla Preistoria ai tempi dei nomadi Tubu / The Central-Oriental Sahara. From Prehistory to the times of the nomadic Tubus** by Vanni Beltrami, BAR S1667, 2007, ISBN 9781407301020

No 72 **Memory and the Mountain** *Environmental Relations of the Wachagga of Kilimanjaro and Implications for Landscape Archaeology* by Timothy A. R. Clack, BAR S1679, 2007, ISBN 9781407301174

"Unlike the specialist who is said to know more and more about less and less until he knows
everything about nothing, I find myself these days, with the additional responsibilities
now devolving upon me, knowing less and less about more and more until one
of these days I stand in danger of knowing nothing about everything."
E.H.D. Arndt, 1950

This book is dedicated to my parents, my husband, Johan Nel and my two children: Calia and Quinn.
In memory of my ancestors, Joseph William Kirby (1874–1932) and Edward Kirby (1915–1993).

Acknowledgements

The loss and destruction of countless important archival records over the years, not only by this institution, but by government, private and public institutions as well, has naturally made the pursuit of research no easy matter. Whether my interpretations, conclusions and deductions about the Mapungubwe Archive and its contested history will stand the test of critique may be doubted by some, but hopefully upheld and pursued by others. Despite the dégringolade of archives that is widespread across not only in South Africa, but in the world, the fact remains that the Mapungubwe Archive is one of our greatest heritage archives and its immense value to South African history should never be underestimated. This monograph is a result of PhD research conducted under the helm of my supervisor, teacher, colleague, Head of Department of Historical and Heritage Studies (Faculty of Humanities at the University of Pretoria), and her "many hats" as also the Director of the University of Pretoria Archives. Professor Karen Harris, my mentor and muse, for her academic guidance, support and encouragement throughout this research. I have been most privileged to benefit from the academic guidance from the staff in the Department of Historical and Heritage Studies: Prof Alois Mlambo, Dr Glen Ncube, Dr Ian Macqueen and Dr Nisa Paleker. Other individuals, institutions, repositories I wish to thank are (in no particular order): Prof Tawana Kupe; Prof Caroline Nicholson; my international PhD examiner, Dr A Cohen (University of Kent), my external examiner's Prof A Mouton (UNISA) and Dr M Oelofse (UFS) and the anonymous peer reviewers of this book. In addition to: Prof Innocent Pikirayi, Prof Theo van Wyk; Nikki Haw, Alett Nel; Dr Ria van der Merwe; Alida Green; Dr. Heidi Fourie; Tersia Perregil, the Ditsong National Museum of Natural History (Transvaal Museum Archives); Dr Justine Wintjes, Fiona Adams; the private E.V. Adams Archive, the Van Graan family archives; Dr André Breedt; Marié Breedt; Dr Masitha Hoeane, Helma Steenkamp, Alexandros Andreou, Maurice Shirinda, Nicole Hoffmann, Lelani Nicolaisen Kgomotso Mathole, Steven Motena and Sandra Markgraaf; Prof Andrie Meyer, Herman Els, Andrea Botha, Sandra Braun, Chriselle Koortzen, Michelle van der Gryp, Janine Somers, Emile Coetzee; Michelle de la Harpe and Anita Dreyer. Special appreciation goes to the US Ambassadors Fund for Cultural Preservation, the US Embassy and diplomatic colleagues: Sheila Goodgall, Kiera Emmons, Jameson de Bose, Frank Whittaker, Todd Haskell, Jessica LaPenn, Martin Perschler, Program Director of the Ambassadors Fund for Cultural Preservation at the U.S. Department of State. Most importantly to my family, my daughter Calia Roslin and son, Quinn Reid. I express heartfelt kindness for their unwavering empathy, patience and unconditional love and to my husband Johan Nel, my familiar, soulmate, and life-long friend, none of this would have been possible and without his love- there is nothing.

UNIVERSITEIT VAN PRETORIA
UNIVERSITY OF PRETORIA
YUNIBESITHI YA PRETORIA

Contents

List of Figures

List of Abbreviations

AAF	Archaeological Archives Forum
AAM	American Alliance of Museums
ACTAG	Arts and Culture Task Group
AFCP	Ambassadors Fund for Cultural Preservation
AGL	*Argeologie* / Archaeology
AGSA	Auditor-General of South Africa
ASEN	Association for the Study of Ethnicity and Nationalism
CALS	Centre for Applied Legal Studies
CBA	Council for British Archaeology
DAC	Department of Arts and Culture
DEAT	Department of Environmental Affairs and Tourism
FAK	*Federasie van Afrikaanse Kultuurvereniginge* / Federation of Afrikaans Cultural Associations
GALA	Gay and Lesbian Archives
GMTFCA	Greater Mapungubwe Transfrontier Conservation Area
HMC	Historical Monuments Commission
HPRA	Historical Papers Research Archive
HSRC	Human Sciences Research Council
ICCROM	International Centre for the Preservation and Restoration of Cultural Property
ICOM	International Council of Museums
ICOMOS	International Council on Monuments and Sites
IKS	Indigenous Knowledge Systems
MCL	Mapungubwe Cultural Landscape
MISTRA	Mapungubwe Institute for Strategic Reflection
NAD	Department of Native Affairs
NARSSA	National Archives and Records Services of South Africa
NASA	National Archives of South Africa
NDT	National Department of Tourism
NHC	National Heritage Council
NHRA	National Heritage Resources Act
NMC	National Monuments Council
NMNH	National Museum of Natural History (Ditsong)
PAIA	Promotion of Access to Information Act
PAS	Portable Antiquities Scheme
RAI	Royal Anthropological Institute (UK)
RGN	*Raad vir Geesteswetenskaplike Navorsing* / Human Sciences Research Council
SABC	South African Broadcasting Company
SADF	South African Defence Force
SAHA	South African History Archive
SAHRA	South African Heritage Resources Act
SANPARKS	South African National Parks
SAP	South African Police
TFCA	Transfrontier Conservation Area
TM	Transvaal Museum
TUC	Transvaal University College
UCT	University of Cape Town
UNESCO	United Nations Education, Scientific and Cultural Organisation
UNISA	University of South Africa
UP	University of Pretoria
UPA	University of Pretoria Archives
USA	United States of America
WITS	University of the Witwatersrand
WHC	World Heritage Committee

Foreword

This publication is on the contested early history of the Mapungubwe Archive held and curated at the University of Pretoria. The Archive preserves materials of enduring historical value associated with the internationally declared site known as Mapungubwe in South Africa, and consequently the Archive forms an integral part of the University of Pretoria's institutional memory. This study interrogates the context as well as the many gaps in the Mapungubwe Archive, by examining specific aspects such as the multiple narratives of Mapungubwe discoveries prior to the traditionally viewed discovery in 1933. Furthermore, it elucidates the University of Pretoria's control of the Mapungubwe gold "treasure trove" during the maiden years of the early 1930s through the lens of the institutional instrument known as the Archaeological Committee (1933–1947) that was governed by the University of Pretoria Council who reported all progress to the State.

The context of the Mapungubwe Archive is considered in lieu of content, particularly through decisions by the University that moved away from its foundations as the English Transvaal University College in 1908 towards the decidedly partisan Afrikaner Capitalise Nationalist University of Pretoria in 1932. Research further delves into those individuals linked with the University of Pretoria Archaeological Committee that reported directly to the University Council and the Minister of the Interior, J.H. Hofmeyr. It is argued that the unsung hero in Mapungubwe history is not necessarily the well-known historian Leo Fouché, but rather the unknown but highly influential figure of Jacob de Villiers Roos, an affluent member closely associated with influential politicians such as J.C. Smuts and J.B.M. Hertzog. Smuts as a founding member of the TUC, and his friend J. de Villiers Roos, played a critical financial and legal role in securing rights to Mapungubwe for the University Council within the milieu of the 1933 general elections and at a time when the University was attempting to buttress the ideals of national unity. Beyond the excavation history which is not covered in this book, is a subaltern history lying within the Mapungubwe Archive that fuelled the contestation debate, expounded by a Committee that controlled much of Mapungubwe on behalf of the University of Pretoria.

Whilst the archaeology of Mapungubwe's past was of great scientific consequence to South Africa, it generated the controversy between the physical biological anthropologists and the cultural anthropologists, including the controversy between archaeologists and anatomists, whilst those same scholar's marginalised local knowledge histories.

The book later focuses on the greater ethical and moral consequence of the questions of legal title, treasure trove (largely unknown in South African contexts and literature), rights of discovery and other legitimate legislative matters that required delicate manoeuvring by the University of Pretoria from the onset of Mapungubwe's gold discovery. In addition were the changes in historical legislation overtime into heritage legislation which contributed to the debates of ownership and stewardship. It is in this historical and political context, that this research seeks to explore the University's perceived status and power over Mapungubwe, questioning how, why and within which political and social settings, critical decisions were made such as securing a national treasure on behalf of the Union of South Africa. Although Mapungubwe's archaeological past has been researched progressively in academia over eight decades, little scholarly attention has been paid to any historical interest in the Mapungubwe Archive.

By interrogating the Mapungubwe Archive, a wealth of untapped historical sources could illuminate the origins of some controversies of Mapungubwe's colonial past and how they mirror present heritage debates and disputes in forming the contemporary history and governance of the Mapungubwe Archive at the University of Pretoria. The central argument is how the Mapungubwe Archive needs to be questioned not only as a historical source, but rather as a discourse within global trends of "reading against the grain". This study focuses on the conceptual notion of history as an imperfect past. The underlying notion of this book is that research argues that Mapungubwe's contested past is inherently unfinished and flawed, because the past constantly challenges many ideas of the present.

A Contested Past and Archive

I want to explore the landscapes of the past, the spaces where archivists and historians struggle with memory, fight with memory, where they see archival records differently … [where] the "archive" is largely perceived as discourse, metaphor, symbol or manifestation of power, as a site of human inscription and intentionality, and of contested memory. Terry Cook, 2010.

1.1. Introduction

Most archival histories consist of reading, accessing and shaping the past in a number of ways. The past can be remembered, recovered or even reinvented, yet no historian can present the "unvarnished truth".[1] Increasingly in the last few decades, the question of what it means to contest the past has become a charged notion, as a contested history, in a basic sense evokes a struggle in the terrain of truth.[2] The idea of contesting the past, poses questions about the present, and what the past means in the present.

Contested history, like memory, is naturally fallible and the past is therefore inherently and most often considered imperfect. Historical debates often revolve around the assumption that "making" history, like the past, is imperfect, biased and flawed, as historians recognise there is no absolute "truth" in history. Similarly, archives have also always been at the intersection of past, present, and future as it is contended that archival "truths" indeed have historical consequences as these "interfaces" or spaces are the focus of power of the present to control what the future will know about the past.[3]

This re-examination of the past is not discipline specific nor is it a novel notion, yet nuanced work on the contested past lies at the heart of many postmodern archival studies.[4] In reconsidering the place of historical knowledge in archival work, it is suggested that "the pendulum is swinging back, not in a simple return to the past… but toward appreciation of the central place of historical knowledge in the distinctive body of knowledge, research, and daily work of the new archival profession which has emerged over the last quarter century".[5] There was growing recognition in the 1980s of the association between academic historical research and the archives, as humanities and social science put into question claims to objectivity as archives offered a way of engaging with knowledge of the past as inevitably partial and subjective.[6]

However, post 1994, the role of postmodern historical knowledge and that of archival scholarship has advanced tremendously both in terms of scope and in the development of many wide-ranging intellectual paradigms. Craven invites scholars to question "what is an archive" and to step away from the "practicalities of keeping archives" and instead consider what they actually "do in a cultural context".[7] Therefore, archives have become sites of contestation as the 'politics of the past' has become increasingly prominent in post democracy eras and the role of archives has to be considered and questioned. Likewise, the past must also be contested, as the question of the archive has risen to greater prominence in South Africa than ever before.[8]

Considering an archive

This book examines the contested early history of the "Mapungubwe Archive" held at the University of Pretoria and how as a manifestation of the institution, it can also be argued that the archive has become a site of contestation in the present. But what is the "Mapungubwe Archive"? Is it a collection of historical papers, a physical construct contained within walls, a university facility or merely a collection of related historical records? Unfortunately, this trajectory of enquiry of when does an archive become an archive is not seemingly simple, but instead poses a rhetorical or philosophical question when attempting to reach a clear definition. Theoretically, the "decolonisation of archival methodology" trend rejects the influences of colonialism and imperialism as well

---

[1] See, for example, E.H. Carr, *What is history?* London: Penguin, 1961.
[2] See, K. Hodgkin and S. Radstone (eds.), *Contested pasts: the politics of memory.* London: Routledge, 2003.
[3] J.M. Schwartz and T. Cook, "Archive, records, and power: from (postmodern) theory to (archival) performance". *Archival Science* 2(3), 2002, pp. 171–185.
[4] See for example, T. Cook, "Electronic records, paper minds: the revolution in information management and archive in the post-custodial and post-modern era". *Archive and Social Studies: A Journal of Interdisciplinary Research* 1(0), 2007, pp. 399–443.
[5] T. Nesmith, "What's history got to do with it? Reconsidering the place of historical knowledge in archival work". *Archivaria* 57, (Spring 2004), pp. 1–2.

[6] T. Nesmith, "Archives from the bottom up: social history and archival scholarship". *Archives and Social Studies: Journal of Interdisciplinary Research* 2 (1), March 2008, pp. 41–82.
[7] L. Craven, *What are archives? Cultural and theoretical perspectives: a reader.* Burlington: Ashgate, 2008.
[8] See for example discussion about the role of archives in a democracy and how heritage has been "valorised", yet the archival system in South Africa is strained and neglected, *Archives at the Crossroads 2007.* Open report to the Minister of Arts and Culture, Archival Conference "National System, Public Interest", co-convened by the national Archives, the Nelson Mandela Foundation and the Constitution of Public Intellectual Life Research Project, April 2007, <https://www.nelsonmandela.org/images/uploads/NMF_Dialogue-Archives_at_the_Crossroads1.pdf> access: 2018.09.26

Figure 1.1. An early photographic view of Mapungubwe Hill from the 1934 archaeological expedition.

as the paternalistic 'western' sense of a Rankian-type definition of an archive.

Therefore, this research acknowledges to an extent, that the "Mapungubwe Archive" is part of the ongoing process or 'turn' of centering archival concerns both practically and theoretically in rejecting the hegemonic environments of defining archives.[9] The Mapungubwe Archive also cannot divorce itself from the Mapungubwe collection under the stewardship of the University of Pretoria nor Mapungubwe as a major heritage site in South Africa.

Considering that the "Mapungubwe Archive" in essence was only retrospectively created in the twenty-first century, broadly speaking then this Archive can be understood to mean anything that it is no longer current, but that has been retained. The Mapungubwe Archive was only launched as a formal repository in February of 2022, post pandemic and only after a major preservation grant from the US Ambassadors Fund for Cultural Preservation which commenced from 2018 and reached its conclusion in November 2021. Compounding the problem, is assigning specific dates for the Archive, although research commenced in 1933, the archive

contains a few records prior to the 1930s, some even dating back to 1900.

However, to overcome the historical tendency of distilling dates, merely for the purposes of research and motivation, the Mapungubwe Archive for the purposes of this book cannot be definitely arranged by date or a chronology. Instead, the Archive should be viewed as a dynamic historical, heritage and contemporary primary resource consisting of irreplaceable records and memory that has evolved from the past into the present and continues evolving. For this reason, the first chapter only at this stage considers and reconsiders "an archive", and for this reason the final chapter concludes the "Mapungubwe Archive" as a modern construct of the twenty-first century. For practical purposes, the Mapungubwe Archive was launched as an African repository at the University of Pretoria on 24 February 2022 and as yet, still has to go through the formal naming process required to allocate its formal name. In addition, all post 2000 archival material, including digital content has yet to be appraised and lodged into the Mapungubwe Archive. Hence, the archive is still in the process of being reimagined and forward-focused for 2026 and beyond.

As a consequence, some of the earliest Mapungubwe records, which later became university departmental records, were identified at some point in time as potential research sources to the archaeologist, and over more time,

---

[9] See T.R. Genovese, "Decolonizing archival methodology: combating hegemony and moving towards a collaborative archival environment". *AlterNative: An International Journal of Indigenous People*, 12(1), 2016, pp. 32–42.

the records acquired deeper meaning and greater value. Evolving over decades and transforming a significant change of name to today, what is referred to as the "Mapungubwe Archive", can be viewed as the archival canon or body of works or narrative of Mapungubwe from the University of Pretoria. More formally, the Mapungubwe Archive serves as both a repository and a depository for materials of enduring historical value associated with the now world-renowned heritage site known as Mapungubwe in South Africa.[10] However, they are also the *fonds d'archives* for the official records of the University of Pretoria thus forming an integral part of institutional memory.

This book is less concerned with the history of the Mapungubwe Archive and is not intended as a history of the subject of Mapungubwe, but rather the ways in which the Archive can be reconsidered, redefined, and thus questions how and why the Archive constitutes part of the collective and institutional memory of the University of Pretoria. This book does interrogate the early historical archival context, as well as gaps in the Mapungubwe Archive, by examining critical aspects of the University of Pretoria's association with Mapungubwe with a focus on the time period of mainly the 1930s. The scope of the Mapungubwe Archive is colossal and the subject of Mapungubwe through many transdisciplinary lenses makes it certainly impossible to cover all research angles. This context of the Mapungubwe Archive in the 1930s is particularly considered, as all decisions on Mapungubwe were taken by the Council of the University of Pretoria under the advice of a sub-committee known as the Archaeological Committee of the University of Pretoria (1933–1947), yet subtly under State control.[11]

This early period of Mapungubwe and the University of Pretoria's parallel history from the "discovery" of gold artefacts in 1933,[12] through to the foundational years of the Archaeological Committee, who "directed" research until its cessation in the 1940s, is re-examined and to an extent deconstructed using a postmodern archival approach. Select members of the Council and the Committee were considered highly influential individuals and were externally well-connected to government administrators who "appear as faceless bodies obscuring the role of the individuals of whom they were constituted."[13] Thus, securing research and legal rights to Mapungubwe and the gold treasure trove that was under the ownership of the University of Pretoria on behalf of the State.

Within the milieu of the 1933 national general elections and at a time when as an institution of higher learning the University of Pretoria supported growing Afrikaner Nationalism.[14] It also buttressed the ideals of national unity and perpetuated the colonial narratives that dominated Mapungubwe research in the early years. The consequences of this primary history directly provides a significant view on why the Mapungubwe Archive was created and how it evolved, backing notions of a contested past into a contested present. It was within this context that concretised the University of Pretoria's perceived status and power over Mapungubwe's history and heritage for more than eight decades. This study's research questions centre on this power of the so-called authority and questions how, why and within which political and social settings, critical legal and institutional decisions were made. For example, securing a national cultural treasure on behalf of the Union of South Africa in 1933 that reverberated into present issues of contestation in heritage legislation and other heritage platforms.

Furthermore, this publication is intended to contribute to the growing research agenda on South African archives and embolden future research into the Mapungubwe Archive. Although Mapungubwe's past has been archaeologically researched progressively in academia for close to eighty-nine years, little scholarly attention or effort has been paid to any historical interest in the Mapungubwe Archive. By unpacking and "peeling back the layers"[15] of the Mapungubwe Archive, a wealth of untapped historical sources can illuminate the origins of some controversies of Mapungubwe's colonial, Afrikaner nationalist and apartheid past and how the contestations mirror present debates and disputes in forming the contemporary history and stewardship of the Mapungubwe Archive by the University of Pretoria.

The central argument remains how the archive needs to be questioned not only as a historical source, but rather as a discourse within global and local archival trends of "reading against the grain".[16] Reading against the grain simply means to read historical records critically and look at the power of the context in which they were written. This book focuses on the conceptual notion of history as

---

[10] The Mapungubwe Archive at the University of Pretoria is the only one of its kind in South Africa and serves as a depository and repository to identify, collect and preserve records of archival value relating to the history/subject of Mapungubwe by the University of Pretoria. Curated and managed by the University of Pretoria Museums, the Mapungubwe Archive maintains and preserves an extensive collection of both documentary and photographic records and includes a broad range of other material in a variety of media, some available for research and access.

[11] See, for example, Mapungubwe Archive, Minutes of Meeting of the Archaeological Committee from 1933 to 1947. The discussion on the Archaeological Committee is however only limited to its early or maiden years.

[12] F.R. Paver, "The mystery grave of Mapungubwe. A remarkable discovery in the Transvaal: a grave of unknown origin containing much gold-work, found on the summit of a natural stronghold in a wild region", *The Illustrated London News*, 8 April 1933.

[13] B.L. Strydom, Broad South Africanism and Higher Education: The Transvaal University College (1909–1919), PhD History, University of Pretoria, 2013, p. 27.

[14] See, F.A. Mouton, "Professor Leo Fouché, the History Department and the Afrikanerization of the University of Pretoria", *Historia* 38(1), 1993, pp. 92–101; See, F.A. Mouton (ed.), *History, historians and Afrikaner nationalism: essays on the history department of the University of Pretoria, 1909–1985.* Vanderbijlpark: Kleio, 2007, pp. 13–43.

[15] V. Harris, "Claiming less, delivering more: a critique of positivist formulations on archives in South Africa". *Archivaria* 44, 1997, p. 136.

[16] See for example, A.L. Stoler, *Along the archival grain: epistemic anxieties and colonial common sense.* New Jersey: Princeton University Press, 2009.

an imperfect past, as it argues that Mapungubwe's past is inherently incomplete, because the past perpetually tests many notions of the present. The Mapungubwe Archive thus evolves to become a metaphor for a past imperfect.

For the purposes of this book, the concept of "past imperfect" has been borrowed from several historical contexts. The idea of an imperfect past has been explored widely over several decades in historical scholarship. There is an emerging interest in this new historical perspective that debates the changing conceptions of time in history.[17] A prime example is the thought-provoking research seminar series at the University College of London titled, "Past Imperfect" which explores recent concerns with the past and its place in the present. The seminar suggests that the present is increasingly over invested and points to:

> [T]he critique of official histories and the conjoining of history and fiction behind us, we now confront new imperatives for what is at stake in thinking across historical, current and future perspectives. We start from the premise of the verb tense 'past imperfect', in which a past that is unfinished constantly challenges the ideas of the "new" and embraces the presentness of the past.[18]

This publication is not about "making" history, but rather how history is "used" as objectively as possible to debate the present. As the title suggests, in the context of research, "past imperfect" is metaphorically applied to the historical time span of the Mapungubwe Archive, thus not "what" happened, but rather "how" it happened. Furthermore, in syntax, the specialised grammatical term of "past imperfect" is both an adjective and a noun. The term is applied to a tense, which denotes "action going on but not completed - usually to the present tense of incomplete or progressive action", also meaning, "not perfect, flawed or can denote damage, containing problems, or having something omitted or missing".[19] The emphasis on imperfection and the flawed nature of history is important in this research, as the boundaries of the past and present are blurred and it is this tension that ensures dialogue with the past and refigures the function of how "an archive" such as the Mapungubwe Archive continues in ever-evolving forms into the present.

Changing archival perspectives

Research draws from broad postmodern approaches and trends in both global perspectives and the emerging South African discourse on archives in theory and in practice. The perception of archives has changed radically since the twentieth century notions of a traditional or classical archive.[20] From the 1990s, the meaning of archives has been challenged by intellectuals such as Jacques Derrida and Ann Stoler who both contended that any theory of the archive must be understood in the context where past, present and future constantly re-articulate each other and in doing so, redefine the archive. The role of archival theory and archival science as developing paradigms are also useful to elucidate contemporary archival challenges as Derrida suggests that:

> [T]he question of the archive is not, I repeat a question of the past...but rather a question of the future, the very question of the future, question of a response, of promise and of a responsibility for tomorrow. The archive: if we want to know what this will have meant, we will only know tomorrow.[21]

Derrida argues that the archive is never fixed and stresses the importance of the archive in historical research. Derrida further claims that the archive affirms the past, present, and future in that it preserves the records of the past and it embodies the promise of the present to the future making the point that archives are also a way of "imagining the future".[22] One way of understanding this shift and considering the temporal qualities of an archive in the framework of research is to examine how the archive and its meaning have changed over time. But how then, does the archive speak to the past, present and future? Such rhetorical questions never have straight forward answers, but most archives continue to expand, yet also their significance, value and use among wider academia also inevitably changes over time. New archival thinking is required to challenge insular views of traditional archives, as changes move the theoretical focus of the archive away from the record towards a functional context behind the record, thus embracing "process rather than product".[23]

Thus, while traditionally an archive was viewed as a physical repository of records pertaining to history, in the last half of the twentieth century a profound conceptual and abstract change shifted the archive from "place" to "process".[24] These recent changing perceptions within

---

[17] See for example: S. Nield, "Past imperfect, present tense: on history as discarded practice" in, M. Blazevic and L. C. Feldman (eds.) *Misperformance: essays in shifting perspectives*. Ljubljana: MASKA Institute of Publishing, Production and Education, 2014, pp. 69–78; L.W. Towner, *Past imperfect: essays on history, libraries and humanities*. Chicago: University of Chicago Press, 1993; C.F. Bryan. Jr., *Imperfect past: history in a new light*. Virginia: Dementi Milestone Publishing, 2015; M.C. Carnes (ed.), *Past imperfect: history according to the movies*. New York: Henry Holt, 1995.

[18] University College of London, "Past Imperfect", 2015, <http://ucl.ac.uk/art-history/news-events/past-imperfect>, access: 2015.09.03.

[19] Definition of "imperfect past" from the Cambridge Advanced Learner's Dictionary and Thesaurus, Cambridge University Press, Cambridge, 2015, <http //dictionary.cambridge.org/dictionary/english/imperfect> access: 2015.10.29.

[20] See for example, T. Cook, "What is past is prologue: a history of archival ideas since 1898 and the future paradigm shift". *Archivaria* 43, 1997, p. 17.

[21] J. Derrida, *Archive fever: a Freudian impression*. Chicago: University of Chicago Press, 1998, p. 36.

[22] J. Derrida, *Archive fever: a Freudian impression*. Chicago: University of Chicago Press, 1998, p. 29.

[23] T. Cook, "What is past is prologue: a history of archival ideas since 1898, and the future paradigm shift". *Archivaria* 43, 1997, pp. 17–63.

[24] B. Brothman, "The past that archives keep: memory, history, and the preservation of archival records". *Archivaria* 51, 2001, p. 79.

archival discourse reverberated in international and national trends and fuelled by a shared preoccupation with the function and fate of the historical record in turn resulted in a "preoccupation of the archive".[25]

This conversion embedded in post colonial theory about what defined an archive was widely regarded as the "archival turn" - first coined by the United States of America (USA) Professor of Anthropology and Historical Studies, Ann Stoler.[26] Since then historical research has focused on "archive science" as a subject of investigation, rather than where research physically takes place.[27] This theoretical change or paradigm shift lies at the heart of the "archival turn" in modern historiography and signified the repositioning and refiguring of archives, not only globally but within a South African archival setting as well.[28]

Nonetheless scepticism arose from modern methodologies, as research shifted from the formation of the archive and extended to the objective recording of history using archives. Influenced by Derrida and Stoler, Terry Cook, a well noted and widely published Canadian archivist, supports the views of analysing the history of archival ideas as a process, as opposed to record or product, and put forward the idea of "making" archives, rather than "keeping" archives.[29]

While many archival intellectuals explore aspects of the "archive" in a philosophical or metaphorical sense, the archive has further become a universal metaphor for all conceivable forms of collective memory as well as other "archival metaphors" surrounding notions of contestation, power and authority.[30] For example, Joan Schwartz and Terry Cook illustrate how archives are inherently viewed as instruments of political and social power that are exercised through the control and dissemination of information, where: archives have the power to privilege and to marginalise. They can be a tool of hegemony; they can be a tool of resistance. They both reflect and constitute power relations. They are a product of society's need for information, and the abundance and circulation of documents reflects the importance placed on information

in society. They are the basis for and validation of the stories we tell ourselves, the story-telling narratives that give cohesion and meaning to individuals, groups, and societies.[31]

Therefore, the archive as an instrument of prevailing relations of power also plays a critical role in the idea that archives have the potential of being contested sites of power struggles. Other historians and archivists also acknowledge the archive's power in determining both what is said and what is silent. F.X. Blouin and W.G. Rosenberg has examined ways of knowledge of history and how custodial practices of archives and historical documents have changed over time, with a particular focus on the nature of contesting authority, authority in history as well as in archives, all signature questions embedded in postmodern archival theory.[32]

In South Africa two leading proponents of the contextual and postmodern critique of the archive, are the historian, Carolyn Hamilton[33] from the University of Cape Town (UCT) and Verne Harris,[34] the Director of Research and Archives at the Nelson Mandela Foundation, both of whose archival perspectives have been widely adopted in a South African setting. Hamilton's approach argues for the concept of the "life of an archive" implying that one needs to look at processes of change within an archive, how it changes and shapes public discourse i.e. the archival life cycle, proposing that it is inadequate to make histories of archives and in fact archives require biographies instead.[35] Increasingly as archives become subjects of historical enquiry, they need to be continually refashioned and forged within social and political "crucibles".[36] Likewise, Harris holds the view that the Rankian nineteenth century positivist paradigm that espoused empirical data and documentary evidence as historical truth-and-proof has dominated most archival discourse in South Africa.[37]

However, both Harris and Hamilton critique such traditional archival practices and instead join the collective

[25] J. Derrida famously called this preoccupation with the archive or tendency *mal d'archive* or archive fever.
[26] See for example, A.L. Stoler, "Colonial archives and the arts of governance". *Archival Science* (2), 2002, 87–109; A.L. Stoler, *Along the archival grain: epistemic anxieties and colonial common sense*. New Jersey: Princeton University Press, 2009.
[27] T. Cook, "Archival science and postmodernism: new formulations for old concepts". *Archival Science* 1, 2001, pp. 21–23; T. Cook, "From information to knowledge: an intellectual paradigm for archives". *Archivaria* 19, winter 1984–1985, pp. 28–49.
[28] C. Hamilton, Harris. V., Taylor, J., Pickover, M., Reid, G. and Saler, R. (eds.), *Refiguring the archive*. Cape Town: David Phillip, 2002.
[29] T. Cook, "Archival science and postmodernism: new formulations for old concepts". *Archival Science* 1, 2001, p. 24; T. Cook, "We are what we keep; we keep what we are: archival appraisal past, present and future". *Journal of the Society of Archivists* 32(2), 2011, pp. 173–189; T. Cook, "Archival principles and cultural diversity: contradiction, convergence or paradigm shift? A Canadian perspective". *International Journal of Archive* 3/4, 2007, pp. 37–38.
[30] J. Taylor, "Refiguring the archive", in C. Hamilton, et al. (eds.), *Refiguring the archive*. Cape Town: David Phillip, 2002, pp. 243–281.

[31] J. Schwartz, and T. Cook, "Archives, records, and power: from (postmodern) theory to (archival) performance". *Archival Science* 2(3), 2002, p. 13.
[32] See, for example, F.X. Blouin, and W.G. Rosenberg, *Processing the past: contesting authorities in history and the archive*. Oxford: Oxford Scholarship, 2011.
[33] See for example, C. Hamilton, Harris. V., Taylor, J., Pickover, M., Reid, G. & Saler, R. (eds.), *Refiguring the Archive*. Cape Town: David Phillip, 2002.
[34] See further readings by V. Harris, *Archives and justice: a South African perspective*. Chicago: Society of American Archivists, 2007; V. Harris "The archival sliver: power, memory, and archives in South Africa". *Archival Science* 2, 2002, pp. 63–86.
[35] See for example, C. Hamilton, The public life of an archive: archival biography as methodology, unpublished paper, presented at the Archive and Public Culture Workshop, University of Cape Town, Cape Town, 2 September 2009.
[36] C. Hamilton, "Forged and continually refashioned in the crucible of ongoing social and political life: archives and custodial practices as subjects of enquiry". *South African Historical Journal* 65(1), 2013, pp. 1–22.
[37] V. Harris, "Redefining archives in South Africa: public archives and society in transition, 1990–1996". *Archivaria* 42 (Fall 1996), pp. 6–27.

call for an archival transformation or re-formation promoting a postmodern or deconstructed paradigm.[38] In this regard, Harris has therefore emerged as one of South Africa's leading social archival thinkers in changing perceptions of archives, postulating a post positivist conception of the archive. Collectively, these two South African scholars, like T. Nesmith urge postmodern archival studies to consciously identify the "cracks that let the light in", allowing the exploration of multiple narratives and perspectives in ways of "seeing archives" beyond mere physical records.[39]

Harris in particular has certainly brought a distinct South African consciousness to archival literature expressed politically within a transformative post democratic context. He argues that the archive is not neutral or impartial territory as Western archive theory has assumed. Instead, the South African archive plays a political and active role in the creation of memory, contemplating the social constructedness of collective memory as part of an ever-changing and evolving political landscape.[40] Harris also posits the modern archive as a political entity and claims a movement out of a custodial era or archival practice and into future movements where archivists are "purveyors of concepts" and social memory.[41]

Although the notion of memory is general rather than abstract, in recent years it has been acknowledged that archive records function as a form of memory, primarily institutional memory. Archives and records therefore also serve as a means to provide or construct a collective or social memory.[42] Historically, archival holdings were recognised for their cultural or historical value and were as a result considered as national "memory banks", this antiquated idea of archives as an organ of national government or state was rejected in lieu of archives as social "spaces of memory" and public memory.[43]

In addition, practically and theoretically, scholarly awareness has matured, particularly where the construct of the archive offers a critical focal point for historical theory and research. In the past decades there has been an increasingly wider and broader range of prevailing schools of thought in archival science than ever before, with early

historical perspectives deeply rooted in positivism.[44] According to Harris, this is the crucible of ideas out of which modern archives – "archival science - emerged in the nineteenth century".[45] The positivist approach assumed the sanctity of evidence whereby archival records were products of administration and diplomatic information, guaranteeing the reliability and authenticity of untainted and empirical historical proof. Therefore, in archival terms, positivism uses as a departure point the objective and fixed nature of records, as well as the impartial and neutral roles played by archivists in the arranging and description thereof.[46]

In the context of research, the archive as a concept is questioned, constructed and deconstructed and it may not be just a concept about dealing with the historical past. It is within such broad perspectives that the archive is examined and questioned, and contested as archives defined by Harris, "demands space for contestation".[47] By using this approach one explores the evidentiary power of archival documentation laying the foundations for radically different approaches to processing the past.

While the archive provides the raw material for writing history, the archive can therefore also be contested and questioned in detail and more acute questions can be formulated about why the archives are either presenting or neglecting certain historical information. It should be further accepted that with all historical research, one can only derive the full value of the archive by acknowledging its limitations and there is also no doubt that the historical record is not impartial and like many archives will always be incomplete, fragmented and imperfect. In this publication, contesting the Mapungubwe Archive is not necessarily about the physical records, but rather contextualising the historical records which form part of the institutional memory of the University of Pretoria.

Contextualizing the archive

The subject of Mapungubwe has fundamentally been pursued by the discipline of archaeology and therefore our understanding of it has largely been insularly archaeological. The Mapungubwe Archive has as a direct result been overlooked and underemphasised in most studies and therefore, has been perpetually unresourced, undervalued and underused. Regrettably, few scholars have ever utilised the Mapungubwe Archive and its associated records as a basis for research nor referred

---

[38] V. Harris, "Claiming less, delivering more: a critique of positivist formulations on archives in South Africa". *Archivaria* 44, 1997, pp. 132–141.

[39] See T. Nesmith, "Seeing archives: postmodernism and changing intellectual place of archives". *The American Archivist* 65, (Spring/Summer 2002), pp. 24–41.

[40] V. Harris, *Exploring archives: an introduction to archival ideas and practice in South Africa*. (2nd ed.) Pretoria: National Archives of South Africa. 2000.

[41] See for example discussion by V. Harris, *Archive and justice: a South African perspective*. Chicago: Society of American Archivists, 2007.

[42] T. Cook, "Archival science and postmodernism: new formulations for old concepts". *Archival Science* 1, 2001, pp. 3–24; M. Hedstrom, "Archives, memory, and interfaces with the past". *Archival Science* 2, 2002, pp. 21–43.

[43] See, E. Ketelaar, "Archives as spaces of memory". *Journal of the Society of Archivists* 29(1), April 2008, p. 10; see also T. Cook "Evidence, memory, identity, and community: four shifting archival paradigms". *Archival Science* 13(2–3), 2013, pp. 95–120.

[44] See for example, P. Mortensen, "The place of theory in archival practice". *Archivaria* 47, 1999, pp. 7–8.

[45] V. Harris, "Claiming less, delivering more: a critique of positivist formulations on archives in South Africa". *Archivaria* 44, 1997, pp. 132–133.

[46] A.J. Gilliland-Swetland and S. McKemmish, "Building an infrastructure for archival research". *Archival Science* 4 (3/4), 2004, pp. 149–197.

[47] V. Harris, *Exploring archives: an introduction to archival ideas and practice in South Africa*. (2nd ed) Pretoria: National Archives of South Africa, 2000.

Figure 1.2. Mapungubwe expedition team of 1934 (left to right) John Schofield, Gerard Lestrade, N Neville Jones, Pieter van Tonder of the University of Pretoria.

to primary sources in order to construct the myriad of theories and approaches to the subject of Mapungubwe, despite over eight decades of scholarship.

The Mapungubwe historical records and documents were first viewed as traditional administrative forms of record-keeping, mainly as an archaeological working tool that produced masses of documentation and an incalculable amount of photographs during the course of excavations and research at Mapungubwe by the University of Pretoria and others.

The University of Pretoria's connection to Mapungubwe followed the period of the Great Depression of 1929, and took place during the rise of Afrikaner nationalism in the 1930s. This era was characterised by a rapidly expanding cultural movement including the adoption of Afrikaans as the single medium of instruction by the University of Pretoria. Institutional politics played a critical role when the University of Pretoria became an Afrikaner institution in 1932, particularly when lecturers were expected to teach "*volks geskiedenis*" or *volks*-history to encourage Afrikaner nationalism.[48] This is evidenced by the publication of the first early history of the University of Pretoria in a source known as *Ad Destinatum. Gedenkboek van die Universiteit van Pretoria* (1910–1960) / Commemorative book of the

University of Pretoria, commissioned by the University Council and edited by C.H. Rautenbach.[49] This historical account is in fact credited to A.N. Pelzer, a member of the Department of History and prominent member of the Afrikaner *Broederbond* (Brotherhood), the elitist once secret organization limited to Afrikaner men.[50]

From the years 1947 to 1967 Mapungubwe research was controlled and directed under the auspices of *Volkekunde* in the Department of Anthropology. Although the early years at Mapungubwe were largely archaeological, research was initially led by the liberal historian, Prof. Leo Fouché. However, the first mention of Mapungubwe within the University of Pretoria's own recorded history falls under the division of the Department of Archaeology, when the discipline of archaeology was formalised in a separate department in 1968.[51] The Department of Archaeology was established under its first lecturer and founder, J.F. Eloff, who was strongly influenced by Afrikaner ethnologists such as J.A. Engelbrecht, W.W.M. Eiselen and P.J Coertze.[52]

---

[48] F.A. Mouton, "Professor Leo Fouché, the history department and the Afrikanerization of the University of Pretoria", *Historia* 38(1), 1993, pp. 92–101.

[49] C.H. Rautenbach, (ed.) et al., *Ad Destinatum. Gedenkboek van die Universiteit van Pretoria*. Johannesburg: Voortrekkerpers Beperk, 1960; University of Pretoria Archive (UPA), A-1, Overview histories.
[50] See, for example, F.A. Mouton, "A.N. Pelzer: a custodian of Afrikanerdom". *South African Historical Journal* 37(1), 1997, pp. 133–155.
[51] C.H. Rautenbach, (ed.) et al., *Ad Destinatum. Gedenkboek van die Universiteit van Pretoria*. Johannesburg: Voortrekkerpers Beperk, 1960.
[52] E. Judson, "A life history of J.F. Eloff", in J.A. van Schalkwyk (ed.), *Studies in honour of Professor J.F. Eloff*. Pretoria: National Cultural History Museum, 1997, pp. 3–4.

According to the South African historian, Jane Carruthers, Afrikaner nationalist politics plagued Mapungubwe as, "institutional politics played a large part of the archaeological history of Mapungubwe". When the language policy of the University exclusively became Afrikaans, so academic freedom became impossible as only the heroes of Afrikanerdom were studied and revered to such an extent that:

> The discipline of History became the Afrikaner battleground and, not surprising in the paradigm of Afrikaner Nationalism and the 'myth of the empty land', Mapungubwe was a political anathema … [Volkekunde] was a questionable discipline in South Africa because of the racism that Volkekunde espoused in its 'scientific' support for atomizing African communities.[53]

The role of *volkekunde* in "controlling" Mapungubwe received wide condemnation by several scholars.[54] This has contributed to the many political views on Mapungubwe. It is further alleged that the University was and remains a "gate-keeper", rather than a custodian, as the institution has been accused of deliberately "hiding" Mapungubwe.[55] Such political opinions persist in the present, as recently reported by *The New Age* discussions in the drive for decolonization of South Africa's higher education claiming that, "it also led the University of Pretoria to perpetuate one of the greatest epistemological cover-ups in South African history, when it hid Mapungubwe artefacts deep in its dungeons" in the 1930s.[56] It is argued that the Mapungubwe Archive serves as a reminder of the University of Pretoria's colonial, Afrikaner nationalist and apartheid history,[57] as the social and political environment within the University of Pretoria has brought Mapungubwe a particular controversial and complex historical reputation.[58]

It took nearly eight decades to recognise the need for the professional "creation of stable, consistent, logical, and accessible archives from fieldwork" as "a fundamental building block of archaeological activity"[59] for an eventual, proper and adequate titled "archaeological archive" to develop.[60] Since the discipline of archaeology emerged within the University of Pretoria in 1968 as previously mentioned, it was only accepted in about the late 1980s that excavation as a method of research is essentially a destructive process. Moreover, no archaeological interpretations were sustainable, until they could be backed up with evidence from field records and post excavation reports. The neglect of historical records is not a new trend as archaeological archives in general are not greatly valued nor used and the state of South African archives in general is no different.[61] Despite the recognition that archives are the "new frontier" for twenty-first century research, there remains in comparison, an obsessive focus instead on material collections storage and other curation challenges.[62] Regarded in fact as a state of crisis, Childs makes this point:

> Little effort has been expended on encouraging the archaeological profession to value its collections as much as the sites from which they are derived … the archaeological profession must take some degree of responsibility for this state of affairs. Archaeologists have learned to value their trowels and shovels more than the collections they create.[63]

Historically, whilst only a few select individuals had access to the Mapungubwe records, which were kept within a departmental vault, even then, these documents were seen as records and not truly for their archival significance. For the purposes of this book it is important to acknowledge that the Mapungubwe Archive is not the creation of a single individual, but reflects a long succession of individuals who have created, shaped and reshaped the Archive within an institutional setting which has been socially and politically influenced over a long period of time. The possibility of establishing dedicated

[53] J. Carruthers, "Mapungubwe: an historical and contemporary analysis of a World Heritage cultural landscape". *Koedoe* 49(1), 2006, p. 7.

[54] See J. Sharp, "The roots and development of *Volkekunde* in South Africa". *Journal of Southern African Studies* 18(1), 1981, pp. 16–36; see also C.S. van der Waal, "Long walk from volkekunde to anthropology: reflections on representing the human in South Africa". *Anthropology Southern Africa* 38(3–4), 2015, pp. 216–234.

[55] A. Rademeyer, "UP ontken artefakte is weggesteek", *Beeld*, 12 January 1999; K. Helfrich, "Tuks denies 'hiding' artefacts", *Pretoria News*, 12 January 1999; A. Dunn, "Historical row", *Pretoria News*, 13 January 1999.

[56] N. Mkhize and I. Lagardien, "How western economics took over", *The New Age*, 2 March 2018.

[57] See articles by, S. Dubow, "Racial irredentism, ethnogenesis, and white supremacy in high-apartheid South Africa". *Kronos* 41(1) 2015, pp. 236–264 S. Dubow, *Scientific racism in modern South Africa*. Cambridge: University Press, Cambridge, 1995.

[58] Other studies, mainly from social archaeology and social anthropology, also use Mapungubwe as case studies that are politically packaged as South African heritage, thus creating and perpetuating political narratives of Mapungubwe and its contested association with the University of Pretoria, even to a point of damage to the institutions reputation see, R. King, "Archaeological naissance at Mapungubwe". *Journal of Social Archaeology* 11(3), 2011, pp. 311–333; L. Meskell, *The nature of heritage: the new South Africa*. Oxford: Wiley-Blackwell, 2012, p. 170.

[59] See, for example the 2003 foreword by H. Swain, Chair of the Archaeological Archives Forum, in, D.H. Brown (ed.), *Archaeological archives: a guide to best practice in creation, compilation, transfer and curation*, London: Institute of Field Archaeologists, 2007; J.A. Baird and L. McFadyen, "Towards an archaeology of archaeological archive". *Archaeological Review* 29(2), 2014, pp. 14–32.

[60] See, for example, the seminal UK study by D.H. Brown, "Archaeological archives: A guide to best practice in creation, compilation, transfer and curation", Archaeological Archives Forum (AAF), London: Institute of Field Archaeologists. 2007, <http: //www.archaeologyuk.org/archives/ aaf_archaeological_archives_2011.pdf.>, access: 2016.06.24.

[61] See other examples such as, N. Merriman and H. Swaine, "Archaeological archives: serving the public interest?" *European Journal of Archaeology* 2(2), 1999, pp. 249–267; G. Lucas, "Time and the archaeological archive". *Journal of Theory and Practice* 14(3), 2010, pp. 343–359.

[62] H. Swaine, "Archive Archaeology", in, R. Skeates, J. Carman and C. McDavid (eds.), *The Oxford Handbook of Public Archaeology*. Oxford: Oxford University Press, 2012, pp. 351–372.

[63] S.T. Childs, "Archaeological collections: valuing and managing an emerging frontier", in, N. Agnew and J. Bridgland (eds.), *Of the past, for the future: integrating archaeology and conservation*. Los Angeles: Getty Publications, 2006, pp. 204–210.

archives for Mapungubwe was largely mooted in the late 1990s by the research need to merely access the early records, and only make use of them for cross reference as research data.[64]

Unfortunately, during the period ranging from the 1950s to the late 1990s, many departmental records went missing or were thrown out, some were negligently discarded and even destroyed, leaving critical gaps in the Mapungubwe Archive.[65] However, it was with the transfer of these 'departmental records' to a museum environment in 1999 that enabled the Mapungubwe Archive to be first formally established and given its official title as an "archive".

It was also only much later that extensive curatorial effort to consolidate and retain as many Mapungubwe records as possible (and scattered collections) from within the University of Pretoria that had become so dispersed over a long period of time, formed part of the permanent museum records. This remains a perpetual challenge as many Mapungubwe records lie in institutional administration and the University's Executive filing systems. However, a positive move was made also in line with larger institutional archival policy as the University of Pretoria Archives (UPA) was established.[66] This was underpinned further by compliance with the Promotion of Access to Information Act, No. 2 of 2000, the National Archives and Record Services of South Africa Act, 1996 (Act 43 of 1996), as amended by the Cultural Laws Amendment Act, No. 36 of 2001 and it was only in 2005 that the Mapungubwe Archive eventually listed as an archival repository.[67]

Reconsidering the Mapungubwe Archive

From the above discussions, it is clear that currently the Mapungubwe Archive needs to be reconsidered. The Archive is unfixed, even though not definitively defined, it remains an institutional historical resource, but not yet a public resource. Furthermore, the Mapungubwe Archive has the potential to become a political tool of the present, though references to the past have resulted in historical narratives that demonstrate notions of contest, control, power, status and ownership that can continue to comment on the present. The significance of this book is to express interest in the future use and role of the Mapungubwe

Archive and encourage that new interdisciplinary discourse take greater cognisance of the Mapungubwe Archive that has been absent so long from historical discourse, archival debates and conventional scholarship.

Moreover, the Mapungubwe Archive is not just an institutional depository, it can and should be viewed as a "space of memory", where knowledge is collected, classified and preserved, and therefore has the ability to be reformed and reconstituted.[68] The trajectory of the Mapungubwe Archive can also be used to inform the institutional practices, as well as the force of politics, within the University of Pretoria's broader scholarship over time and space. The apparent neglect of the Mapungubwe Archive for decades has perhaps both allowed and alluded to ways in which the archive continues to accrue different meanings, perspectives and interpretations over time. This mirrors the notion of "an archive having a life" and does not assume once "safely cloistered" in the archive, a record, an object or a collection is preserved relatively unchanged for posterity.[69]

Nonetheless, their creation, organisation, preservation and the omission of some records in the Mapungubwe Archive is far from perfect, neutral or impartial. Instead, it reflects the University of Pretoria's fundamental and institutional preoccupations and priorities, as well as potential "hidden histories".[70] The Archive has immense potential to reveal a great deal about changing notions of the institution's sense of justice, ethics, power, status and control as retaining records was also a deeply subjective decision.[71] The understanding of Mapungubwe's contested early history can be shaped by the Archive and can reveal why some records were kept and others not, and more importantly what can be further extracted and elucidated from the many omissions, silences and absences? There are also minor private contributors to the Archive which are critical unravelling the narrative such as the private archives of E. V. Adams and the family records of the Van Graan family, among the unknown records tied up in the former Transvaal Museum Archive in Pretoria.

---

[64] See cross-referencing method and use of archive records in, A. Meyer, *The Iron Age sites of Greefswald: stratigraphy and chronology of the sites and a history of investigations*, Pretoria: University of Pretoria, 1998, pp. 50–55.

[65] Personal interview and discussions with A. Meyer in Pretoria, 15 May 2015.

[66] The University of Pretoria Archives (UPA) serves as the memory bank of the institution, it preserves and maintains access to records from all sectors of the University as well as associated institutions and communities. This institutional archive was only formally established in 1999, <https://www.up.ac.za/up-archives>, access: 2016.06.25.

[67] Mapungubwe Archive, copy of Directory Entries of Archival Repositories 2005, <http://www.national.archives.gov.za/dir_entries_pg7_2005.html>, access: 2016.05.26.

[68] See, E. Ketelaar, "Archives as spaces of memory". *Journal of the Society of Archivists* 29(1) April 2008, pp. 9–27.

[69] See, C. Hamilton, "Backstory, biography, and the life of James Stuart". *History in Africa* 38, 2011, pp. 319–341.

[70] The linking of archives and hidden history is interesting and is gaining more attention in modern international archival studies, see S. Roff, "Archives, documents, and hidden history: a course to teach undergraduates the thrill of historical discovery real and virtual". *The History Teacher* 40(4), 2007, pp. 551–558. See also, University of Oxford, 2017, "Hidden histories in the archives", <https://www.history.ox.ac.uk/article/hidden-histories-archives>, access: 2018.04.03.

[71] The archivist, record-keepers, or individuals making calls of what records to keep as "evidence" and which to not is an important point where the 'archivist' becomes the point of discussion, as does the archive itself. Many scholars such as Terry Cook, Verne Harris, Mark Greene and others discuss and debate of making archives, rather than keeping archives and the creation of records in archival practice and the construction of evidence, see for example, B. Brothman, "The past that archives keep: memory, history, and the preservation of archival records". *Archivaria* 51, 2001, pp. 48–70.

Figure 1.3. Early photograph of University of Pretoria camp among mopane bushveld near Mapungubwe Hill, with Prof. Leo Fouché sitting and his back turned.

Such difficult questions are important in raising the scholarly potential of a largely untapped archive. It is argued that a critical investigation of the Mapungubwe Archive can shed further light on deeper nuances of the contests or multiple pasts associated with Mapungubwe and the University of Pretoria. More importantly, this publication sets out to highlight the importance of these historical records and the potential of the Mapungubwe Archive to enhance our understanding of the early history of Mapungubwe's contested past and how the Archive can be used to inform present debates. This is particularly relevant to the Mapungubwe Archive, which is seen both as an institutional archive (or institutional instrument) as well as a primary repository of archaeological, cultural, historical and heritage resource, whereas the archive is still conventionally viewed by some scholars as just "artefacts of archaeological knowledge" and thus as "artefacts of history".[72]

Similarly, this view aligns with the emerging postmodern pattern of the growing importance, relevance and future of archives and not necessarily just as historical records of the past but critically also the dire need to save the

historical record due to the alarming and growing neglect of South Africa's archives.[73] More broadly, this further relates to the contribution and legitimacy of the archive, to not only the discipline of history but to anthropology, social studies, the arts and literature, and collectively these disciplines share a common concern about the debate and fate of the historical record or "the postmodern suspicion of the historical record".[74]

Book outline

The book comprises of five chapters, outlining the key themes of the research on the Mapungubwe Archive and how they get unpacked, as well as how they fit together. Each chapter addresses particular aspects of the main research question. This first chapter as the introduction presents an outline and context of the University of Pretoria to the subject of Mapungubwe and the Mapungubwe Archive specifically. It highlights the concept of "contestation", a continuing theme supporting the book's title as a "past imperfect". It reviews select key texts surrounding changing perspectives in archival discourse.

This brief theory is necessary in order for the Mapungubwe Archive to be "theorised" about, and for the archive to

---

[72] S. Guha re-examines the way in which the past is recalled and historicised, with a focus upon issues of historiography, the notions of the archive as an artefact of evidence and the changing needs of archaeological academia towards archives and the increasing role archives play in research. See for example, S. Guha, *Artefacts of history: archaeology, historiography and Indian pasts.* London: Sage Publications Pty. Ltd, 2015.

[73] See article by R. Pather, "Activists fight to keep SA's historical documents safe", *Mail & Guardian*, 6 March 2016.
[74] M. Manoff, "Theories of the archive from across the disciplines". *Libraries and the Academy* 4(1) 2004, p. 14.

find its place in current historical archival discourse on the topic. Leading global and South African archival scholars such as Terry Cook, Joan Schwartz, Tom Nesmith, Ann Stoler, Verne Harris and Carolyn Hamilton's perspectives are discussed. It aims to provide an overview of the changing perceptions of an archive with a focus on the notion of history as "flawed" which embodies all pasts as "imperfect". The Introduction therefore summarises the contextual foundation in which the research questions are formulated. It further outlines the general scope and highlights the focus, gaps and contribution of the book, as well as the significance of the Mapungubwe Archive for future research.

Chapter two revisits Mapungubwe literature presented in broad chronological themes. Time shifts range from early literature that includes largely colonial narratives that cover the early period 1933 until 1940; followed by an overview of post War studies that are limited and sporadic and which waned between the 1950s and 1960s. These following decades provided the political backbone to the scholarly flourish of stratigraphic and Iron Age studies which marked the 1980s, strongly influenced by *Volkekunde* or Cultural Anthropology and later entrenched, by when Archaeology became an accepted field of study at the institution The literature review then expands to the proliferation of post 1994 research which is largely very critical of previous studies and interpretatively based social studies, mainly within the discipline of social anthropology and social archaeology in reaction against cultural approaches.

This literature chapter provides the setting of how research on the archive fits within broader disciplinary conversations, synthesising and summarising arguments about how wide-ranging and transdisciplinary the subject of Mapungubwe can be. This shift between time periods allows for historical clarity of the chronological progression to augment and spark the contestation of Mapungubwe's early history and at the same time tracks the intellectual trajectory of the Mapungubwe Archive.

Continuing the theme of contestation, chapter three introduces the argument that there were multiple discoveries of Mapungubwe, prior to the primary discovery of gold on Mapungubwe in 1932, which in 1933 fell under the helm of the University of Pretoria's early history. This section is devoted to the parallel narratives of the early history before 1933 and highlights the ignored Indigenous histories, the nineteenth century discovery of Mapungubwe by an elusive historical figure by the name of F.B. Lotrie, as well as, the ecological significance and history of Dongola near Mapungubwe and the German discovery of Mapungubwe by Leo Frobenius in 1928. This chapter delves further into the main gold discovery by the five discoverers which led to the declaration of Mapungubwe as a "treasure trove". It sets out the initial contact between the discoverers and the University of Pretoria and what transpired. It also uncovers many of the controversies and irregularities of

the "discovery" and provides clarity of what occurred before 1933 and what emerged just after, including what was shared in the public domain, what was published and what was chosen not to be shared.

The emphasis in chapter four is the second main focus of the early history of the University of Pretoria from the viewpoint of the Mapungubwe Archaeological Committee. From its maiden years in 1933, the University was a major instrument of institutional power and authority over Mapungubwe influencing the State and vice versa, the direction of research as well as the research results and interpretations made about the archaeological site. This chapter does not cover the archaeological excavation history of Mapungubwe for this period. Instead, this section elucidates the fact that Mapungubwe's early history was controlled more or less by the Committee fronted by a lesser known individual, J. de Villiers Roos whose influence was exponentially greater than that of the historian Prof. Leo Fouché to whom much of Mapungubwe's traditional history is ascribed and accredited to.

Fouché and Roos as contesting personalities in Mapungubwe's history is delved into, separating those that "make" history from those who "partake" and the consequences thereof that influenced and controlled the power of the Mapungubwe narrative, both colonial and nationalist. This chapter argues that the Committee's role was much more than mere excavation, and points to their institutional influence and responsibility towards the State. In addition, the little known role of the Transvaal Museum in the public exhibition of the Mapungubwe Collection under their curatorship for nearly thirty years is further highlighted and supported by Mapungubwe records traced to the Transvaal Museum Archive.

Following the kaleidoscope of discoveries and state claims to the "treasure trove", chapter five illuminates the legal chartering by the University of Pretoria that shaped the colonial and nationalist claims to Mapungubwe. This chapter charts the trajectory of historical legislation from the Historical Monuments Commission in 1926 to the later workings of the National Monuments Council into the newly transformed National Heritage Resources Act of 1999, its effects and deficiencies as the current heritage legislation.

This evolution of failed legislation and discord around selective heritage is the result of which gave unintentional or intentional rise to the early notions of "ownership" and what is referred to in the present as "stewardship".

Finally, the epilogue considers the purpose of seeing the Mapungubwe Archive and its transformative life-cycle. It reflects back on its overall history, evolving from archaeological records that were first viewed as administrative documents, merely as field records and correspondence. The Archive is then only considered

Figure 1.4. Prof Leo Fouché, Head of History and excavations, acting as agent on behalf of the University of Pretoria, accompanied by E.V. Adams, the Attorney during February 1933 negotiations with discoverers and the gold in their possession of the treasure trove. © E. V. Adams Archive.

again briefly between the 1960s and 1980s, the select-and-neglect era as mere data research sources. From the late 1990s, institutionally, the historical records are taken slightly more seriously for their value as having potentially important historical content.

There are also intentional gaps and silences during the height of apartheid, mainly the 1980s and even post 1994, largely as a result of departmental agendas, academic struggles and internal institutional politics. The future and fate of the Mapungubwe Archive that forms an integral part of the institutional memory of the University of Pretoria in the coming century is considered. It demonstrates current reconsiderations of why the Mapungubwe Archive is contested and imperfect providing conclusions.

Revisiting Mapungubwe Literature

It is as if we have a secret code for communicating with one another, which is unintelligible to the world at large ... Add to this the generally appalling standards of writing in archaeology, and it's easy to understand the huge chasm between archaeological research at the technical level and our wider audience. Brian Fagan, 2006.

2.1. Previous research

The secondary literature on the subject of Mapungubwe is expansive and covers about eighty-five years of research, with a majority of scholars writing from within the discipline of South African archaeology. Much of what is known about Mapungubwe since the early 1930s has been derived from archaeological studies, yet vastly differing perspectives illustrate just how deeply divided scholars are in South Africa over Mapungubwe's precolonial past. Prior to this period, the ignored African histories and studies thereof are dealt with later in chapter 3. Yet, the twentieth century studies engaged cursorily in theory, with fieldwork research mainly derived from the archaeological excavations at Mapungubwe that focused on the period of the late first millennium AD.[75]

However, a handful of historical studies have filled gaps in the historical record by constructing some more of the recent histories of Mapungubwe from the fourteenth century onwards.[76] From the onset of the twenty-first century, there has been a bourgeoning of literature production characterised by global perspectives, but rooted in the politics of the past. The increasing international interest in Mapungubwe and its wider cultural landscape precipitated an outbreak of more diverse research beyond the confines of archaeology into southern Africa's prehistory.[77]

Given the extreme and diverse nature of the literature produced on Mapungubwe over the past eight and half decades, this literature review will indicate an overview of the type of research as well as provide select key examples in the footnotes. However, within the parameters of the book which focuses on the archive per se, the literature review will not be able to encompass the vastness of this literature. Moreover, the literature overview is focussed more on the earlier publications which are of relevance to this book of the early historical period 1933–1940, while the later, existing literature takes no cognisance of the Mapungubwe Archive as previously expressed.

Thus, although Mapungubwe literature is very extensive, it is not the intention of this chapter to cover all the studies, but rather provide a synthesis of the kinds of Mapungubwe knowledge prevalent to relate what has been done previously on the subject. These studies range, for example, from excavation reports;[78] stratigraphy and site chronologies;[79] typological ceramic (pottery) studies;[80]

---

[75] This Iron Age (Middle to Late Iron Age) is regarded broadly as covering the period AD 1000 - AD 1300, see, for example, B.M. Fagan, "The Greefswald sequence: Bambandyanalo and Mapungubwe". In, J.D. Fage and R. Oliver, (eds.), *Papers in African Prehistory*. Cambridge: Cambridge University Press, 1970, pp. 173–199; For an overview of the archaeology of the two main sites known as K2 and Mapungubwe see, for example, A. Meyer, "K2 and Mapungubwe". *South African Archaeological Society Goodwin Series* 8, 2000, pp. 4–13.

[76] See for example, P. Bonner and J. Carruthers, The recent history of the Mapungubwe area, Mapungubwe Cultural Heritage Resources Survey, Report commissioned by the Department of Environmental Affairs and Tourism, 2003; T.N. Huffman, "Historical archaeology of the Mapungubwe area: Boer, Birwa and Machete". *Southern Africa Humanities* 24(1), 2012, pp. 33–59; S. Tiley-Nel, "Sermons in stone, poetry in potsherds: the history of the Mapungubwe collection". In S. Tiley-Nel (ed.) *Mapungubwe remembered: contributions to Mapungubwe by the University of Pretoria*. Johannesburg: Chris van Rensburg Publications (Pty) Ltd, 2011, pp. 174–195; J. Wintjes, "Frobenius discovered before crossing Limpopo ruins: ancient fortificated settlements, beautiful pottery mountains stop". *De arte* 52(1), 2017, pp. 31–67.

[77] For a more concise overview of Mapungubwe and its context within precolonial African archaeology see for example, P. Mitchell, *The*

archaeology of Southern Africa. Cambridge: Cambridge University Press, 2002.

[78] Mapungubwe Archive, C. van Riet Lowe, "Mapungubwe: first report on excavations in the Northern Transvaal". *Antiquity* 10(39), 1936, pp. 282–291; J.F. Eloff and A. Meyer, "The Greefswald sites". In E.A. Voigt (ed.) *Guide to archaeological sites in the northern and eastern Transvaal*. Pretoria: Transvaal Museum, 1981, pp. 7–22.

[79] A. Meyer, *The Iron Age sites of Greefswald: stratigraphy and chronology of the sites and a history of investigations*, Pretoria: University of Pretoria, 1998; E.M.O. Hanisch, An archaeological interpretation of certain Iron Age sites in the Limpopo/Shashi valley. Unpublished MA dissertation, University of Pretoria, 1980; B.M. Fagan, "The Greefswald sequence: Bambandyanalo and Mapungubwe". *Journal of African History* 5(3), 1964, pp. 337–361.

[80] J.F. Schofield, "The pottery of the Mapungubwe district". In L. Fouché (ed.), *Mapungubwe: ancient Bantu civilization on the Limpopo: reports on excavations at Mapungubwe (Northern Transvaal) from February 1933 to June 1935*. Vol. I, Cambridge: Cambridge University Press, 1937, pp. 32–102; J. F. Schofield, *Primitive pottery: an introduction to the South African ceramics, prehistoric and protohistoric*. Cape Town: South African Archaeology Society, 1948; I. Pikirayi, "Ceramics and group identities; towards a social archaeology in southern African Iron Age studies". *Journal of Social Archaeology* 7, 2007, pp. 286–301; S. Tiley-Nel, A technological study and manufacture of ceramic vessels from K2 and Mapungubwe Hill, South Africa. Unpublished MA thesis, University of Pretoria, 2013.

dating sequences;[81] rock art studies;[82] stone age studies;[83] ethnographic and oral history studies;[84] conservation studies;[85] to research on landscape dynamics;[86] rainmaking rituals;[87] climate change;[88] and other studies on the economic, political and social complexity for constructing the numerous theories and interpretations of the origin, rise and decline of the Mapungubwe state towards the end of the thirteenth century.[89] In addition, scholars from the natural science disciplines have further contributed to a large body of knowledge on Mapungubwe. This research emanates from physical anthropology;[90] zooarchaeology;[91] physics and chemistry;[92] to metallurgy;[93] as well as several other types of studies, including theses which have resulted in specialist research that has generated multitudes of more knowledge into the Mapungubwe literature.[94]

This chapter provides a brief examination of Mapungubwe literature as background information and introduces the context of how the Mapungubwe Archive fits into the wider Mapungubwe historical narrative. It further provides a sympathetic exposition of some of the most relevant, seminal works and land mark studies within four broad chronological eras: the earliest literature of the 1930s and 1940s; post War studies from 1950s to the late 1960s, (the discipline years of archaeological studies); the apartheid era studies from the 1970s and 1980s; and lastly, post democracy studies from 1994 onwards to the present. This chapter therefore offers an overview of the historical and contextual knowledge on Mapungubwe, demonstrating that one of the gaps and weak points of both past and existing secondary literature as a whole lacks attention paid to the Mapungubwe Archive.

[81] J.C. Vogel, "Radiocarbon dating of the Iron Age sequence in the Limpopo Valley". *South African Archaeological Society Goodwin Series* 8, 2000, pp. 51–57; S. Woodborne, M. Pienaar and S. Tiley-Nel, "Dating the Mapungubwe Hill Gold". *Journal of African Archaeology* 7(1), 1999, pp. 99–103.

[82] E.B. Eastwood and G. Blundell, "Re-discovering the rock art of the Limpopo-Shashe confluence area, southern Africa". *Southern African Field Archaeology* 8, 1999, pp. 17–27; M. Schoonraad, "Preliminary survey of the rock-art of the Limpopo Valley". *The South African Archaeological Bulletin* 15(57), 1960, pp. 10–13; A.R. Willcox, "Painted petroglyphs at Balerno in the Limpopo Valley, Transvaal." *South African Journal of Science* 56, 1963, pp. 108–110; A.R. Willcox and H. Pager, "More petroglyphs from the Limpopo valley, Transvaal." *South African Archaeological Bulletin* 23, 1968, pp. 50–51.

[83] K. Kuman, J.C. Baron and R.J. Gibbon, "Earlier Stone Age archaeology of the Vhembe-Dongola National Park (South Africa) and vicinity". *Quaternary International* 129, 2005, pp. 23–32; T.R. Forssman, The Later Stone Age occupation and sequence of the Mapungubwe landscape, MSc. Dissertation. University of Witwatersrand, 2010.

[84] G.F Lestrade, "Some notes on the ethnic history of the VhaVenda and their Rhodesian affinities". *South African Journal of Science* 24, 1927, pp. 486–495; G.P. Lestrade, "Report on certain ethnological investigations in connection with the archaeological discoveries at Mapungubwe" in, L. Fouché (ed.), *Mapungubwe: ancient Bantu civilization on the Limpopo: Reports on excavations at Mapungubwe (Northern Transvaal) from February 1933 to June 1935*, Vol. I, Cambridge: Cambridge University Press. 1937, pp. 119–124; see also N.M.N. Ralushai, Preliminary report on the oral history of the Mapungubwe area, unpublished report for the Department of Environmental Affairs and Tourism, 2002.

[85] S. Tiley-Nel and H. Botha, "The conservation of the Mapungubwe gold collection, South Africa". *Journal of the Institute of Conservation* 36(1) 2013, pp. 65–80; J. Carruthers, "Mapungubwe: an historical and contemporary analysis of a World Heritage landscape". *Koedoe* 49, 2006, pp. 1–13; M. Berry and M. Cadman, *Dongola to Mapungubwe: the 80-year battle to conserve the Limpopo valley*. Swartwater: Mmabolela Press. 2007; F. Koleini, Mapungubwe metals revisited: a technical and historical study of Mapungubwe material culture with an emphasis on conservation, PhD thesis, University of Pretoria, 2014.

[86] M. Manyanga, Resilient landscapes: socio-environmental dynamics in the Shashe-Limpopo basin, Southern Zimbabwe c. AD to the present. *Studies in Global Archaeology* 11. Uppsala: Uppsala University, 2007; B. van Doornum, Changing places, spaces and identity in the Shashe-Limpopo region of Limpopo Province, South Africa. PhD thesis, University of Witwatersrand, 2005.

[87] M.H. Schoeman, "Imagining rain-places: rain control and changing ritual landscapes in the Shashe-Limpopo confluence area, South Africa". *South African Archaeological Bulletin* 61(184), 2006, pp. 152– 65; M. Murimbika, Sacred powers and rituals of transformation: an ethnoarchaeological study of rainmaking rituals and agricultural productivity during the evolution of the Mapungubwe state, AD 1000 to AD 1300. Unpublished PhD thesis. University of Witwatersrand, 2006.

[88] J. Smith, J. Lee-Thorp and S. Hall, "Climate change and agropastoralist settlements in the Shashe-Limpopo river basin, southern Africa AD 880 to 1700". *South African Archaeological Bulletin* 62(186), 2007, pp. 115–125; T.N. Huffman, "Climate change during the Iron Age in the Shashe Limpopo Basin, southern Africa". *Journal of Archaeological Science* 35(7), 2008, pp. 2032–2047; T.N. Huffman and S. Woodborne, "Archaeology, baobabs and drought: cultural proxies and environmental data from the Mapungubwe landscape, southern Africa". *The Holocene* 26(3). 2016, pp. 464–470.

[89] T.N. Huffman, "Mapungubwe and Great Zimbabwe: the origin and spread of social complexity in southern Africa". *Journal of Anthropological Archaeology* 28(1), 2009, pp. 37–54; J.A. Calabrese, *The emergence of social and political complexity in the Shashi-Limpopo Valley of southern Africa, AD 900 to AD 1300: ethnicity, class and polity*. Oxford: BAR Publishing, International Series 1617, 2007.

[90] Mapungubwe Archive, A. Galloway, *The skeletal remains of Bambandyanalo*. Johannesburg: Witwatersrand University Press, 1959; M. Steyn, An assessment of the health status and physical characteristics of the prehistoric population from Mapungubwe. PhD dissertation, University of the Witwatersrand, 1994.

[91] Mapungubwe Archive, E.A. Voigt, The faunal remains from Greefswald as a reflection of Iron Age economic and cultural activities. MA dissertation, University of Pretoria, 1978; E.A. Voigt, *Mapungubwe: an archaeo-zoological interpretation of an Iron Age community*. Pretoria: Transvaal Museum, 1983.

[92] M. Wood, "Making connections: relationships between international trade and glass beads from the Shashe Limpopo Area". *The South African Archaeological Society Goodwin Series* 8, 2000, pp. 78–90; A. Tournié, L.C. Prinsloo and P. Colomban, "Raman classification of glass beads excavated on Mapungubwe Hill and K2, two archaeological sites in South Africa". *Journal of Raman Spectroscopy* 43(4), 2012, pp. 532–542; L.C. Prinsloo and P. Colomban, "A Raman spectroscopic study of the Mapungubwe oblates: glass trade beads excavated at an Iron Age archaeological site in South Africa". *Journal of Raman Spectroscopy* 39(1), 2008, pp. 79–90; H.C. Beck, "The beads of the Mapungubwe district", in, L. Fouché (ed.), *Mapungubwe: ancient Bantu civilization on the Limpopo: Reports on excavations at Mapungubwe (Northern Transvaal) from February 1933 to June 1935*. Cambridge: Cambridge University Press, 1937, pp. 104–113; see also C. van Riet Lowe, "Beads of the water". *Journal of Bantu Studies* 11(1), 1937, pp. 367–372; C.C. Davison, "Chemical resemblance of garden roller and M1 glass beads". *Journal of African Studies* 32(4), 1973, pp. 247–257.

[93] D. Miller, "Metal assemblages from Greefswald areas, K2, Mapungubwe Hill and Mapungubwe southern Terrace". *South African Archaeological Bulletin* 56, 2001, pp. 83–103; A. Oddy, "On the trail of Iron Age gold". *Transvaal Museum Bulletin* 19, (November 1983), pp. 24–26; S. Chirikure, "Metals in society: iron production and its position in Iron Age communities of southern Africa". *Journal of Social Archaeology* 7, 2007, pp. 72–100.

[94] F. Koleini, de Beer, M.H. Schoeman, I. Pikirayi, S. Chirikure, G. Nothnagel and J.M. Radebe, "Efficiency of neutron tomography in visualizing the internal structure of metal artefacts from Mapungubwe Museum Collection with the aim of conservation". *Journal of Cultural Heritage* 13, 2012, pp. 246–253; L.C. Prinsloo, N. Wood, M. Loubser, S.M.C. Verryn and S. Tiley, "Re-dating of Chinese celadon sherds excavated on Mapungubwe Hill, a thirteenth century Iron Age site in South Africa, using Raman spectroscopy, XRF and XRF". *Journal of Raman Spectroscopy* 36(8), 2005, pp. 806–816; A.R. Antonites, J. Bradfield and T. Forssman, "Technological, functional and contextual aspects of K2 and Mapungubwe worked bone industries". *African Archaeological Review* 33(4), 2016, pp. 437–463.

Figure 2.1. Group photograph on site in 1934 (seated from left to right): Clarence van Riet Lowe, General Jan Smuts, Dr. I B. Pole-Evans and Mr Smuts. (Standing): Unidentified, Neville Jones and Mr Schuster.

2.2. Early literature: 1930s to 1940s

The first studies of Mapungubwe's history were under the auspices of the University of Pretoria, forming the initial foundations upon which all other research on the subject is based. The volume on Mapungubwe by Leo Fouché, *Mapungubwe: ancient Bantu civilization on the Limpopo: reports on excavations at Mapungubwe (Northern Transvaal) from February 1933 to June 1935 Volume I*, was published in 1937 and is regarded as the first comprehensive study on the subject of Mapungubwe.[95] Although considered a seminal work, this first volume relied mainly on report contributions by other scholars, under the editorship of Fouché.[96] *Mapungubwe Volume I* provided the early accounts of the first season of excavations on Mapungubwe from February 1933 to June

1935, and outlined a presentation of initial findings and ascribed Mapungubwe's origins to "the Bantu".[97]

Moreover, this view was underpinned by the title, *Ancient Bantu civilisation on the Limpopo* together with ceramic and metal analyses and the first recording of Mapungubwe oral traditions and ethnographic investigations by G.P. Lestrade a linguist at the University of Cape Town.[98] Not only did Fouché's volume lack early historical insight, very little interpretation and offered no theoretical basis,[99]

---

[95] Mapungubwe Archive, L. Fouché, (ed.), *Mapungubwe: ancient Bantu civilization on the Limpopo: Reports on excavations at Mapungubwe (Northern Transvaal) from February 1933 to June 1935*, Cambridge: Cambridge University Press, 1937.

[96] See for example, L.J. Krige, "Geological report on Mapungubwe". In L. Fouché (ed.), *Mapungubwe: ancient Bantu civilization on the Limpopo: reports on excavations at Mapungubwe (Northern Transvaal) from February 1933 to June 1935*. Cambridge: Cambridge University Press, 1937, pp. 3–4; J.F. Schofield, "The pottery of the Mapungubwe district". In L. Fouché (ed.), *Mapungubwe: ancient Bantu civilization on the Limpopo: Reports on excavations at Mapungubwe (Northern Transvaal) from February 1933 to June 1935*. Cambridge: Cambridge University Press, 1937, pp. 32–102.

[97] Although the term "Bantu" was used commonly in the disciplines of anthropology, history and archaeology in the 1930s, it is no longer accepted unless it has its original context in reference to Bantu languages. Historically, it was a generally accepted colonial term referring to the major linguistic group of Nguni languages in South Africa widely used in sub-Saharan Africa. Bantu-speaking people are not a homogenous group. Nonetheless, the word Bantu is associated with colonialism and apartheid and from 1977, the term "Bantu" was replaced by preferable term "black". "Abantu" is derived from the Zulu word meaning, "people", the plural is "umuntu" meaning person. See, C. Saunders and N. Southey, *A dictionary of South African history*. Cape Town: David Philip, 1998; South African History Online, "Defining the term 'Bantu'", 2011, <http://www.sahistory.org.za/article/defining-term-bantu>, access: 2018.05.30.

[98] G.P. Lestrade, "Report on certain ethnological investigations in connection with the archaeological discoveries at Mapungubwe". In L. Fouché (ed.), *Mapungubwe: ancient Bantu civilization on the Limpopo: Reports on excavations at Mapungubwe (Northern Transvaal) from February 1933 to June 1935*. Cambridge: Cambridge University Press, 1937, pp. 119–124

[99] See Fouché's biography by S. Tiley-Nel, "Leo Fouché (1880–1949)". In S. Tiley-Nel (ed.) *Mapungubwe Remembered: Contributions to*

but Smuts Professor of Commonwealth History at the University of Cambridge, Saul Dubow criticised "the avowedly 'cultural' approach favoured by most of the contributors" that is clearly "not free of the influence of diffusionist thinking and 'tribal' differences" as merely exploratory notes regarding the origins of Mapungubwe.[100]

Fouché, as a historian in the Department of History, had a sound reputation and a recognised academic career. However, as South African Professor Alex Mouton points out, he maintained that history had to be seen as a neutral and an objective science, yet, he was known to neglect the role of interpretation in writing history.[101] Nonetheless, Leo Fouché was not an archaeologist by training and so the Archaeological Committee of the University of Pretoria considered that a preliminary account of the first Mapungubwe excavations should rather be published worldwide by the well-known southern African archaeologist, Clarence van Riet Lowe. As a result in September 1936, *Mapungubwe: first report on the excavations in the Northern Transvaal* was first published in the journal of *Antiquity*.[102] This is in fact the first publication on Mapungubwe and not Fouché's 1937 volume which is often mistaken to be the first publication.

Van Riet Lowe was a Chief Engineer in the Department of Public Works and was appointed as an ad hoc member of the Archaeological Committee earlier in 1933. Many of van Riet Lowe's contributions to Mapungubwe provided the groundwork for directing much of the archaeological excavations which the Committee subsequently followed for years.[103] Even so, Fouché's seminal work on *Mapungubwe Volume I* was endorsed by the Archaeological Committee and received both national and many international peer reviews. It was considered a welcomed publication as an introduction to Mapungubwe.[104]

The second seminal work entitled, *Mapungubwe, Volume II Report on excavations at Mapungubwe and Bambandyanalo in the Transvaal from 1935–1940* was

produced by Capt. Guy A. Gardner.[105] Gardner, of British origin, was regarded as an amateur archaeologist, despite the fact that he had previously excavated in Egypt and in South Africa and also later held the esteemed position of President of South African Archaeological Society.[106] He was appointed by the University of Pretoria to take charge of the second season of excavations at Mapungubwe from 1934 to 1940.

International interest was further stimulated by the publication of this second monumental volume on Mapungubwe and was considered an influential study, since it contained valuable archaeological information for many of Gardner's successors and continues today to be regarded as a pivotal reference, despite the fact that results were published twenty years later in 1963. Unlike *Volume I* by Fouché (1937) which relied on contributions of other authors, it should not go unnoticed that Gardner wrote up his entire findings for *Volume II*.

Numerous factors contributed to the delay of publication: the beginning of World War II, when Gardner was called up for military service in July 1940; a malaria outbreak along the Limpopo which halted excavations; no funding from government; as well as a further delay to accommodate the first C14 radiocarbon dates for Mapungubwe by Phillip Tobias in 1959.[107] Furthermore, by 1950 the Director of the Archaeological Survey, C. van Riet Lowe distanced himself from Mapungubwe research withdrawing his editorship of Gardner's publication perhaps as a sign of his disapproval of Gardner's racial views or owing to his decline in health. Van Riet Lowe suggested that the University of Pretoria rather terminate excavations at Mapungubwe.[108]

More significantly, P.J. Coertze, a leading exponent of *volkekunde* and the Head of the Department of Anthropology at the University of Pretoria, as a cultural anthropologist took over editorship. This resulted in much contention between Gardner's intended original manuscript and that which was strictly edited at the hands of an anthropologist who often disregarded the archaeological evidence in lieu of his own cultural approach and racial agenda to the origins of Mapungubwe. Coertze approached his research as a *volksdiens* (service to the *volk*, or Afrikaner people), he viewed racial purity

Mapungubwe by the University of Pretoria. Johannesburg: Chris van Rensburg Publications (Pty) Ltd, 2011, pp. 15–18.

[100] S. Dubow, *Scientific racism in modern South Africa*. Cambridge: Cambridge University Press, 1995, p. 96.

[101] F.A. Mouton "Professor Leo Fouché, the History Department and the Afrikanerization of the University of Pretoria". *Historia*, 38(1), 1993, pp. 92–101.

[102] Mapungubwe Archive, C. van Riet Lowe, "Mapungubwe: First report on excavations in the Northern Transvaal". *Antiquity* 10(39), 1936, pp. 282–291.

[103] See van Riet Lowe's biography by S. Tiley-Nel, "Clarence van Riet Lowe (1894–1956)". In S. Tiley-Nel (ed.) *Mapungubwe remembered: contributions to Mapungubwe by the University of Pretoria*. Johannesburg: Chris van Rensburg Publications (Pty) Ltd, 2011, pp. 26–28.

[104] See list of other newspapers and journals such as, *The Star*, 23 November 1937; *Sunday Times*, 28 November 1937; *Cape Times*, 4 February 1938; *Manchester Guardian*, 16 November 1937; *The Museum News*, 15 December 1937; *Nature Magazine*, 15 December 1938; *London Geographic Journal*, February 1938, *Life and Letters* 30 March 1938; *Science Newsletter*, 12 March 1938; *Museums Journal*, March 1938; *L'Antropologie* 1939; *Internationales Archive For Ethnography*, 1938; *Mecvre de France*, 1938.

[105] G.A. Gardner, *Mapungubwe, Volume II, Report on excavations at Mapungubwe and Bambandyanalo in the Transvaal from 1935–1940*. P.J. Coertze (ed.), Pretoria: Van Schaik Publishers, 1963.

[106] For more about Gardner's historical background and formal training, see for example, S. Tiley-Nel, "Guy Atwater Gardner (1881–1959)". In S. Tiley-Nel (ed.) *Mapungubwe remembered: contributions to Mapungubwe by the University of Pretoria*. Johannesburg: Chris van Rensburg Publications (Pty) Ltd, 2011, pp. 22–24.

[107] Mapungubwe Archive, copy of P. Tobias, "Note on carbon-14 dates". In A. Galloway (ed.), *The skeletal remains of Bambandyanalo*. Johannesburg: University of the Witwatersrand, 1959, p. xi.

[108] Mapungubwe Archive, UP/AGL/D/1372/2, letter from Van Riet Lowe to the Registrar of the University of Pretoria, 6 May 1950; see also A. Meyer, *The Iron Age sites of Greefswald: stratigraphy and chronology of the sites and a history of investigations*, Pretoria: University of Pretoria, 1998, p. 24.

Figure 2.2. Early excavations at the site of K2 in 1936 by Capt. G. A Gardner.

of paramount importance, and had hoped to include race and the importance of cultural traditions of people as core Mapungubwe concepts. Coertze influenced and controlled not only Gardner's published findings as well as much of the Mapungubwe literature that followed during the post War period and thus, underlying racially motivated research continued.[109]

In *Mapungubwe Volume I*, Fouché accepted without empirical evidence that the Mapungubwe inhabitants were of Sotho or Shona origin and refused to consider the findings of the Witwatersrand University physical anthropologist, Alexander Galloway. He concluded that the Mapungubwe human remains were classified as Boskopoid, hence not of black African or Bantu descent, but instead proposed a Khoisan ancestry.[110] Whilst the argument of a biological basis for Mapungubwe culture fuelled physical anthropologists views and academic rivalry, the strains of Mapungubwe's racial theories were institutionalised. This historical contestation, whether directly or indirectly only, later influenced future literature

as well as further research about Mapungubwe's racial affiliations.[111]

Debates around the human remains and race continued also during the time when P.J. Coertze had requested Gardner to rewrite entire chapters to accommodate the new C14 radiocarbon dates acquired for Mapungubwe. Despite suffering severely from throat cancer, Gardner finished the draft of *Volume II* and re-typed sixteen pages, a mere few hours before his death in December 1959.[112] Gardner's Mapungubwe volume was criticised not only for its delay, but similarly his obscure interpretations of the site. For example, he suggested a Bronze Age culture and presented his own interpretations of North African Hamitic origins for Mapungubwe as a Neolithic site. These obscure conclusions unfortunately eventually reached the public domain.[113] According to Dubow, Gardner's results

---

[109] See opinion article by Stellenbosch social anthropologist, C.S. van der Waal, "Apartheid thinking in academia", *Die Burger*, 8 June 2013.
[110] A. Galloway, "The skeletal remains of Mapungubwe". In L. Fouché (ed.), *Mapungubwe: ancient Bantu civilization on the Limpopo: reports on excavations at Mapungubwe (Northern Transvaal) from February 1933 to June 1935.* Cambridge: Cambridge University Press, 1937, pp. 32–101; A. Galloway, *The skeletal remains of Bambandyanalo.* Johannesburg: Witwatersrand University Press, 1959.

[111] Other physical anthropologists later re-examined the human skeletal material and concluded that they did have distinct Negroid affiliations, see, G.P. Rightmire, "Iron Age skulls from southern Africa re-assessed by multiple discriminant analysis, *African Journal of Physical Anthropology* 33 (2), 1970, pp. 147–168.
[112] See biography of Gardner by S. Tiley-Nel, "Guy Atwater Gardner (1881–1959)". In S. Tiley-Nel (ed.) *Mapungubwe remembered: contributions to Mapungubwe by the University of Pretoria.* Johannesburg: Chris van Rensburg Publications (Pty) Ltd, 2011, pp. 22–24.
[113] "First Transvaal Bantu? Bronze Age site' new development in the Limpopo Valley", *The Star*, 12 October 1935.

ought to be contextualised, "as a product of the pre-war era of archaeological and anthropological thought".[114]

During the time of the delayed publication of *Volume II*, Gardner had continued to publish, presenting his Hamitic ancient Egyptian origins, and misinterpretations of pre-Bantu origins, thus fuelling the race migration paradigms.[115] Whilst Gardner had previously practiced archaeology in Egypt and in England, he did not have much or enough experience of South African archaeology.[116] Some scholars were sympathetic about the delay in publication, which was beyond Gardner's control, as well as the conditions under which he worked with seasonal outbreaks of malaria. Although in Brian Fagan's review of Gardner's research, he claimed that *Mapungubwe Volume II* was, "a landmark in Iron Age Studies in southern Africa", he doubted that the idea of Mapungubwe as an Iron Age culture could be exclusively identified with any one particular race.[117]

Despite evident criticism of Gardner's work for several decades, this did not dampen his research record on the subject of Mapungubwe and he published several other important papers.[118] In 1955, Gardner did however acknowledge that "the failure to publish even a preliminary report on the excavations at the farm named *Greefswald 37 MS* in the northern Transvaal during the years 1935–40" lead towards a misapprehension of what was excavated and the conclusions". Gardner went on to add that, "it would be tragic indeed if the Phoenician, Sabaens, Galla and Sardinians, danced an impossible historical fandango on the sandy summit of Mapungubwe Hill" and stated that if his six years of carefully excavating the site "without some written record of what was accomplished all our work is likely to be relegated to the limbo of the lost".[119]

Compounding problems increased as news at the University of Pretoria arrived from the Department of the Interior that they were no longer prepared to continue funding the archaeological research for the years 1941 and 1942. Although the archaeological work on Mapungubwe Hill remained incomplete, Van Riet Lowe recommended instead a "stronger ethnological flavour" and endorsed the appointment of the linguist and ethnologist, J.A. Engelbrecht replaced him as the new Director of Field

Operations.[120] Van Riet Lowe emphasised the following in a letter to the Archaeological Committee:

> Nonetheless I must repeat that I am satisfied that from an archaeological point of view, further work on the hill not add materially to what we already know... I have no doubt that Prof. Engelbrecht... will give the Committee a stronger ethnological flavour-which is now more necessary than ever.[121]

As a result, Mapungubwe research soon became ineluctably shaped by studies in ethnology and *volkekunde* as anthropologists and ethnologists such as J.A. Engelbrecht, N.J. van Warmelo,[122] and W.T.H. Beukes[123] sat as members on the University of Pretoria Mapungubwe Committee. Collectively they decided on the future direction of Mapungubwe research. Yet, following the aftermath of the Second World War, together with the National Party taking over power in 1948 and apartheid becoming institutionalised in South Africa, research faded. The Archaeological Committee of the University of Pretoria was eventually dissolved in 1947 and since the Committee was responsible for research funds, Mapungubwe research and publications temporarily ceased.[124]

2.3. Post war studies: 1950s to 1960s

The 1950s signalled a major turning point as research moved deliberately away from archaeological enquiry towards ethnological investigations, and by 1954 it was envisaged that research could continue for at least another eight years at Mapungubwe. Early in 1954, J.G. Strijdom, then the Minister of Lands and leader of the Transvaal group of Afrikaner Nationalists, proposed that the University of Pretoria needed to reinvestigate the farm *Greefswald* on condition that archaeological enquiry was done by the Department of Volkekunde.[125] In the interim,

---

[114] S. Dubow, *Scientific racism in modern South Africa*. Cambridge: Cambridge University Press, 1995, p. 100.

[115] G.A. Gardner, "Hottentot culture on the Limpopo". *South African Archaeological Bulletin*, 4(16), 1949, pp. 116–12.

[116] S. Tiley-Nel, "Guy Atwater Gardner (1881–1959)". In S. Tiley-Nel (ed.) *Mapungubwe remembered: contributions to Mapungubwe by the University of Pretoria*. Johannesburg: Chris van Rensburg Publications (Pty) Ltd, 2011, pp. 22–24.

[117] See B. Fagan, "Review of Mapungubwe, Volume II by G.A. Gardner". *Journal of African History* 5(2), 1964, pp. 314–316.

[118] G.A. Gardner, "Mapungubwe and Bambandyanalo". *South African Archaeological Bulletin* 11(42), 1956, pp. 55–56; G.A. Gardner, "The shallow bowls of Mapungubwe". *South African Archaeological Bulletin* 14(53), 1959, pp. 35–37.

[119] G.A. Gardner, "Mapungubwe 1935–1940". *South African Archaeological Bulletin* 10(39), 1955, p. 73.

[120] J.A. Engelbrecht, an expert in Korana studies, and a linguist by training founded the Department of Ethnology at the University of Pretoria and together with other Afrikaner *volkekundiges*, or "ethnic scientists" focused on the concept of culture, race, traditions and the social order of African people, see A. Kuper, "The work of anthropologists in Southern Africa". In, B. de L'Estoile, F. Neiburg and L. Sigaud (eds.), *Empires, nations and natives: anthropology and state-making*. Durham & London: Duke University Press, 2002, pp. 277–297.

[121] Transvaal Museum Archive, T.M. 10/39 (File 100) UP/MA/TVL/004, C. van Riet Lowe, letter to the Registrar of the University of Pretoria, 9 September 1940.

[122] Dr. Nicholas Jacobus van Warmelo was the Chief Ethnologist of the Department of Native Affairs (NAD) from 1930 until 1969, he sat on the Mapungubwe Committee briefly and contributed to recording some of the oral history and accounted at the time that certain traditions recalled occupation of come communities at Mapungubwe. The Van Warmelo archives are a wealth of untapped archival and historical information that have the potential to add value to the Mapungubwe narrative.

[123] W.T.H. (Wiets) Beukes was an anthropologist who held the position of honorary Curator of the Ethnological division at the Transvaal Museum from 1934 and was a Senior Lecturer at the University of Pretoria as Head of Bantu Administration until 1951.

[124] S. Tiley-Nel, "Sermons in stone, poetry in potsherds: the history of the Mapungubwe collection". In S. Tiley-Nel (ed.) *Mapungubwe remembered: contributions to Mapungubwe by the University of Pretoria*. Johannesburg: Chris van Rensburg Publications (Pty) Ltd, 2011, pp. 174–195.

[125] In 1952, the University of Pretoria had awarded J.G. Strijdom an honorary Doctorate in Public Administration. The year that Mapungubwe

Figure 2.3. Heinrich Sentker (1915-1983) excavations on the Southern Terrace in 1953.

presumably due to the absence of an internal professional archaeologist, students were relied upon to conduct further Mapungubwe research. Under permissions from the Historical Monuments Commission (1923–1969) intermittent research managed to continue in 1953 and 1954 by a student named, H.F. Sentker who undertook limited, but detailed excavations during this period.[126]

Sentker's research results, which were never published, only appeared fifteen years later in an Afrikaans field report.[127] This very brief field report (the only one produced in the 1950s) outlined basic, limited and systematic excavations covering a stratigraphic study of the area on the base of Mapungubwe Hill known as the southern Terrace, yet provided no interpretation or conclusive findings. Surprisingly the report provided neither interpretation nor any additional ethnological or anthropological knowledge about Mapungubwe. In 1956 there was a "sudden growth" and "re-arrangement of personnel" in the Department of *Volkekunde* at the University which brought any temporary excavations to

a halt.[128] After the Second World War however, other than Gardner's papers already mentioned, a few important archaeological papers on Mapungubwe's trade glass beads were published in 1956[129] and the first preliminary survey of the rock art of the Mapungubwe region appeared only in 1960.[130] Furthermore, this post War period further perpetuated the controversy of Mapungubwe's origins, marking the climax of the "racial diffusion" tradition in South African anthropology.[131]

The ethnological emphasis of a "Mapungubwe Culture" firmly took root from the early 1960s onwards when cultural anthropologists such as P.J. Coertze theoretically equated culture with racial ethnicity.[132] In 1950, P.J. Coertze had been appointed as the Head of *Volkekunde* at the University of Pretoria, which resulted in his control of the Mapungubwe excavations, yet under the guise of *volkekunde* or anthropology. Coertze took on an openly cultural approach and as the Head of the Department heavily influenced and prejudiced the Mapungubwe research findings at a time when *Volkekunde* took

---

research was renewed also coincided with J.G. Strijdom was elected leader of the National Party on 30 November 1954 and then became Prime Minister of South Africa. Strijdom was regarded as the "Lion of the North" and upheld very strong racial policies perpetuating white minority rule and carried on the implementation of ethnic segregation and apartheid.

[126] See more information by F.H. Boot, "Obituary: H F Sentker". *The South African Archaeological Bulletin* 39(140), Dec.1984, p. 143.

[127] H.F. Sentker, Mapungubwe 1953–1954. Ongepubliseerde verslag. Pretoria: Universiteit van Pretoria, 1969.

[128] C.H. Rautenbach, (ed.) et al., *Ad Destinatum. Gedenkboek van die Universiteit van Pretoria*. Johannesburg: Voortrekkerpers Beperk, 1960, p. 123.

[129] W.G.N. Sleen, "Trade-wind beads". *Man* 65 (Feb. 1956), pp. 27–29.

[130] M. Schoonraad, "Preliminary survey of rock art of the Limpopo Valley". *South African Archaeological Bulletin* 15 (57), 1960, pp. 10–13.

[131] S. Dubow, *Scientific racism in modern South Africa*. Cambridge: Cambridge University Press, 1995, p. 102.

[132] P.J. Coertze, "Ras en Kultuur". *Hertzog-Annale van die Suid-Afrikaanse Akademie vir Wetenskap en Kuns: Jaarboek* V. Pretoria: Suid-Afrikaanse Akademie vir Wetenskap en Kuns, 1958, pp. 53–56.

institutional rooting at the University of Pretoria.[133] Furthermore, the "muting of the role played by racism and racial ideology in twentieth century South Africa" had to some extent been reflected and filtered through in the literature on the history of *volkekunde*.[134]

Although the University of Pretoria was considered one of the major seats or "bastions"[135] of *volkekunde* (only later referred to as anthropology) the literature demonstrated a clearly distinctive Afrikaner nationalist ethnological tradition.[136] Nonetheless, despite the overwhelming influence of *volkekundiges*, ethnologists and anthropologists, there was a literary silence or deliberate stillness to be found in the Mapungubwe literature of this particular period. This might have been because Archaeology as a discipline was not an independent department as it was rather sub-assumed under the discipline of *volkekunde* in the early 1960s. Criticism of the scientific merits of *volkekunde* was much more rife than it was in archaeology, as this was considered a "questionable discipline in South Africa because of the racism that *volkekunde* espoused in its 'scientific' support for atomizing African communities into 'ethnic' groups and thus relegating them to Bantustans in terms of apartheid policy".[137] This is reflected in the total absence of cultural anthropological literature in post War Mapungubwe studies.

Although P.J. Coertze never published among the *volkekunde* fraternity on Mapungubwe, he strongly supported connections between racial differences and cultural achievement. He was overwhelmingly concerned with cultural and social aspects of ethnicity, and suggested that race was inherent and linked to levels of civilisation.[138] While this was a period of political instability and the University's recognition as an academic institution was epitomised by Afrikaner nationalist authority, the focus on Mapungubwe research shifted somewhat to avoid the question of "race". Instead, the South African Iron Age was investigated from social and economic points of view, particularly from a materialist position directing attention to Mapungubwe's material culture. At this time, a few specialist reports mainly by scholars from the University of

the Witwatersrand focused on the Mapungubwe ceramics and glass beads.[139]

Towards the end of the 1950s and early 1960s, Mapungubwe had moreover highlighted a distinct rift between the physical anthropologists and the cultural anthropologists and the 'new archaeology'. Fagan in particular challenged the racial undertones of Mapungubwe's previous studies, but ignored the obvious discrepancies between the evidence derived from physical anthropology and archaeology.[140]

The professionalization of archaeology in South Africa only truly flourished from the 1960s onwards, which coincided with a period of economic boom at many South African universities. Before this, the discipline had a relatively low profile.[141] This post War period also included the abandonment of the "Bantu Period" in favour of the adaptation of the Iron Age and according to Dubow, was "liberated from the paralysis of an unchanging past and incorporated fully into the broad reach of pre-colonial southern African prehistory."[142] Dubow claims that having been "stung by criticism of Gardner's report", Roger Summers, the Zimbabwean archaeologist was approached by the University of Pretoria in 1966 to examine the collection and review the archaeological research at Mapungubwe.

According to Dubow, Summers declined the position because his methods and interpretations would perhaps be "in conflict" with those of the University of Pretoria.[143] However, correspondence indicates that Summers was willing and intended on first viewing the Mapungubwe collection and making excavation recommendations to J.F. Eloff who would then submit them for P.J. Coertze's consideration, the then Head of the Department.[144] Perhaps it was intended that Summers could aim at working on Mapungubwe in conjunction with his research in Rhodesia. Summers examined the early files and historical records as an archival foundation to eventually produce a manuscript entitled, *Mapungubwe Reconsidered* unfortunately and sadly it was never published.[145]

[133] C.H. Rautenbach, (ed.) et al., *Ad Destinatum. Gedenkboek van die Universiteit van Pretoria*. Johannesburg: Voortrekkerpers Beperk, 1960, p. 123.

[134] A. Banks, "Fathering *volkekunde*: race and culture in the ethnological writings of Werner Eiselen, Stellenbosch University, and 1926–1936." *Anthropology Southern Africa* 38(3), 2015, pp. 163–179.

[135] J. Sharp, "The roots and development of *Volkekunde* in South Africa". *Journal of Southern African Studies* 18(1), 1981, pp. 16–36.

[136] For an overview of the intellectual journey from *volkekunde* to anthropology, see C.S. (Kees) van der Waal, "Long walk from volkekunde to anthropology: reflections on representing the human in South Africa". *Anthropology Southern Africa* 38(3 & 4), 2015, pp. 216–234.

[137] J. Carruthers, "Mapungubwe: an historical and contemporary analysis of a World Heritage cultural landscape". *Koedoe* 49(1), 2006, p. 8.

[138] See, P.J. Coertze, "'n Prinsipiële en feitelike inleiding tot studie van die bevolkingsverhoudingsvraagstuk in Suid-Afrika". *Tydskrif vir Rasse-Aangeleenthede* 22(3), 1971, pp. 106–108.

[139] C. van Riet Lowe, *The glass beads of Mapungubwe*. Union of South Africa, Department of Education, Arts and Science Archaeological Survey, 1955; J.F. Schofield, *Primitive Pottery*. Cape Town: South African Archaeological Society, 1948.

[140] B.M. Fagan, "The Greefswald sequence: Bambandyanalo and Mapungubwe". In J.D. Fage and R. Oliver (eds.), *Papers in African Prehistory*. Cambridge: Cambridge University Press, 1970, p. 173.

[141] J. Deacon, "The professionalization of archaeology in the 1960". In P. Robertshaw (ed.), *A history of African archaeology*. London: James Currey Ltd. 1990, pp. 50–51.

[142] S. Dubow, *Scientific racism in modern South Africa*. Cambridge: Cambridge University Press, 1995, p. 103; also see for example, M. Hall, *The changing past: farmers, kings, and traders in southern Africa, 200–1869*. Cape Town: David Philip, 1987.

[143] S. Dubow, *Scientific racism in modern South Africa*. Cambridge: Cambridge University Press, 1995, p. 103.

[144] Mapungubwe Archive, UP/AGL/D/2055, letter from R. Summers, The National Museums of Southern Rhodesia to J. F. Eloff, Department of Archaeology, 31 December 1965.

[145] Mapungubwe Archive, UP/AGL/D/2054, R. Summers unpublished paper titled, "Mapungubwe Reconsidered", 1966.

Beyond its archaeological value, Summers's manuscript is historically insightful from an interpretation perspective as he methodically compiled notes about the excavations, research gaps and the Mapungubwe controversy. Summers viewed the controversy as mainly legal, anthropological and archaeological, stating that Mapungubwe had become "a grave" to some archaeological reputations. This is also the first time that the early historical records are referred to as an "archive", as Summers also reviewed the personalities involved in Mapungubwe's early history. This is a poignant moment in the deliberate "turn" towards an archive. Eventually, due to the lack of suitably trained Iron Age archaeologists in South Africa and a decline in government support, all research and excavations ceased at Mapungubwe and Coertze instead focused rather on the editorship of Gardner's *Mapungubwe Volume II*, which was eventually published in 1967.[146]

2.4. Discipline years of Archaeology: 1970s to 1980s

Although the conclusions drawn about Mapungubwe over thirty years (1930–1960), point to a rich African Iron Age "culture" that invigorated South African archaeology at the time, the proposed dates of Mapungubwe's origins to AD 1200 provided the first empirical challenge to the myth of the empty land.[147] At the University of Cape Town, the subsequent appointment of an international and Cambridge trained archaeologist, Ray Inskeep, followed in the footsteps of A.J.H. Goodwin, South Africa's first professional archaeologist in prehistory. Inskeep belonged to the first generation of academic archaeologists in southern Africa and made serious attempts to address the issue of ethics in archaeology, the development of sound theoretical approaches, and claimed that there was a lack of professionalism within the discipline.[148]

Inskeep produced an influential work, *The peopling of southern Africa* in which he reviewed the advances of South African archaeology both conceptually and theoretically, interpreting aspects of Mapungubwe within the Iron Age focus, which was central to the peopling of Africa.[149] By 1968, archaeology was accepted as a scientific discipline in the Department of Anthropology at the University of Pretoria further spurring improved conditions for professional archaeology at Mapungubwe.[150]

Advances in the discipline enabled the University of Pretoria the opportunity to resume research at Mapungubwe, this time under permission from the South African Defence Force (SADF) as the archaeological site was located on the border of South Africa. This apartheid period was characterised by an increase in military protection with security and patrols by the infantry of the SADF, together with the South African Police (SAP) who controlled the area due to its geographic intersection along South Africa's borderline due to the large scale Border War of 1975–1989. Historically, the SADF had controlled the area from 1933 until 1969, when the terrain was used as a base for artillery units. In 1969, the South African government handed over the farm, *Greefswald*, for military control and access, with the provision that archaeological research remained exclusively with the University of Pretoria.[151]

Prof. Andrie Meyer, then a young lecturer in the Department of Archaeology, stated that the SADF in fact granted the University of Pretoria full access to the archaeological sites and further undertook to erect fences round the sites, which were (apparently) out of bounds to military personnel.[152] After 1974, the Vhembe Military Terrain, as it was known, continued to be used as an infantry (foot soldiers) base and from 1976 the Soutpansberg Military Area Headquarters at Messina were responsible for managing the property.[153]

2.5. Interjection of Greefswald's dark history: 1970-1974

Furthermore, a darker past about Mapungubwe has since come to light, in that from 1970 until 1974,[154] the farm *Greefswald* served as a drug rehabilitation centre and psychiatric "torture residence" for homosexual and drug-abusing conscripts under the treatment of Dr. Aubrey Levine, the chief military psychiatrist for the SADF military forces.[155] *Greefswald* was purportedly Levine's

---

[146] G.A. Gardner, *Mapungubwe, Volume II, Report on excavations at Mapungubwe and Bambandyanalo in the Transvaal from 1935–1940*. P.J. Coertze (ed.), Pretoria: Van Schaik Publishers, 1963.

[147] S. Marks, "South Africa: the myth of the empty land". *History Today* 30(1), 1980, pp. 7–12.

[148] J. Deacon, "The professionalization of archaeology in the 1960". In P. Robertshaw (ed.), *A history of African archaeology*. London: James Currey Ltd. 1990, pp. 42–50.

[149] R.R. Inskeep, *The peopling of southern Africa*. Cape Town: David Philip, 1978.

[150] A. Meyer, *The Iron Age sites of Greefswald: stratigraphy and chronology of the sites and a history of investigations*. Pretoria: University of Pretoria, 1998, p. 25.

[151] Mapungubwe Archive, see letter from the Department of Agricultural Credit and Land Tenure to the Chief of Logistic Services of the South African Defence Force (SADF), 21 November 1968.

[152] A. Meyer, *The Iron Age sites of Greefswald: stratigraphy and chronology of the sites and a history of investigations*. Pretoria: University of Pretoria, 1998, p. 26.

[153] On 25 July 1967, Mapungubwe and the surrounding environs of *Greefswald*, together with the neighbouring farms *Samaria* and *Den Staat* were proclaimed as the Vhembe Nature Reserve. Later the property was transferred to the Transvaal Provincial Administration, under the Chief Directorate of Nature and Environmental Conservation until 1992, to form part of the future nucleus for a larger Limpopo conservation area.

[154] Mapungubwe Archive, unappraised, a SADF Vhembe Military Terrain 25 years (1967–1992) commemorative card for their silver jubilee contains this information which confirms these dates for *Greefswald*. The SADF's environmental services emblem as a water-mark forms the background for the text, 1992.

[155] L. Pollecut, 2009, "Unlocking South Africa's military archives". In K. Allan (ed.), *Paper Wars: Access to information in South Africa*. Johannesburg: Witwatersrand University Press, 2009, p. 136; see also South African History Archives (SAHA), <http://foip.saha.org.za/static/paper-wars-access-to-information-in-south-africa>, access: 2018.06.06. Pollecut makes specific reference to documents held by the Department of Defence (DOD) Archives, Volume 47 *War Resister*, "*Greefswald* Works Committee File nos. GG521/3/5/2/2 Jan-Nov 1977.

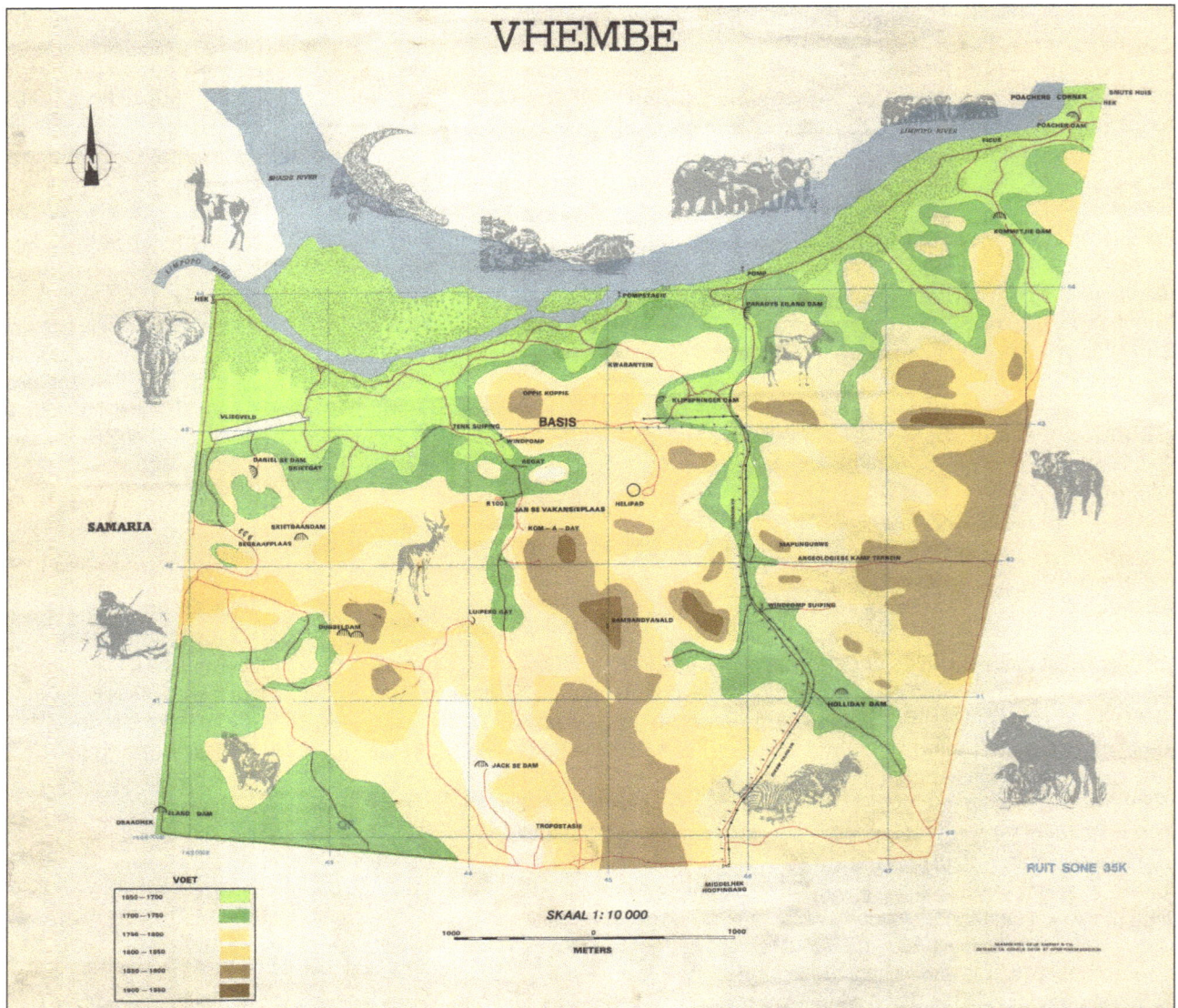

Figure 2.4. Map of Vhembe Base at Greefswald indicating quarantine and other military areas by 47 Survey Squadron compiled by the Commandant of the Northern Transvaal, ca.1975.

"bizarre project", where according to R.M. Kaplan, Levine "coerced army drug users into forced hard labour" to "cure" their addiction.[156] Medical abuse utilising aversion therapy was punitive and coercive shock therapy used on *Greefswald* in the drug treatment programme. According to V. Reddy, inmates were detained in isolation for about three months and during the time *Greefswald* operated, the farm was used as some form of implicit threat to give patients the choice of going there, or "consenting" to aversion therapy. *Greefswald* was considered the most feared camp by most conscripts, it was a despicable

"military prison where suffering, horror and deprivation was the norm".[157]

In his doctoral study, R. Sinclair states that, "certainly in the *Greefswald* file, [Levine's] name comes repeatedly as the person *Greefswald* staff perceived as being in charge".[158] Other accounts of *Greefswald* atrocities have since surfaced on popular platforms, such as the 2014 book by Gordon Torr titled, *Kill Yourself & Count to 10*.[159] This semi-autobiographical work is by a former SADF

---

[156] R.M. Kaplan, "The Aversion Project - psychiatric abuses in the South African Defence Force during the apartheid era". *South African Medical Journal* 91(3), 2001, pp. 216–217; R.M. Kaplan, "The bizarre career of Aubrey Levin: from abuser of homosexual conscripts to molester of male prisoners". *Forensic Research & Criminological International Journal* 2(5), 2016, p. 69; see also R. Poplak, "Dr Shock: how an apartheid-era psychiatrist went from torturing gay soldiers in South Africa to sexually abusing patients in Alberta", *The Walrus*, 19 September 2015, <https://thewalrus.ca/doctor-shock/>, access: 2018.06.06.

[157] V. Reddy, Moffies, stabanis, and lesbos: the political construction of queer identities in Southern Africa. PhD dissertation, University of Kwa-Zulu Natal, 2005. p. 144; see also for example, M. van Zyl, et al. *The aVersion Project: Human rights abuses of gays and lesbians in the SADF by health workers during the apartheid era*, Cape Town: Simply Said and Done, 1999, p. 67.
[158] R. Sinclair, The office treatment of white, South African, homosexual men and the consequent reaction of Gay liberation from the 1930s to 2000. Unpublished PhD thesis, Rand Afrikaans University, 2004, p.170.
[159] See, G. Torr, *Kill yourself and count to 10*. Cape Town: Penguin Random House, 2014.

VHEMBE MILITARY TERRAIN

1. The farm Greefswald is situated at the confluence of the Limpopo and the Shashi rivers where South Africa, Zimbabwe and Botswana meet. The South African Defence Force controls the area since 1933.

2. From 1933 to 1969 the terrain was used as a base for artillery units, from 1970 to 1974 as a rehabilitation centre for drug addicts, and since 1974 as an infantry base. The Soutpansberg Military Area Headquarters at Messina, whose emblem appears on the envelope, is responsible for managing the property.

3. Due to its particular environmental assets Greefswald, together with the neighbouring farms Samaria and Den Staat, was proclaimed as the Vhembe Nature Reserve on 25 July 1967. The name "Vhembe" originates from a post office which was situated on the farm Den Staat. Vhembe is the Venda name for the Limpopo River and means "the river that digs deep down", refering to the underground water flow of the Limpopo.

4. Vhembe is renowned for the Mapungubwe koppie which is of particular archaeological value. Two archaeological sites on the property were proclaimed National monuments in 1983 and 1984. Bushmen paintings also occur. A cottage which General Jan Smuts used for relaxation and for his own "bush deliberations" is situated just within the eastern boundary.

5. Vhembe is home to some of the few remaining patches of riverine forest along the Limpopo. Large wild fig trees occur, the largest of which has a canopy diameter of 48m and a stem circumference of 11m. Numerous rare mammal, bird and reptile species as well as a variety of game species occur at Vhembe. Impressive sandstone formations add to the environmental value of the property. On 11 June 1987 Vhembe was registered as a Natural Heritage Site.

6. The property is being transferred to the Transvaal Provincial Administration (Chief Directorate of Nature and Environmental Conservation) during 1992 to be managed as a nucleus area for a future larger Limpopo conservation area.

7. The SADF's environmental services emblem forms the background for this text. The castle portrays the SADF's environmental involvement, whilst the zebra, which occurs in all the provinces, simbolizes the countrywide conservation effort of the SADF. *"Conservamus"* means *"We Conserve"*.

Figure 2.5. Vhembe Military Terrain South African Defence Force.

conscript who has novelised the account of the time he spent in *Greefswald* detention barracks under the apartheid regime. Cynically, however, A. Smith has argued that this is only a work of "fiction" and that testimonial literature as historical documentation should be viewed as an "unreliable source".[160] Nonetheless, it must be taken into account that military records are confidential, and whilst testimonial has the potential to shed light on some aspects of the historical period, one should further recognise interpretational freedom and its ability to possibly distort history or events of the past. There have been no academic interventions on this very critical part of Mapungubwe's "secret history" and the Mapungubwe Archive remains silent on many of the SADF activities, particularly since many of the *Greefswald* files still remain classified and embargoed as South African secret military documents.[161]

2.6. Archaeological Iron Age studies continued

During the apartheid era, Iron Age studies flourished, coupled with the strengthening of South African internal security forces and the expanding apartheid regime, any new developments in South African archaeology coincided with the general increase in improved archaeological methodology, as the value of professional archaeology also enjoyed better government funding particularly for Iron Age research.[162] Andrew Zipkin from Cornell University states that under apartheid, Iron Age research at Mapungubwe invigorated archaeology to the extent that conclusions provided the empirical challenge to the myth of the empty land, but also had the potential to reveal discoveries and results that had critical political implications. Zipkin affirms that, "the renaissance for archaeology in South Africa began in the late 1960s, spurred by economic development and an increasing culture and educational conscious government".[163]

Nonetheless, Martin Hall, a historical archaeologist from the University of Cape Town also argued that Iron Age archaeology exhibited pronounced political and social influence and posited that previous literature about the Iron Age of southern Africa focused mainly on the "Africaness" of the Iron Age and the diversity of African Iron Age culture. He further alluded to the personal politics of professional archaeologists, but is not specific about any literature and fails to provide factual evidence for his assumptions which appear to be rather based on a researcher's personal views on apartheid.[164]

---

[160] A. Smith, see the full article on slide share, <https://www.slideshare.net/AdrianLloydSmith1/kill-yourself-count-to-10-the-unreliability-of-testimonial-literature-as-historical-documantation-south-african-literature-49915181>, *s.a.* access: 2016.05.28.

[161] There are several records now accessible pertaining to the SADF and Greefswald as a notorious forced-labour camp for gay conscripts, some are available in the South African History Archive (SAHA) and Gay and Lesbian Archive (GALA), but Greefswald was certainly perceived as Dr Levine's sole creation. First exposed by the magazine, *Resister* in the *Journal of the Committee on South African War Resistance*, Dec. 1986- Jan 1987 (No.47.), pp. 11–17; see for example, M. van Zyl, et al. *The aVersion Project: Human rights abuses of gays and lesbians in the SADF by health workers during the apartheid era*, Cape Town: Simply Said and Done, 1999; Sentinel Projects, "The abuse of psychiatry in the SADF: I am first a soldier & then a psychiatrist", reproduced from 'Resister' magazine <sadf.sentinelprojects.com/1mil/thug1.html>, access: 2016.05.26; *Business Day*, "The horrors of the Vault", 9 December 2014; *Daily Maverick*, "Dr Shock is in the dock- and now his wife in under lock", 29 January 2013.

[162] A. Meyer, *The Iron Age sites of Greefswald: stratigraphy and chronology of the sites and a history of investigations.* Pretoria: University of Pretoria, 1998, pp. 25–26.

[163] A. Zipkin, Archaeology under apartheid: a preliminary investigation into the potential politicization of science in South Africa. Unpublished Honors thesis, New York, Cornell University, 2009, p. 27.

[164] See, for example: M. Hall, "Hidden history: Iron Age archaeology in Southern Africa". In P. Robertshaw (ed.), *A history of African archaeology*. London: James Currey Ltd., 1990; M. Hall, "The burden of tribalism: the Social Context of Southern African Iron Age Studies". *American Antiquity* 49(3), 1984, pp. 455–467.

Similar to Hall's hypotheses, Nick Shepherd, based at the Centre for African Studies at the University of Cape Town, shares views that archaeology in South Africa was certainly politicised in the 1960s. He argues that archaeology as a profession was closely connected to the minority rule government that had control over funding and excavation permits.[165] Both Cape Town-based scholars, Hall and Shepherd, are known to be critical commentators on South Africa archaeology and its history. Both held strong views on the social and political contexts of Iron Age archaeology, but never worked at Mapungubwe nor published papers specifically on the subject. Yet, they both inferred to the growing the rift between English- and Afrikaans speaking academics and exposed the ideological contexts i.e. colonialism and apartheid, within which 'prehistories' were written and are being written.[166] Between the 1960s, 1970s and late 1980s (even delving into the early 1990s), archaeological literature on the Iron Age in South Africa definitely thrived a period labelled by Zipkin, as the "Apartheid-Professional Period". In his thesis, Zipkin tested the specific assertions made about Iron Age archaeology during apartheid, particularly Hall and Shepherd's perspectives. He further explored the various links on how and why archaeology thrived under the apartheid regime during the 1960s and 1970s, and suggests that the support from State in fact aided in the modernization of archaeology in South Africa and concludes that the politics of the discipline are incorrectly claimed.[167] Zipkin states that:

> These processes occurred in concert with the increasing legislative elaboration of the apartheid system by the National Party government ... seeking all the trappings of a modern state, the government spent huge sums of boom time money on cultural and scientific institutions including archaeological endeavours.[168]

Responding to this period of resurgence in the discipline of archaeology and new government patronage, the University of Pretoria as partial beneficiaries of the National Party government from the 1960s onwards, fully supported Iron Age research which they mainly stated as "*Greefswald*", not always attributing the name "Mapungubwe". J.F. Eloff's *Greefswald* research was funded by the *Raad vir Geesteswetenskaplike Navorsing* (RGN) or the Human Sciences Research Council (HSRC) which largely focused on pioneering regional histories.[169]

Eloff's five volume series reports, *Die Kulture van Greefswald*[170] (The Cultures of *Greefswald*) was obviously produced in Afrikaans, suggesting that research for Mapungubwe was largely supported by the political context of the University during this time and likewise inaccessible to many English-speaking academics. Eloff was regarded as a sound academic, with a broad knowledge in archaeology, anthropology and conservation. He held several professional positions and served as President of the Southern African Archaeological Society, a member of the Historical Monuments Council, and later the National Monuments Council and was also a member of the Human Sciences Research Council and a Faculty member of the Academy of Arts and Science.[171] Although Eloff's research on Mapungubwe spanned from the 1960s until 1983, his subsequent field reports on excavations at *Greefswald* were for reasons unknown, never published.[172] However, it is acknowledged that academics in this period were mainly tasked to teach and not to publish. Yet, a scant publication record further gave the impression that Afrikaans-speaking academics operated inside myopic structures and outside international academia discourse, particularly on Mapungubwe Iron Age research.

According to the University of Cape Town based archaeologist, Janette Deacon, archaeology in South Africa only truly came of age in the 1970s, as research was influenced by several changes. These included the revised legislation in the National Monuments Act No. 28 of 1969; tightening laws on those governing collections and excavations on prehistoric sites; as well as the need for recognition of professional status. In 1969, the Southern Society for Quaternary Research was established, and in the same year a Department of Archaeology was established at the Transvaal Museum and in 1970, the Southern African Association of Archaeologists. These developments furthered Mapungubwe research, as the effects of social and political events influenced Iron Age research goals. In particular, generous financial support for archaeological research by government agencies such as the Council for Scientific Industrial Research (CSIR) ensued.[173]

As a direct result of the financial economic boom, there was a professional surge in archaeological research throughout

---

[165] N. Shepherd, "The politics of archaeology in Africa". *Annual Review of Anthropology* 31, 2002, pp. 189–209.

[166] See for example, M. Hall, "The burden of tribalism: the social context of southern African Iron Age studies". *American Antiquity* 49(3), 1984, pp. 455–467.

[167] A. Zipkin, Archaeology under apartheid: a preliminary investigation into the potential politicization of science in South Africa. Unpublished Honors thesis, New York, Cornell University, 2009, pp. 27–28; 48–55.

[168] A. Zipkin, Archaeology under apartheid: a preliminary investigation into the potential politicization of science in South Africa. Unpublished Honors thesis, New York, Cornell University, 2009, p. 27.

[169] E.S. van Eeden, "Pioneering regional history studies in South Africa: reflections within the former section for regional history at the Human Sciences Research Council (HSRC). *Historia* 59(1) 2014, pp. 118–140.

[170] Mapungubwe Archive, J.F. Eloff, *Die Kulture van Greefswald*, Volumes I-V, Ongepubliseerde verslag aan die Raad vir Geesteswetenskaplike Navorsing. Pretoria: Universiteit van Pretoria, 1979.

[171] E. Judson, "A life history of J.F. Eloff". In J.A. van Schalkwyk (ed.), *Studies in honour of Professor J.F. Eloff*. Pretoria: Research by the National Cultural History Museum, Vol. 3, 1997, pp. 2–8.

[172] See J.F. Eloff, Greefswald-opgrawing 1980, Ongepubliseerde verslag, Pretoria: Universiteit van Pretoria, 1980; J.F. Eloff, Verslag oor opgrawingswerk op die plaas Greefswald gedurende April 1981, Ongepubliseerde verslag, Pretoria: Universiteit van Pretoria, 1981; J.F. Eloff, Verslag oor argeologiese navorsing op Greefswald gedurende April 1982, Ongepubliseerde verslag, Pretoria: Universiteit van Pretoria, 1982; J.F. Eloff, Verslag oor argeologiese navorsing op Greefswald gedurende April 1983, Ongepubliseerde verslag, Pretoria: Universiteit van Pretoria, 1983.

[173] J. Deacon, "The professionalization of archaeology in the 1960". In P. Robertshaw (ed.) *A history of African archaeology*. London: James Currey Ltd. 1990, pp. 52–53.

the late 1970s and 1980s at the University of Pretoria. Research by a new lead archaeologist Prof. A. Meyer filled the research gaps left by J.F. Eloff. Meyer continued systematic excavations and his research goals focused largely on cultural historical perspectives which included the cultural identification; reconstructing of the economy; technology and aspects of settlement; the description of stratification; settlement chronology; site features and artefact typologies, with the aim of understanding Mapungubwe within the context of the southern African Iron Age.[174] A number of specialist reports were produced on the Mapungubwe faunal remains, largely spearheaded by Elizabeth Voigt from the Archaeology Department within the Transvaal Museum.[175] There were also other reports from the British Museum by Dr Andrew Oddy on the technological analyses of the Mapungubwe gold[176] and Claire Davidson's chemical analysis of trade glass beads.[177]

Throughout the 1970s, and initially funded by the *Raad vir Geesteswetenskaplike Navorsing* (RGN), Meyer continued to conduct research under the guidance of Eloff, but they only co-authored one publication together in their twenty-years of collaboration.[178] Meyer, influenced by Inskeep's ethical approach and desire to improve professionalism, developed and applied new standards to archaeological fieldwork at Mapungubwe with a focus on detailed stratigraphic recording and meticulous excavation techniques.[179] The merging of the Department of Anthropology and the Department of Archaeology during the 1980s at the University intended to improve research support for *Greefswald*. According to Meyer though, research had to be postponed in 1988 mainly as a result of increased military activity on the northern border, as well as for the purpose of site maintenance until 1990.[180]

Figure 2.6. View of the University of Pretoria archaeological camp on Greefswald during the 1970s.

While research by both Eloff and Meyer from the University of Pretoria was descriptive and later shifted to explanatory models within cultural historical frameworks, there was a focus on specialist archaeological studies as Iron Age research became highly specialised. In general, Mapungubwe literature lacked theoretical rigour and wider interpretations to engage discourse with other institutions and Mapungubwe was not viewed within wider global contexts. Other emerging critical approaches towards archaeology arose in academia as socio-political disputes surfaced within the domains of Martin Hall's historical research as well as the structuralist approaches developed by Tom Huffman (1944–2022), an American-trained archaeologist at the University of the Witwatersrand, as cognitive archaeology. These interpretations were mostly from more liberal universities at the time, such as the University of the Witwatersrand and the University of Cape Town and thus contrasted starkly with those views held by the University of Pretoria. Compounding the critique was that many of the publications from the University of Pretoria during this period were published in Afrikaans. This further resulted in the isolation of Mapungubwe research results from popular consciousness, and as academics felt the effects of apartheid, they almost exclusively worked in segregated research institutions.[181]

Even though early 1990s Mapungubwe literature is somewhat sparse, there is an exception of specialised studies worth noting. These mainly stemmed from physical anthropology and biological literature regarding the paleodemography, health status and physical

---

[174] For a detailed outline of archaeological research on the Greefswald project and its phases see, A. Meyer, *The Iron Age sites of Greefswald: stratigraphy and chronology of the sites and a history of investigations*. Pretoria: University of Pretoria, 1998, pp. 24–34.

[175] E.A. Voigt, The faunal remains from Greefswald as a reflection of Iron Age economic and cultural activities. MA dissertation, University of Pretoria, 1978; E.A. Voigt, *Mapungubwe: an archaeo-zoological interpretation of an Iron Age community*. Pretoria: Transvaal Museum, 1983.

[176] A. Oddy, "On the trail of Iron Age Gold". *Transvaal Museum Bulletin* 19 (November 1983); A. Oddy, "Gold in the southern African Iron Age". *Gold Bulletin* 17(2), 1984, pp. 70–78.

[177] C.C. Davidson, "Three chemical groups of glass beads at the Greefswald sites", In J.F. Eloff (ed.), *Die Kulture van Greefswald* Vol. II, Ongepubliseerde verslag aan die Raad vir Geesteswetenskaplike Navorsing, Pretoria: Universiteit van Pretoria, 1979.

[178] J.F. Eloff and A. Meyer, "The Greefswald sites". In E.A. Voigt (ed.), *Guide to archaeological sites in the northern and eastern Transvaal*. Pretoria: Transvaal Museum, 1981.

[179] See for example, A. Meyer, *Navorsingsmetodiek. Inligtingformate vir argeologie veldwerk*. Pretoria: Universiteit van Pretoria, 2003; A. Meyer, "Stratigrafie van die ystertydperkterreine op Greefswald". *Suid-Afrikaanse Tydskrif vir Etnologie* 17(4) 1994, pp. 137–160; A. Meyer, "Stand van argeologiese insig in die volkerebewegings in Suid Afrika". *Suid-Afrikaanse Tydskrif vir Etnologie* 12(2), 1989, pp. 69–75.

[180] A. Meyer, *The Iron Age sites of Greefswald: stratigraphy and chronology of the sites and a history of investigations*. Pretoria: University of Pretoria, 1998, p. 33.

[181] M. Hall, "Hidden history: Iron Age archaeology in Southern Africa". In P. Robertshaw (ed.) *A history of African archaeology*. London: James Currey Ltd, 1990, p. 73.

characteristics of the Mapungubwe populations.[182] In fact, the 1990s witnessed a comparative boom in publication on the human remains specifically, despite the contributions of previous studies.[183] Knowledge about the human skeletal remains were required to be reassessed, as many questions remained unanswered about the biological affinities between the populations that occupied the two main sites of K2 and Mapungubwe.[184] Other research areas not previously considered, now included lifeways; health in the Iron Age; growth of children; dental and bone diseases, as well as population dynamics and for the first time, hints at the need for future research on aspects such as genetic or DNA analysis on the Mapungubwe human remains was recommended, perhaps as a solution to the ongoing contestations of origins.[185]

2.7. Post democracy years: 1994 to the 21st century

South African democracy in 1994 activated a stronger social and political focus on Mapungubwe studies from a diversity of post-colonial and post apartheid perspectives. This provided Mapungubwe literature the impetus for a growing emphasis on transdisciplinary, multidisciplinary and interdisciplinary research that was absent in previous research. The complexity and scale of Mapungubwe's research problems accumulated over nearly eight decades demanded a radical change in attitude and approach in moving researchers beyond the confines of their own discipline in order to explore new trajectories more apt for twenty-first century thinking.

Furthermore, as a result of emerging democratization, heritization and globalization, Mapungubwe literature now occupies a much larger place in historical, social and political consciousness than it did at the beginning of the decade. Open debates and discussions around Mapungubwe and its wider landscapes (both cultural and natural) and the role of communities ensued particularly during the post apartheid period.[186] In general, these studies addressed more complex ethical and social issues, as post colonial archaeological and archaeological ethnographic approaches unpacked the "micro-politics of archaeology"[187] and brought about new knowledge and

the desperately needed set of renewed conversations in literature about Mapungubwe.[188]

Conventional archaeological studies on Mapungubwe continued to flourish post 1994, however with a greater focus on re-considered, re-examined, re-interpreted, re-visited, and re-imagined approaches to the subject. This re-thinking or naissance of Mapungubwe was critically explored from several theoretical threads such as postmodern, post colonial, post apartheid and neoliberal views, perhaps as a means of attempting to unpack Mapungubwe's contested past to have meaning in contemporary society. The reconsideration of the past attempted to embrace the socio-political dimensionality that had been absent in South African archaeology and previous Mapungubwe studies. This period comprised a broad range of specialised studies, such as reassessments of the human burials and reviews of the skeletal remains,[189] to revisiting the faunal assemblages[190] and re-dating the Chinese celadon from Mapungubwe Hill.[191] It is important to mention that dating of the site was increasingly becoming more important, beyond the scientific merits of radiocarbon dating, of which there are only seven for Mapungubwe Hill. The imported items such as trade glass beads and Chinese celadon were used to also serve as social and chronological indicators as well as reliance on only ceramic typology for change as indications of chronology was waning and more scientific techniques and new types of analyses became more readily available in South Africa.

Two key archaeological studies post 1994 require specific mention as they have become standard reference Mapungubwe books. The first is Meyer's (1998), *The Iron Age sites of Greefswald: stratigraphy and chronology of the sites and a history of investigations*.[192] The second key book is Huffman's (2007), *Handbook to the Iron Age: the archaeology of pre-colonial farming societies in southern Africa*.[193] Likewise, post democracy literature argued that too much emphasis had been placed on ceramic

[182] For example, see M. Steyn and M. Henneberg, "Preliminary report on the paleodemography of the K2 and Mapungubwe populations (South Africa). *Human Biology* 66(1), 1994, pp. 105–120.

[183] M. Steyn and M. Henneberg, "Odontometric characteristics of the people from the Iron Age sites at Mapungubwe and K2 (South Africa). *Homo, Journal of Comparative Human Biology* 48(3), 1997, pp. 215–226; see also, M. Steyn and M. Henneberg, "Cranial growth in the prehistoric sample from K2 at Mapungubwe (South Africa) is population specific". *Homo, Journal of Comparative Human Biology* 48(1), 1997, pp. 62–71.

[184] M. Steyn, An assessment of the health status and physical characteristics of the prehistoric population from Mapungubwe. PhD thesis, University of Witwatersrand, 1994.

[185] M. Steyn, "A reassessment of the human skeletal remains from K2 and Mapungubwe". *South African Archaeological Bulletin* 52(165), 1997, pp. 14–20.

[186] I. Pikirayi, "Sharing the past: archaeology and community engagement in Southern Africa". In P. Stone and Z. Hui (eds.), *Academe, practice and the public*. London: Routledge, 2014, pp. 157–159.

[187] See N. Shepherd, "The politics of archaeology in Africa". *Annual Review of Anthropology* 31, 2002, pp. 189–209.

[188] See for example, R. King, "Archaeological naissance at Mapungubwe". *Journal of Social Archaeology* 11(3), 2011, pp. 311–333; R. King, "Teaching archaeological pasts in South Africa: historical and contemporary considerations of archaeological education". *Archaeologies* 8(2), 2012, pp. 85–115.

[189] M. Steyn, "A reassessment of the human skeletal remains from Mapungubwe and K2 (South Africa)". *South African Archaeological Bulletin* 52 (165), 1997, pp. 14–20; M. Steyn, "A review of the human skeletal remains from the Greefswald sites". In A. Meyer (ed.), *The archaeological sites of Greefswald*. Pretoria: University of Pretoria, 1998, pp. 287–291; M. Steyn, "The Mapungubwe gold graves revisited". *South African Archaeological Bulletin* 62(186), 2007, pp. 140–146.

[190] L. Hutten, K2 revisited: an archaeozoological study of an Iron Age site in the Northern Province, South Africa. Unpublished Msc dissertation, University of Pretoria, 2005.

[191] L.C. Prinsloo, N. Wood, M. Loubser, S.M.C. Verryn and S. Tiley, "The re-examination of Chinese celadon sherds from Mapungubwe a thirteenth century Iron Age site in South Africa using Raman spectroscopy, XRD and XRF". *Journal of Raman Spectroscopy* 36, 2005, pp. 806–816.

[192] A. Meyer, *The Iron Age sites of Greefswald: stratigraphy and chronology of the sites and a history of investigations*. Pretoria: University of Pretoria, 1998.

[193] T.N. Huffman, *Handbook to the Iron Age: the archaeology of pre-colonial farming societies in southern Africa*. Kwa-Zulu Natal: University of Kwa-Zulu Natal Press, 2007.

and associated typological studies and much of the archaeological literature that had dominated Mapungubwe for decades had been on the subject of Iron Age ceramics. While this is partly true, ceramic classification has established a vigorous structure for ordering of time and space, thus providing Mapungubwe's essential chronology together with the calibrated radiocarbon dates for the chronological dating sequence of Iron Age settlements in the Limpopo region.[194] However, there is a general cognisance of the parochial use of archaeological ceramics as the only means to understand Mapungubwe, but studies have significantly changed over recent decades. This is reflective in the diversity of literature on other material culture such as glass trade beads studies[195] and the research of metals,[196] as well as other insights into the economic, political and social changes which moulded increasingly complex societies between AD 900 and AD 1300.[197]

Another landmark publication dedicated to "rethinking" Mapungubwe is the *African Naissance* (2000) Goodwin Series by The South African Archaeological Society.[198] This collectors-type volume comprises twelve research papers devoted to Mapungubwe, and is the first time that such a wide range of research and up-to-date information with informed insight from well-recognised contributors, some of South Africa's most foremost archaeologists at the time, is presented in a single work. Considered as an important chapter in the history of southern Africa, this volume further aimed to serve wider interest than just academia, but also as an educational source book for teachers and has since become a Mapungubwe source book for researchers. The introduction to *African Naissance* by a leading and well-respected archaeologist, Tim Maggs, a leading archaeological authority from the University of Cape Town states, that:

> The term 'African Renaissance' carries great resonance, but for the historians and archaeologists the question will inevitably arise: what was the original African 'Golden Age' that will inspire the Renaissance - the rebirth of society and culture - in the new millennium? What is it that we in southern Africa can call upon in the post colonial era to serve as an appropriate model

from the past? The simple answer to this question is the theme and title of this volume.[199]

The second key volume presented as a research report committed to "rethinking" Mapungubwe as a "living legacy" is *Mapungubwe Reconsidered* (2013) produced by the Mapungubwe Institute for Strategic Reflection (MISTRA).[200] The report is a dedicated series exploring the complexity and working of the rise and decline of the Mapungubwe state combining methodologies of archaeology, political science, economic history and international relations. This collaborative work applied a trans-disciplinary approach and investigated the key dynamics of Mapungubwe as a pre-colonial society and reflected on the typical post 2000 debates concerning issues of oral traditions and oral history, Indigenous knowledge systems (IKS), ethnicity, conflicts and cleavages within past societies.

MISTRA's publication further aimed to address pertinent questions ranging from the interplay of Mapungubwe's society on the economy, global trade and the environment to the protection of its heritage and state legitimacy. MISTRA was founded in 2010 by an array of private, academic and government partners with experience in research, academic policy and politics and serves as an independent group that takes a long-term view on the strategic challenges facing South Africa. MISTRA is constructed on the foundations of the past and "combines research and rigorous discourse" and seeks to deepen debate and broaden avenues of enquiry on a plethora of issues relating to history, economics, governance, art, natural sciences and culture. MISTRA further endeavours to provide platforms for dialogue and forge intellectual partnerships that "bolster a fledgling democracy, and push the boundaries of limited expectation of our fractured history".[201]

Literature was further proliferated as a direct result of Mapungubwe's increased elevated national and legal status following its declaration as Vhembe Dongola National Park in April 1998 and when the Mapungubwe Cultural Landscape (MCL) was gazetted as a National Heritage Site in December 2001.[202] In addition, the National Order of Mapungubwe inspired with design elements of Mapungubwe Hill, the gold rhino and gold sceptre, was instituted in December 2002 by the South African government and awarded by the Presidency to

[194] J.C. Vogel, "Radiocarbon dating of the Iron Age sequence in the Limpopo Valley". In M. Leslie and T. Maggs (eds.), African Naissance: the Limpopo Valley 1000 years ago. Johannesburg: *The South African Archaeological Society Goodwin Series* No. 8, 2000, pp. 51–57.
[195] M. Wood, "Making connections: relationships between international trade and glass beads from the Shashe-Limpopo area". In M. Leslie and T. Maggs (eds.), *African naissance: the Limpopo Valley 1000 years ago*. Johannesburg, South African Archaeological Society Goodwin Series; No. 8, 2000, pp. 78–90.
[196] S. Chirikure, "Metals in society: iron production and its position in Iron Age communities of southern Africa". *Journal of Social Archaeology* 7(1), 2007, pp. 72–100.
[197] See for example, T.N. Huffman, "Mapungubwe and Great Zimbabwe: the origin and spread of social complexity in southern Africa". *Journal of Anthropological Archaeology* 28, 2009, pp. 37–54.
[198] M. Leslie and T. Maggs (eds.), *African naissance: the Limpopo Valley 1000 years ago*. The South African Archaeological Society Goodwin Series No. 8, 2000.

[199] T. Maggs, "African naissance: an introduction". In M. Leslie and T. Maggs (eds.), *African naissance: the Limpopo Valley 1000 years ago*. Johannesburg: South African Archaeological Society Goodwin Series No.8, 2000, pp. 1–3.
[200] MISTRA, A. Schoeman and M. Hay, (eds.), *Mapungubwe reconsidered: a living legacy- exploring beyond the rise and decline of the Mapungubwe state*. Johannesburg: Mapungubwe Institute for Strategic Reflection (MISTRA), 2013.
[201] See MISTRA, "Why Mapungubwe", <http://www.mistra.org.za>, *s.a.* access: 2017.06.07.
[202] Refer to SANParks Mapungubwe National Park and World Heritage Site Management Plan, 2017. <https://www.sanparks.org/assets/docs/conservation/park_man/mapungubwe-draft-plan.pdf>, *s.a.* access: 22.06. 2017.

South African citizens for excellence and exceptional achievement on the international stage currently remains South Africa's highest honour.[203]

Mapungubwe's value to the world was further recognised by its inscription by the United Nations Educational, Scientific and Cultural Organisation (UNESCO), as a specialised agency of the United Nations World Heritage list in July 2003.[204] This included the newly named Mapungubwe National Park in September 2004 under the management of South African National Parks (SANParks) and later by its formal declaration in 2009 as a proclaimed World Heritage Site.[205] This exponentially elevated status shone a spotlight specifically on the Mapungubwe Cultural Landscape. As a result, there was subsequent attention paid to Mapungubwe in cultural heritage studies[206] as the heritage site's potential became evident as a major tourism hub.[207]

Progress was made when the Peace Parks Foundation Limpopo-Shashe Transfrontier Conservation Area (TFCA) was renamed in June 2009, as the Greater Mapungubwe Transfrontier Conservation Area (GMTFCA).[208] With increasing demand to access Mapungubwe's heritage from all sectors, there was also now a dire need to protect the heritage of Mapungubwe. In 2001, civil society made calls with the awareness campaign such as the "Save Mapungubwe Coalition"[209] in response to the mining industry threatening Mapungubwe since extractive economies[210] such as mining endangered what was now regarded as an ecologically and culturally sensitive region.[211]

Owing to the plethora of recent and existing studies, there is in fact an abundance of Mapungubwe literature not possible to be fully discussed or disclosed within the confines of this book. Many delve into the national resonances that are further reflective of a struggling democracy coming to grips with Mapungubwe's heritage, its meaning, value, access and its conservation, as well as the countless imperfections that face contemporary post apartheid South Africa today and in general, wider heritage in Africa. Plaguing issues such as the protection of heritage, whose heritage it is, post apartheid archaeology challenges, including aspects of historical dispossession, disputes on the origins of Mapungubwe, repatriation, restitution, mineral exploitation, land claims, embroiled international border politics, institutional monopoly, destructive mining enterprises and state agendas have increased the literature ten-fold in the past two decades.[212]

Perhaps one of the most pertinent aspects to highlight in any Mapungubwe literature review is the decade-old contestation surrounding the human skeletal remains, even following their repatriation by the University of Pretoria and other involved institutions in November 2007.[213] Only a handful of studies on the repatriation were produced, some acknowledging that, "apartheid's lingering ghosts ensures that repatriation processes in South African are complex".[214] However, other studies followed a more bureaucratic or top-down approach to the Mapungubwe reburial as mere "processes and procedures".[215] Justified criticism was levelled at the repatriation process as it was not considered widely publicised due to inadequate public consultation.[216]

[203] E. Jenkins, *Symbols of nationhood*. Braamfontein: South African Institute of Race Relations, 2003.

[204] See, UNESCO, "Mapungubwe Cultural Landscape", <http://whc.unesco.org/en/list/1099>, access: 22.06.2017.

[205] The South African World Heritage Convention Act, No. 49 of 1999.

[206] M. Cocks, S. Vetter and K.F. Wiersum, "From universal to local: perspectives on cultural landscape heritage in South Africa". *International Journal of Heritage Studies* 24(1), 2017, pp. 35–52; L. Meskell, "Mapungubwe Cultural Landscape: extractive economies and endangerment on South Africa's borders". In C. Brumann and D. Berliner (eds.), *World heritage on the ground: ethnographic perspectives*. New York: Berghahn Books, 2016, pp. 273–293.

[207] L. Leonard and T. Lebogang, "Exploring the impacts of mining on tourism growth and local sustainability: the care of Mapungubwe Heritage site, Limpopo, South Africa, *Sustainable Development*, Wiley Online Library, 2017, <https://doi.org/10.1002.sd.1695>, access: 2018.04.04

[208] D.N. Evans, "An eco-tourism perspective of the Limpopo River Basin with particular reference to the Greater Mapungubwe Trans-Frontier Conservation Area given the impact thereon by the proposed Vele colliery". Tourism Working Group of the GMTFCA 18, 2010.

[209] The Save the Mapungubwe Coalition was formed in early 2010 in response to the mining rights granted to the Limpopo Coal Company (Pty) Ltd. (Limpopo Coal) in March 2010 for its proposed Vele Colliery near Mapungubwe; See also, "Dispute between coal miner and conservation coalition". *Farmer's Weekly*, 11 December 2012; "Fight to save 'SA's lost city of gold'". *Sunday Argus*, 1 June 2015.

[210] Archaeology and mining are both viewed as extractive processes with negative historical legacies in South Africa, see for example, L. Meskell, "Mapungubwe Cultural Landscape: extractive economies and endangerment on South Africa's borders". In C. Brumann and D. Berliner (eds.), *World heritage on the ground: ethnographic perspectives*. New York: Berghahn Books, 2016; S. Chirikure, "'Where angels fear to tread': ethics, commercial archaeology, and extractive industries in southern Africa". *Azania: Archaeological Research in Africa* 49(2), 2014, pp. 218–231.

[211] See for example the research report by Centre for Applied Legal Studies (CALS). Changing corporate behaviour: the Mapungubwe case study. University of the Witwatersrand, Johannesburg: Raith Foundation, 2014.

[212] See discussions for example highlighted by L. Meskell, "Negative heritage and past mastering in archaeology". *Anthropological Quarterly* 75, 2002, pp. 557–574; L. Meskell, "Recognition, restitution and the potentials of post colonial liberalism for South African heritage". *South African Archaeological Bulletin* 60, 2005, pp. 72–78; see also N. Shepherd, "The politics of archaeology in Africa". *Annual review of Anthropology* 31, 2002, pp. 189–209; N. Shepherd, "Who is doing courses in archaeology at South African universities? And what are they studying?" *South African Archaeological Bulletin* 60, 2005, pp. 123–126.

[213] Mapungubwe Archive, unappraised current records on Mapungubwe repatriation process, November 2007.

[214] M.H. Schoeman and I. Pikirayi, "Repatriating more than Mapungubwe human remains: archaeological material culture, a shared future and an artificially divided past". *Journal of Contemporary African Studies* 29(4), 2011, pp. 389–403.

[215] W.C. Nienaber, N. Keough, M. Steyn and J.H. Meiring, "Reburial of the Mapungubwe human remains: An overview of process and procedure". *South African Archaeological Bulletin* 63(188), 2008, pp. 164–169.

[216] J. Nel, "Gods, graves and scholars: the return of human remains to their resting place". In S. Tiley-Nel (ed.) *Mapungubwe remembered: contributions to Mapungubwe by the University of Pretoria*. Johannesburg: Chris van Rensburg Publications (Pty) Ltd, 2011, pp. 230–239.

Furthermore, not surprising, but due to the deficiency of community participation (including local knowledge); institutional agendas, government's top-down approach and the poor control of process due to lack of adequate legislation, the manner in which the Mapungubwe repatriation played out eventually in both public and scholarly discourse was further viewed as a bone of contention.[217] Alarmingly, more about Mapungubwe's repatriation lies available in the public domain than it does in the academic sphere, despite being one of the most singularly important events in Mapungubwe's history.[218]

Newspaper articles covered the repatriation process albeit with some inaccuracies, which gave rise to emotions being exuded by negotiating communities and produced much renewed sensitivity about the contested excavated human skeletal remains, as well as the reburied remains.[219] To some community members the act of reburial was viewed as a cleansing ceremony, to such an extent that Mapungubwe is now considered the "New Mecca" implying that going to the site hopes to become a cultural pilgrimage.[220] The fact remains that scholars from all disciplines have failed to contribute more knowledge about the Mapungubwe human remains and their repatriation, particularly at a time when scholars are encouraged to take greater cognisance of communities as part of a national healing process and historical redress.[221]

The post 1994 period is predominantly marked by archaeological Iron Age studies.[222] In comparison to the non-existent studies of Mapungubwe's earliest prehistory such as the fossil record or palaeontology, knowledge of the Stone Age period has also markedly improved somewhat.[223] Despite, many points of disagreement that still exist among archaeologists concerning the prehistory of the early precolonial farming and forager communities of this period, existing literature appears to be less isolated

than before. Previously research focused only on the key sites of Mapungubwe and K2, but more recently research engaged with the wider landscape of the Shashe Limpopo River valley with work done across the borders in Botswana and Zimbabwe about Mapungubwe and its relationship further afield to other sites such as Mapela in Zimbabwe.[224]

Archaeological studies from the Universities of Pretoria, the Witwatersrand and Cape Town remain on-going and have yielded new results and an increasing body of knowledge about Mapungubwe's origins, spread and decline.[225] Expanded ideas about the transformation of socio-political complexity of Mapungubwe as an early state, and the political and economic interactions in Mapungubwe's hinterland,[226] and the socio-environmental dynamics of the wider Shashe Limpopo landscape have also come to the forefront of contemporary research studies.[227] After the democratic transition, twenty-first century literature actively sought more collaborative approaches beyond the discipline of archaeology to a more holistic and wider regard for Mapungubwe's heritage. In general, heritage studies have demonstrated how archaeological heritage (and the past) has struggled to be of service and relevant to present society, as scholars have failed to articulate its relevance to multiple audiences. Some academics remain ever embedded within their ivory-tower structures, refusing to engage with public archaeology and entrenched in what was once scorned as "armchair archaeology".[228]

Involvement with traditional communities, public and community participation efforts have been deemed half-hearted, with scholars employing a top-down approach, and in some cases ignoring local knowledge realities. Unfortunately, Mapungubwe as a case study frequently crops up in existing literature, as yet another poor example of failed cultural heritage and dissonance is continually expressed in terms of the neglect of local knowledge. Pikirayi, in defence of local community voices states that:

Although memory has become a prolific area of enquiry in history and archaeology, this is largely absent in the

[217] See X. Kashe-Katiya, Carefully hidden away: excavating the archive of the Mapungubwe dead and their possessions. Unpublished MA minor dissertation, University of Cape Town, 2013.

[218] See SABC Education, "Mapungubwe: echoes in the valley" (July 2017) by award-winning Director Mandla Dube. This trilogy retells the history of Mapungubwe through the eyes of the Indigenous people of southern Africa, debunking colonial views and aims to raise the bar in historical visual documentation. See, <https://www.mediaupdate.co.za/media/139923/sabc-3-announces-the-arrival-of-mapungubwe-echoes-in-the-valley>, s.a. access: 2017.04.17.

[219] See for example, newspaper articles by T. Mogakane, "Ancient rulers remains to return to royal graves: famed gold pieces go 'home' too", *City Press*, 28 October 2007; K. Nandipha, "A joyful welcome for ancient rulers returning home". *City Press*, 4 November 2007; P. Hlahla, "Remains returned to Mapungubwe descendants: families celebrate symbolic gesture by Tuks and others". *Pretoria News*, 31 October 2007.

[220] I. Pikirayi, *Tradition, archaeological heritage protection and communities in the Limpopo Province of South Africa*, Addis Ababa, Ethiopia: Organisation for Social Science Research in Eastern and Southern Africa, 2011, p. 59.

[221] M. Legassick and C. Rassool, *Skeletons in the cupboard: South African museums and the trade in human remains, 1907–1917*. Cape Town: South African Museum, 2000.

[222] T.N. Huffman, *Handbook to the Iron Age: the archaeology of pre-colonial farming societies in southern Africa*: KwaZulu-Natal: University of KwaZulu-Natal Press, 2007.

[223] T. Forssmann, "Missing pieces: Later Stone Age surface assemblages on the greater Mapungubwe landscape, South Africa". *Southern African Humanities* 25(1), 2013, pp. 65–85.

[224] S. Chirikure, M. Manyanga, A.M. Pollard, F. Bandama, G. Mahachi and I. Pikirayi, "Zimbabwe culture before Mapungubwe: new evidence from Mapela Hill, south-western Zimbabwe". *PloS One* 9(10), 2014; T.N. Huffman, "Mapela, Mapungubwe and the origins of states in southern Africa". *South African Archaeological Bulletin*, 2015, pp. 15–27.

[225] T.N. Huffman, "Mapungubwe and Great Zimbabwe: the origin and spread of social complexity in southern Africa". *Journal of Anthropological Archaeology* 28(1), 2009, pp. 37–54.

[226] A. Antonites, Political and economic interactions in the hinterland of the Mapungubwe polity, c. AD 1220–1300, South Africa. PhD dissertation, Yale University, 2012.

[227] M. Manyanga, Resilient landscapes: socio-environmental dynamics in the Shashe-Limpopo basin, Southern Zimbabwe c. AD to the present, *Studies in Global Archaeology* (11). Uppsala: Uppsala University, 2007.

[228] See use of this adjective by R. Summers, "Armchair archaeology". *South African Archaeological Bulletin* 5(19), 1950, pp. 101–104. The necessity of "armchair" research in the 21st century is fundamentally different, particularly since researchers are using free satellite imagery from Google earth to expose discoveries, develop fieldwork and theories. Realistically, research is no longer just about fieldwork, see online article Armchair archaeology, 2008, *The Economist*, <https://www.economist.com/node/11999379>, access: 2018.06.06.

study and interpretation of Mapungubwe and other sites in the Limpopo Province of South Africa. Although social memory is disparate and fragmented, it serves to challenge authoritative, dominant, and highly contested narratives about the past of these communities... what communities expect... is a platform to challenge competing monolithic post-apartheid narratives about their pasts.[229]

Compounding the many challenges is the long, almost eighty-five year history of excavations at Mapungubwe, that has "left major scars on the fabric and landscape" of this heritage site and broader issues of heritage conservation are under debate and discussion in existing literature.[230] Currently, as the year 2020 approaches, it is also apparent that the notion of thinking beyond traditional archaeology is stronger in existing studies, as there are attempts to redefine, deconstruct and merge social disciplines such as archaeology and history in modern South Africa. Some scholars are blurring the boundaries of untransformed disciplines, employing post apartheid approaches as a means of engaging more with communities and demonstrating concentrated efforts to bring Mapungubwe research more into line with the disciplines of social anthropology and ethnoarchaeology.[231] This is perhaps in response to redress of past imbalances and a means of attempting to address the past more in the present. The politicization of heritage and the archaeological politics in the post apartheid era continue to be shaped by several studies such as that from academics such as Shepherd.[232] Furthermore, within the context of contemporary heritage debates and the characteristic criticism of South African archaeological studies, Meskell further acknowledges the failings of heritage and that the Mapungubwe Cultural Landscape has a long, diverse and contested history.[233] Meskell is particularly scathing in reviewing the historical position of Mapungubwe's excavations and claims the following:

Mapungubwe was a major site for deploying apartheid doctrine but one that was to ultimately confound a racist program through material evidence of black achievement and identity... Afrikaner archaeologists at the University of Pretoria were bestowed exclusive rights to excavate Mapungubwe. Pretoria was an Afrikaans university with strong associations with Afrikaner ideology and many anthropologists and archaeologists bolstered and perpetuated apartheid ideology.[234]

As the turn of the twenty-first century endures, one cannot deny nor notice the "anthropologization" of archaeological heritage and the politicisation of Mapungubwe as highlighted in many of the mentioned studies as well as in the profusion of a whole corpus of other diverse Mapungubwe-related literature.[235] This is perhaps a resilient response to offer a diversity of post colonial and post apartheid views in the re-processing of South African history (the unmaking and making of the past) since heritage is broadly defined by history.

Even after the recent two decades, South African scholars still appear to be struggling with Mapungubwe's past and its role in present society, as discipline boundaries are disappearing and blurring. Mapungubwe's sedimented legacies have waxed and waned, but the past iniquities continue to linger and somehow always resurface. This is exemplified as Meskell rightly states in her conclusions in, *The nature of heritage: the new South Africa*, "past mastering is always an ongoing project, always unfinished and future perfect".[236] The limited number of studies on the early history of Mapungubwe and the glaring paucity of any studies in utilising the Mapungubwe Archive demonstrates that this book certainly merits local and global attention. The passage of time affords any scholar a change in perspective and an opportunity to look upon history differently as did our predecessors.

[229] I. Pikirayi, "Archaeology, local knowledge, and tradition: the quest for relevant approaches to the study and use of the past in Southern Africa". In P.R. Schmidt and I. Pikirayi (eds.), *Community archaeology and heritage in Africa: decolonizing practice*. London: Routledge, 2016, p. 123.

[230] See for example, S. Chirikure., M. Manyanga., W. Ndoro, and G. Pwiti, "Unfulfilled promises? Heritage management and community participation at some of Africa's cultural heritage sites". *International Journal of Heritage Studies* 16(1–2), 2010, pp. 30–44. See discussions by W. Ndoro, S. Chirikure and J. Deacon (eds.), *Managing heritage in Africa: who cares?* New York: Routledge, 2017.

[231] I. Pikirayi, *Tradition, archaeological heritage protection and communities in the Limpopo Province of South Africa*. Addis Ababa: Ethiopia: Organisation for Social Science Research in eastern and Southern Africa, 2011.

[232] N. Shepherd, "Heading south, looking north: why we need a post-colonial archaeology". *Archaeological Dialogues* 9, 2002, pp. 74–82; N. Shepherd, "Who is doing courses in archaeology at South African universities? And what are they studying?" *South African Archaeological Bulletin* 60, 2005, pp. 123–126.

[233] L. Meskell, "Falling walls and mending fences: archaeological ethnography in the Limpopo". *Journal of Southern African Studies* 33, 2007 pp. 383–400.

[234] L. Meskell, "Mapungubwe Cultural Landscape: extractive economies and endangerment on South Africa's borders. In C. Brumann and D. Berliner (eds.), *World heritage on the ground: ethnographic perspectives*. New York: Berghahn Books, 2016, p. 276.

[235] See, J. Kolen, "The 'anthropologization' of archaeological heritage". *Archaeological Dialogues* 16(2), 2009, pp. 209–225.

[236] L. Meskell, *The nature of heritage: the new South Africa*. Oxford: Wiley-Blackwell, 2012, p. 203.

3

The Transvaal Treasure Trove: A Contested Discovery

Who owns the golden treasure recovered by excavators sent from the Pretoria University to the Northern Transvaal? Reports to hand show that doubts have already risen regarding the disposable of the valuables found to date. Cases on this subject are exceedingly rare in South African law, and precedents several hundreds of years old have to be followed. It would however appear as though the Government has a very strong claim to the ownership of the relics.[237]

3.1. 'Finders Keepers'[238]

Archaeological discoveries in South Africa began with the pioneers in the middle of the nineteenth century. From the early twentieth century, colonial views of archaeology as a frontier of prehistory prevailed under political patronage, as South Africa increasingly became a country of many remarkable discoveries.[239] For instance, at the time, the Prime Minister J.C. Smuts, was a "keen supporter of all things archaeological and under his patronage archaeology became part of civil service".[240] Moreover, only in the 1920s did the discipline of archaeology become established in Cape Town.[241] This period was further characterised by universities becoming nationalised forces as the ideals of South Africanism set in.[242]

Against this backdrop and through the lens of the term "treasure trove" this chapter will briefly look at the definition, origins, history and trajectory of treasure trove law from ancient times up to the present, and to the rationale of declaring the discovery of the Mapungubwe gold as a treasure trove. Specific attention will furthermore be focused on the multiplicity of oral and historical narratives around knowledge of Mapungubwe prior to the 1933 discovery. These "discoveries" range from the ignored histories of local knowledge about Mapungubwe

Hill, the first so-called "European" late nineteenth century discovery by F.B. Lotrie, the role of the Dongola Botanical Reserve in 1922 close to Mapungubwe Hill to the German discovery by the Anthropologist, L. Frobenius in 1928 and the final traditional gold discovery in 1932. In this chapter the Archive's historical sources will be closely examined since they are the only available documentary evidence which retraces and refigures the historical and complex threads, both before and after the 1933 gold discovery on Mapungubwe Hill.

In 1933, the discovery of Mapungubwe was popularised by the University of Pretoria historian Leo Fouché, as a resonant search for "hidden treasure" by "five fossickers" evinced as a treasure trove.[243] This set in motion the justification of a discovery of immense archaeological value and scientific ownership dating back to colonial times.[244] The discovery was regarded as the first find of wrought or refined gold in the Transvaal and attracted formal scientific enquiry early in February 1933 by the University of Pretoria. It laid claim to the discovery at Mapungubwe as historically rooted in colonial explanations of an "ancient Bantu civilisation".[245]

This archaeological discovery gave rise to immense public appeal of Mapungubwe as a "vast treasure house of ancient Bantu relics", but within the walls of scholarship, there was a fundamental preoccupation with racial origins that played a role in "legitimising" early research. While the academic pursuit of the "treasure trove" received scholarly attention, it nonetheless assigned this major archaeological discovery a historical meaning that is presently considered a heavily contested process in South

---

[237] J. de Villiers Roos, "Transvaal treasure ownership puzzle: whose are the gold ornaments found in the north". *The Star*, 26 March 1933.

[238] This old English adage is borrowed from the children's common rhyme of "finders, keepers, losers, weepers". In many ways, it denotes childish possession of discovering a lost object and centres on the premise that if something is lost, unowned or abandoned, whoever finds it first can claim it. There is no doubt its legal and ethical application dates back centuries and relates to the ancient Roman law of possession.

[239] For example, in the 1920s J.C. Smuts was a supporter of John Goodwin, the first professional Stone Age archaeologist in South Africa who was Cambridge trained and later, in 1925, when Raymond Dart discovered the Taung fossil, this too was supported by Smuts. Smuts supported prehistory and archaeology using his political connections, influential leverage and personal relationships to such an extent that South African archaeology as a branch of prehistory enjoyed much of his support over the periods from the 1920s to the late 1940s.

[240] Refer to A. Zipkin, Archaeology under apartheid: a preliminary investigation into the potential politicization of science in South Africa. Honors thesis, Cornell University, 2009, pp. 18–19.

[241] See for example, B.D. Malan, "Remarks and reminiscences on the history of archaeology in South Africa". *South African Archaeological Bulletin* 25 (99/100), 1970, pp. 88–92.

[242] Refer to B.L. Strydom, Broad South Africanism and Higher Education: The Transvaal University College (1909–1919), PhD History, University of Pretoria, 2013.

[243] It is worthy to note that Fouché *Mapungubwe Volume I* referred to the discoverers as the "five fossickers". The term fossicking originated in the days of the Australian Gold Rush in the early 1850s and is defined as searching for artefacts and natural deposits such as gemstones and minerals, such as gold in or on the ground for enjoyment or recreational reasons. Furthermore, the term has extended to mean to "rummage" for a purpose other than for commercial gain.

[244] L. Fouché, (ed.), *Mapungubwe: ancient Bantu civilization on the Limpopo: Reports on excavations at Mapungubwe (Northern Transvaal) from February 1933 to June 1935,* Volume I. Cambridge: Cambridge University Press, 1937, p. 2.

[245] In Fouché's preface to *Mapungubwe Volume I*, written on 23 October 1936, he points to the matter of terminology explaining the term "Bantu" to denote a linguistic family not only as a language and culture, but also race.

Figure 3.1. Unexcavated and exposed original gold grave from the summit of Mapungubwe Hill.

Africa. The idea that Mapungubwe's past could only be understood by archaeology and the declaration of gold finds as a "treasure trove" were claimed purely on the basis of archaeological research on the back of neglected local histories about knowledge of Mapungubwe.

In addition, through use of the Archive, this chapter will also emphasise that the declaration as a treasure trove heightened the historical complexities and legal tensions between the government, the University of Pretoria and the discoverers who actually uncovered the treasure trove. The "finders' keepers" rule did not apply, but instead invoked legal control and controversy over the discovery of Mapungubwe gold by the University of Pretoria. As the multiplicity of narratives around Mapungubwe unfolded, local knowledge was ignored and instead used and abused, ever manipulated as a lead-up to one of South Africa's greatest discoveries. This discounting of oral history and archival evidence is emphasised in the narrative of the early history of Mapungubwe.

This chapter provides the background to the archaeological discovery as well as a unique window into institutional possession and control, which will be further discussed in later chapters. In the final chapter this will inevitably bring into question the discussions of ownership, stewardship and contestation. By also briefly highlighting the path of legislation over time to the eventual protection of heritage towards the end of this chapter, it further suggests the idea

that this "control" over the discovery stems to an extent from the imperial treasure trove rule. It is argued that the treasure trove served as a stimulus to the politicisation and contestation, instead of serving as an ethical and moral compass of stewardship over Mapungubwe by the University of Pretoria.

3.2. Treasure trove: a brief history

According to the Oxford English Dictionary the definition of "treasure trove" has its origins in the medieval English term that literally means "found treasure".[246] The term "treasure trove" is derived from the Anglo-French *tresor trové*, the equivalent of the Roman word for *thesaurus* meaning "treasure" in Latin.[247] The definition of treasure trove has been legally held throughout centuries but differs from country to country and from one era to the next. However, it would appear to be Germanic or Roman in

---

[246] Definition of "treasure trove" from the Oxford English Dictionary, Oxford University Press, Oxford, 2018, <https://en.oxforddictionaries.com/definition/treasure_trove>, access: 2018.06.06.

[247] R.W. Lee, *The elements of Roman law: with a translation of the Institute of Justinian*. (4th Ed.). London: Sweet & Maxwell, 1956, p. 139. Under Roman imperial law the treasure trove made reference to ancient deposits of money, of which no memory exists, so that it has no present owner. Although this definition was confined to money and no reference was made to abandonment of ownership, if treasure was found the finder was entitled to keep it. As a consequence, if such treasure was fortuitously found and not by direct search, on another person's land, half went to the finder and half went to the owner of the land.

origin as its adoption in England goes back to the Anglo-Saxon period. The fundamental difference is that "treasure trove" in England decreed in principle that all ownerless objects of treasure belong to the Crown, whereas Latin law viewed that treasure trove belonged equally to the finder and landowner.[248]

Described in the twelfth and thirteenth centuries account of the English Cleric and Jurist, Henry de Bracton, in *De Legibus et Consuetudinibus Angliae* (ca.1250), (*On the Laws and Customs of England*), treasure trove was limited to objects of precious metal buried with the intention of recovery, and of which the owner could not be traced. Treasure trove thus only extended to objects that were buried with the intention of recovery rather than being lost or abandoned or placed in a grave. The origin of the law was to discourage people from trying to avoid paying tax by concealing their wealth. These origins of treasure trove lay in Common Law, as determined by the judiciary and not in Statute Law as determined by government or parliament.[249]

In September 1194, the office of the Coroner was formally established in England by the *Articles of the Eyre*, to "keep the pleas of the Crown" which stated that, "a coroner shall continue as heretofore, to have jurisdiction to enquire treasure that is found, who were the finders - and who is suspected thereof". In 1276, the King of England, Edward I (1272–1307) issued the Apocryphal Statute, the *De Officio Coronatis* which contained specific instructions to coroners about treasure trove, thus making them solely responsible to safeguard rights to the Crown in the matter of buried treasure.[250] This old feudal right to treasure trove, under which the King claimed all finds of gold or silver that had been buried in the ground, had been adapted as an antiquities law in 1886 when the government paid finders rewards for valuable finds. Mainly viewed as an administrative act, there was no law ever passed that set out a definitive written version of treasure trove.[251]

By the mid-nineteenth century, in the Western world, the Common law of treasure trove was the only legal protection afforded to archaeological discoveries and in part extended to the protection of valuable antiquities offered to museums.[252] However, this protection was still limited to gold and silver objects for which owners were unknown and which had been deliberately buried with the intention of recovery and could be declared treasure trove

but nonetheless became property of the Crown.[253] The Crown in turn offered museums the opportunity to acquire treasure trove finds, and the finder received the full market value as a reward. Historically, refined gold and other valuables such as silver coins, or bullion, precious stones and other undiscovered valuables were of considerable fiscal importance as a source of Crown revenue.[254] In Adam Smith's classic, *The Wealth of Nations*, he claimed that treasure trove "found concealed in the earth, and to which no particular person could prove any right" was thus considered as "no contemptible part of the revenue of the greatest sovereigns of Europe, and was founded solely and fundamentally on the principles of classic economics".[255]

By the late nineteenth century, Lord Talbot de Malahide introduced a Private Member's Bill in 1858 to reform the treasure trove, to ensure that finds of treasure were reported, as long as the treasure trove served its purpose and added substantially to the royal reserves. Unfortunately, the Bill was never passed, as objects claimed as treasure troves were melted down into bullion, and clearly provided no incentive to a finder's keeper's fee as such discoveries would not be reported. Eventually gold and silver finds were valued for their antiquity, so pressure grew on the Crown to pay rewards for precious metal, mainly the more important finds. Talbot's Bill paved the way for the Ancient Monuments Act, which was introduced in England in 1882 and served as the first attempt to introduce any kinds of protection and legislation to archaeological heritage.[256] In 1886, a motion was finally passed by the government of a new policy whereby finds claimed as treasure trove were offered to museums and finders were eventually paid a financial reward.[257]

In the twentieth century, discoveries of treasure trove abounded, particularly of refined gold, as such finds were often romanticised about and largely ended up in private patronage.[258] Soon judicial attempts were made to change the law of treasure trove and in 1944, the reform began in earnest soon after the Second World War.

A motion was put forward by the Council for British Archaeology (CBA), but the government was not persuaded to take action and archaeological consensus could not be

[248] R. Bland, "Treasure trove and the case for reform". *Art, Antiquity and Law* 1, (February 2006), pp. 11–26.

[249] R. Bland, "Rescuing our neglected heritage: the evolution of the government's policy on portable antiquities in England and Wales". *Cultural Trends* 14(4), 2005, pp. 257–296.

[250] B. Knight, 1999, History of the Medieval English Coroner System, Crowner Part 6: Treasure trove and nautical activities, <www.britannia.com/history/articles/coroner6>, access: 2018.03.27.

[251] R. Bland, "Response: the Treasure Act and Portable Antiquities Scheme". *Internet Archaeology* 33, 2013.

[252] W. Martin and G. Lushington, "The law of treasure trove". *Journal of the Royal Society of Arts* 56(2883), 1908, pp. 348–359.

[253] R. Bland, "Treasure trove and the case for reform". *Art, Antiquity and Law* 1 (February 2006), pp. 11–26

[254] In terms of treasure trove, the seminal work of Sir George Hill is widely regarded see for example, G.F. Hill, *Treasure trove in law and practice, from the earliest time to the present day*. Oxford: Clarendon Press, 1936.

[255] A. Smith, *An inquiry into the nature and causes of the wealth of nations* (1776). S.M. Soares (ed.) MetaLibri Digital Library, 2007, p. 219.

[256] J. Carman, *Valuing ancient things*. Leicester: Leicester University Press, 1996, pp. 49–55.

[257] G.F. Hill, *Treasure trove in law and practice, from the earliest time to the present day*. Oxford: Clarendon Press, 1936, pp. 239–240; R. Bland, "Rescuing our neglected heritage: the evolution of the government's policy on portable antiquities in England and Wales. *Cultural Trends* 14(4), 2005, p. 258.

[258] See illustrated edition by, C.R. Beard, *The romance of treasure trove*. London: Sampson Low, Marston & Co Ltd, 1933.

reached, so no progress was made.[259] Decades later, the concept of treasure trove eventually moved out of English Common law and into Statute law when the Treasure Act of 1996 was passed in England, which dropped the title of "trove", but retained the notion of "treasure". This was followed by the adoption of the Portable Antiquities Scheme (PAS), in England and in Wales, which today continues to bring about greater awareness and higher levels of reported found treasure, that in a majority of cases still fill museum coffers on behalf of the English nation.[260]

The notions of treasure trove law strongly persist into the twenty-first century, yet remain remarkably entrenched in western legal doctrines.[261] According to N.E. Palmer, treasure trove was "an archaic concept, rife with anomalies and unanswerable questions" and has "evolved for a different purpose from that which it now serves, and it serves its present purpose dismally".[262] Worldwide, treasure trove law is still legally recognised in international cultural property law, however in contrast, in America, the "slow death of treasure trove" is welcomed as, "modern law has recognised and resolved the problem, leaving no room for royal prerogatives. The old rules of treasure trove may make good theatre, but its poor law, and its death can come none too soon".[263]

Nonetheless as emphasised by N. Cookson, it is important to bear in mind that the doctrine of "treasure trove was conceived long before archaeology gave cultural value to old things, and considers valuables from an essentially financial perspective, not an artistic or historical one".[264] It is within the context of this narrative that the Mapungubwe gold discovery of 1933 as a treasure trove gave rise to the notion of contestation.

3.3. Ignored Indigenous histories

Scholars have long been aware that there exist a handful of early records, in conjunction with fragmented oral and local histories that allude to knowledge of Mapungubwe before 1933. Much of the colonial history that has been generated by academic research often overlooked or simply ignored the merits of local knowledge. S. Lekgoathi, Professor

Figure 3.2. Portrait of Petty Chief Tshiwana one of the oral history informants to Lestrade in 1933.

of History at the University of the Witwatersrand makes the point that, "the studies that have been carried out throughout the years have contributed to the scholarly advantage of archaeology, but to the disadvantage of oral history".[265]

The earliest recorded oral traditions assert that the last descendant who lived at Mapungubwe was a legendary chief named Petty Chief Tshiwana.[266] Other archival records suggest that he occupied a place referred to as *Manopi,*[267] a smaller hill which lies to the south of

---

[259] H Cleere, "The CBA: the first fifty years". *Council for British Archaeology Annual Report* 44, 1994, pp. 108–109.

[260] J. Carleton, "Protecting the national heritage: the implications of the British Treasure Act 1996". *International Journal of Cultural Property* 6(2), 1997, pp. 343–352.

[261] See for example, C. Sparrow, "Treasure trove: a lawyer's view". *Antiquity* 56, 1982, pp. 199–201.

[262] Norman Palmer was a Barrister and Professor of Commercial Law at the University College of London and was regarded as a distinguished art lawyer and leading legal authority in the world of cultural property and trove law within the context of international property law. See for example, N.E. Palmer, "Treasure trove and title to discovered antiquities", *International Journal of Cultural Property* 2(2), 1993, p. 275.

[263] R B. Cunningham is a professor of law at the University of California, in the Hasting College of Law in San Francisco. Legal reliance on the treasure trove rule was last applied in 1948 by an American court. See R.B. Cunningham, 2000, "The slow death of treasure trove", The Archaeological Institute of America, Archaeology Archive, <https://archive.archaeology.org/online/features/trove/>, access: 2018.06.11.

[264] N Cookson, "Treasure trove: dumb enchantment or new law?" *Antiquity* 66, 1992, p. 401.

[265] See for example the interview dialogue between O. Ntsoane and V. Neluvhalani, moderated by the historian, Prof. S. Lekgoathi from the University of the Witwatersrand in exploring Indigenous knowledge and historical sources about Mapungubwe, In MISTRA, *Mapungubwe reconsidered: a living legacy- exploring beyond the rise and decline of the Mapungubwe state.* Johannesburg: Mapungubwe Institute for Strategic Reflection (MISTRA), 2013, pp. 13–17.

[266] In September 1933, the government ethnologist G.P. Lestrade interviewed two informants named Tshiwana and Ditjane, so-called petty chiefs that lived in the immediate vicinity of the site. Tshiwana claimed to be one the last descendants at Mapungubwe and the half-brother of Mowena or Mabina (Mavhina) who reputedly led the 1933 Van Graan discovery to its location. Chief Tshiwana (see Fouché, 1937, Plate V) claimed his daughter named Mahobe lived at the base of Mapungubwe Hill and was the last resident of the area, see L. Fouché, (ed.), *Mapungubwe: ancient Bantu civilization on the Limpopo: reports on excavations at Mapungubwe (Northern Transvaal) from February 1933 to June 1935,* Volume I. Cambridge: Cambridge University Press, 1937, pp. 8, 18.

[267] The name, *Manopi* is located on the farm Greefswald, but is mentioned not as a specific place, but rather refers to a wider landscape of what appears to reference the main Mapungubwe valley area, see recent article by J. Wintjes, "Frobenius discovered before crossing Limpopo ruins: ancient fortificated settlements, beautiful pottery mountains stop", *De arte* 52(1), 2017, pp. 41–42.

Mapungubwe Hill.[268] Many of the oral traditions from the 1930s that were recorded as "native traditions", sometimes as verbatim, vernacular manuscripts, resulted from direct interviews with informants from local communities. These records were produced by ethnologists such as N.J. van Warmelo[269] and G.P. Lestrade,[270] who both interviewed and gathered information from elder community members in the immediate vicinity, as well as other local communities, with the aim of tracing any oral sources to knowledge of Mapungubwe.[271]

The 1920s and 1930s of post War South Africa were marked by a distinct knowledge and segregationist philosophy regarding African customs and culture. Lestrade was a government archetype who supported the politicised notions of "cultural adaptation" and Bantu "culture" which became evident in many of the new courses of African studies offered at universities. Within the fields of anthropology[272] and ethnology,[273] "culture" was popularly used and was employed as a synonym for "civilisation" and other times, as "race" classification. Lestrade's ideology of "cultural adaptation" became crucial in the government's Economic Commission's advocacy for segregation.[274] Nonetheless, according to R. Thornton, Professor of Anthropology at the University of the Witwatersrand, as much as these particularistic cultural studies are now criticised and wholly rejected, the ethnography that was published in this period was historically essential to the institutionalisation of the discipline of anthropology as a science, and indeed "helped to make academic anthropology" possible in the first place.[275]

During the decade of 1926 and 1936, the Afrikaner ethnological tradition was founded, and established roots for *volkekunde* which was based on classification rather than on the trajectory of social anthropology which was established on participant observation. This polarization of two radically different traditions evident in early studies contrasted the political orientations of the anti-segregation social anthropologists with the J.B.M. Hertzog-aligned *volkekundiges*. This dichotomy affected the way in which South African society was perceived at the time by these "imperfect interpreters".[276]

However, an advantage of the early ethnological reports, such as those of Lestrade, provided critical geographical clues to early place names that potentially connected historical oral memory to Mapungubwe's landscape. Although it was confirmed at that time that "Mapungubwe" was not the name of a person or chief, but rather the name of a place, several oral references also allude to the origins and meaning of Mapungubwe.[277] Historical references are also made to Little Mapungubwe or *Maphungubyana* (small Mapungubwe) a minor but distinctive stone-capped hill which is situated to the south-east of Mapungubwe Hill. Described as "the small conical hillock with towering rock cap a little way to the south-east from the hill is called *Nyindi* (in Sotho, *Nyete*) and a reference by Dzivhani and Van Warmelo to its name is first recorded as follows in a Tshivenda praise poem:

A dzimela a ende Nyindi,
A konou ku vhona Maphungubyana
Maphungubye ndi dya ka Huvhi.

One who loses his way, let him to Nyindi
From where he will see Maphungubyana (Small Maphungubye), Mapungubwe is the country of Huvhi.[278]

While none of the oral histories disclaim any direct knowledge of Mapungubwe, it was nonetheless regarded as a sacred hill and site of the ancestors. One of the elders,

---

[268] Mapungubwe Archive, UP/AGL/D/217, specific reference to Manopi and other local names indicated on a hand-drawn map based on the recorded oral traditions, 4 August 1933; Mapungubwe Archive, UP/AGL/D/213/1, G.P Lestrade typed interview notes with Siwana (Tshiwana), dated 1 September 1933; and UP/AGL/D/213/2, interview notes with Ditjane, dated 3 September 1933.

[269] Nicholaas Jacobus van Warmelo (1904–1989) was an internationally recognised anthropologist who served as the Chief Ethnologist of the Ethnological section in the Native Affairs Department of the State from 1930–1969. The Van Warmelo manuscript collection comprises more than 57 000 pages was donated to the University of Pretoria Library now held in Special Collections and is a large untapped archival source of his unpublished legacy, for a detailed list of this collection, see, <https://repository.up.ac.za/handle/2263/52076>, access: 2018.06.20; See also, R.D. Coertze, "Obituary N.J. van Warmelo 1904–1989". *South African Journal of Ethnology* 12(3), 1989, pp. 85–90.

[270] Gérard Paul Lestrade (1897–1962) was born in Holland, and immigrated to South Africa in 1902; he was well-known for his mastery of languages and his unrivalled linguistic talents. Initially a language Harvard scholar, he was appointed as the first ethnologist in the department of Native Affairs and in 1930 took up a position at the University of Pretoria as Professor of Bantu Studies and in 1935 was appointed as Chair of Bantu Languages at the University of Cape Town, see Obituary, "Gérard Paul Lestrade: 1897–1962". *African Studies* 22 (2), 2007, pp. 91–95.

[271] L. Fouché, (ed.), *Mapungubwe: ancient Bantu civilization on the Limpopo: Reports on excavations at Mapungubwe (Northern Transvaal) from February 1933 to June 1935,* Volume I. Cambridge: Cambridge University Press, 1937, pp. 119–124.

[272] Anthropology only became a university subject in South Africa around the 1920s, although the field of ethnology predates this development by decades, this discipline was largely led by colonial missionaries and government officials.

[273] For the purposes of clarity, ethnology at Afrikaans-speaking universities was referred to as *volkekunde* and as social anthropology by English-speaking universities.

[274] See for example, W. Beinart and S. Dubow (eds.), *Segregation and apartheid in twentieth century South Africa: rewriting histories.* London: Routledge, 1995, pp. 161–161.

[275] See for example argument by R. Thornton, "Evolution, salvation and history in the rise of the ethnographic monograph in Southern Africa 1860–1920". *Social Dynamics* 6(2), 1981, p. 14.

[276] W.D. Hammond-Tooke, *Imperfect interpreters: South Africa's anthropologists 1920–1990.* Johannesburg: Witwatersrand University Press, 1997.

[277] Oral records assert that Mapungubwe can alternatively be spelt as: *Maphungubwe, Mapunguhwe, Mapungupye,* or *Mapunguwe* (see V. Ralushai, 2002, p. 6). Fouché (1937, p. 1) claimed that "Mapungubwe" means "the hill of the jackals" or "place of many jackals" but oral history does not support this interpretation and instead Ralushai suggested the correct meaning of Mapungubwe to be "place of stones". Mapungubwe Archive, UP/AGL/D/213, see recorded interview with Siwana (probably Tshiwana) stating that the name "Mapungubwe" is of Karanga origin meaning "silver jackal", 1 September 1933.

[278] N.J. van Warmelo (ed.), *Copper miners of Messina and the early history of the Zoutpansberg.* Vernacular accounts by S.M. Dzivhani, M.F. Mamadi, M.M. Motenda and E. Modau. Pretoria: Department of Native Affairs, Union of South Africa, 1940, pp. 94–95.

recorded only by the name Ditjane, who was interviewed in September 1933 stated the following:

> Mapungubwe was a sacred place, the graves of ancestors and the official residence of chiefs. Ceremonies were performed there e.g. praying for rain, for safety and victory in war... the chief and his doctors used to go to it to make things right, with the help of the spirits of departed ancestors.[279]

According to more recent oral sources, informants did not suggest that Mapungubwe was a religious centre either. Rather it was regarded as a once powerful political capital or *musanda* characterised by its impregnable hill with steep slopes and limited access, reserved for the ruler who would have possessed both religious and political powers.[280] In support of this view, the *Bakalanga Sketches*, a brief history of the Bakalanga compiled in 1935 by the historian, Peter M. Sebina, made direct reference to Mapungubwe. He described it as a stronghold with soldiers "who guarded the borders of the land" as "sentries posted on the hill-top" and related details even about the ritual death and burial of the king or *Mambo*.[281] However, there are hints at scholarly bias to Sebina's version of this oral history, as Van Riet Lowe remained doubtful about any truths and points to contestation of his claim.[282] Whether or not Sebina's version can be confirmed, or if such claims had been refuted or supported by other oral histories, remains unexplored historically. Many of the Mapungubwe oral histories were, and remain, unpublished and may be part of other scattered institutional archives, perhaps under the guise of ethnological reports and unpublished anthropological manuscripts.[283]

In the 1930s, Lestrade's ethnological approach to Mapungubwe's local knowledge was fourfold: to investigate the ethnic history of the area; to obtain knowledge to recognise any excavated material by physical samples (i.e. gold and beads); to obtain descriptions of technology and the manufacture of objects (e.g. pottery) and to investigate the origins, explanations or parallels of artefacts and other objects.[284] He also took several portrait photographs of the informants he interviewed. The communities that Lestrade interviewed lived in and around Mapungubwe in September 1933, and he also followed up interviews in August 1934 into western Venda at the Headquarters of Chief Mphepu, as well as some of the Tsonga-Shangaan communities that stayed at the Elim Mission Station. Further afield, Lestrade interviewed both Shona and Lemba communities that lived in the Belingwe region of southern Rhodesia (present-day Zimbabwe) and in October 1934 he continued informant interviews in eastern Venda with Chief Tshivhasa, Petty Chief Tshirundu and other communities in the region in proximity to Mapungubwe.[285] Lestrade spent close to a year on ethnological enquiries, yet only published his results on the oral traditions in Fouché's 1937 *Mapungubwe Volume I*, but nowhere else. His final ethnological report historically supported the mixed occupation of the Mapungubwe area by the Shona, Venda and Kalanga, which included some Tswana/Sotho groups. This was not so much in contrast with the present communities of Mapungubwe, as supported by recent historical archaeological studies that indicate the Twamamba (Venda) and Birwa (N. Sotho) occupation.[286] Written, somewhat apologetically in 1935, in his ethnological report to the University of Pretoria, Lestrade acknowledged:

> ... [B]oth chiefs and tribesmen and women, who came, sometimes long and weary distances, to give information that was sought... with willingness to being plied with hosts of questions about their tribal lore and usages, in many cases of an intimate and sacred nature, such as natives are usually most loth to communicate to a white man, and who, for little or no reward, spent endless time and trouble, and extended hospitality which in many cases they could ill afford, for the benefit of white men who at first sight they must have instinctively heartily distrusted, and who had, as it appeared to them, committed grave desecration of sacred precincts and sacred objects for the sake of satisfying what must have been little else than a curious and irrational whim, boding no good to themselves... and give such a harmonious, if scant and broken picture of the facts of the case.[287]

---

[279] Mapungubwe Archive, UP/AGL/D/116, hand-written notes of the original interview by G.P. Lestrade with Ditjane, dated 2 September 1933, Messina.

[280] N.M.N. Ralushai, Preliminary report on the oral history of the Mapungubwe area. Unpublished report for the Department of Environmental Affairs and Tourism, Pretoria, 2002, pp. 12–13.

[281] Peter M. Sebina wrote *Ka ga Makalaka* or the *Bakalanga Sketches* (Part II) which won the second book prize in African Languages awarded by the International African Institute in 1935. Sebina (1894–1962) was a reputed educator and historian in Botswana, he also served as the Bamangwato Tribal Secretary and personal secretary to Tsheke Khama for over twenty-five years, and served on the Area Council of Bamangwato and the African Advisory Council.

[282] Mapungubwe Archive, UP/AGL/D/453, Extracts from, "Bakalanga Sketches" by the Historian, Peter M. Sebina, Serowe, Bechuanaland (Botswana). A note is scribbled in the corner by C. van Riet Lowe to G.P Lestrade, "I don't like the ring of it", 3 May 1935.

[283] For example, there are references to G.P. Lestrade papers at the University of Cape Town Libraries: Special Collections (Manuscripts and Archives), Fonds BC255, this collection consists mostly of unpublished papers relating to Lestrade's lifetime study of Bantu languages and his correspondences, as well as his archaeological papers on Mapungubwe in 1934, including photographs of various tribes and the site. Other Lestrade Archives (Ref MS 276) are located at the Royal Anthropological Institute (RAI) in the UK.

[284] See G.P. Lestrade, "Report on certain ethnological investigations in connection with the archaeological discoveries at Mapungubwe". In L. Fouché (ed.), *Mapungubwe: ancient Bantu civilization on the Limpopo: Reports on excavations at Mapungubwe (Northern Transvaal) from February 1933 to June 1935*. Cambridge: Cambridge University Press, 1937, pp. 119–124.

[285] Mapungubwe Archive, UP/AGL/D/487, Report on certain ethnological investigations in connection with the archaeological discoveries at Mapungubwe, G.P. Lestrade, 1935; see also L. Fouché, (ed.), *Mapungubwe: ancient Bantu civilization on the Limpopo: Reports on excavations at Mapungubwe (Northern Transvaal) from February 1933 to June 1935*, Volume I. Cambridge: Cambridge University Press, 1937, pp. 119–124.

[286] See recent history of the area by T.N. Huffman, "Historical archaeology of the Mapungubwe area: Boer, Birwa and Machete". *Southern Africa Humanities* 24(1), 2012, pp. 33–59.

[287] Mapungubwe Archive, UP/AGL/D/487, Report on certain ethnological investigations in connection with the archaeological discoveries at Mapungubwe, G.P. Lestrade, 1935.

Figure 3.3. Group portrait of local informants from a Lemba village, Southern Rhodesia 1934.

Prof. Victor Ralushai (1935–2011), an industrious scholar of African knowledge systems and a distinguished oral historian, provided the only comprehensive yet incomplete report on Mapungubwe's oral history.[288] In 2002, he admitted that he had had only two months to produce the report commissioned by the Department of Environmental Affairs and Tourism. However, for reasons unknown, perhaps time constraints, he did not consult the Mapungubwe Archive nor the N.J. van Warmelo nor the G.P. Lestrade archival records. Nonetheless, his research aimed to track down informants that he interviewed and concluded in his oral report that:

> By studying the history of Mapungubwe and the neighbouring areas using music, folklore, traditional literature etc. as a source of information we now have got more information on the history and customs of the inhabitants of Mapungubwe and the neighbouring areas. However, it is important to note that it is certainly not enough. What is needed now is a detailed work on the history and customs of people, with all researchers of related disciplines working together rather than in isolation…. Indeed, the whole world would have known a lot about this famous pre-historic

site had researchers on Mapungubwe started much earlier.[289]

There remain many contradictions and inconsistencies from secondary oral sources, and unfortunately the evidence remains scant and circumstantial as none of the oral histories make direct reference to Mapungubwe. These oral records, interviews and personal memories (some passed down over generations, some through myths and stories) are critical in recognising the early history of Mapungubwe, albeit alluding to the communities that lived in and around the area. Local knowledge makes reference to a sacred burial site on a summit, and some oral sources offer discrepancies on the origin of the name "Mapungubwe" and its meaning.[290]

---

[288] At the time Prof. Ralushai compiled these reports he was elderly and although very unwell, did complete additional information on the oral history and did intend on extending his research, see N.M.N. Ralushai, Additional information on the oral history of Mapungubwe, unpublished addendum to the World Heritage Nomination Dossier for Mapungubwe, Department of Environmental Affairs and Tourism, Pretoria, 2003.

[289] N.M.N. Ralushai, Preliminary report on the oral history of the Mapungubwe area, unpublished report for the Department of Environmental Affairs and Tourism, Pretoria, 2002, p. 25.

[290] The Ralushai's reports aimed to record oral history mainly from living memory, praise songs and folk tales of how local black inhabitants interacted with the Mapungubwe landscape before white settlers in the 20th century. He also focused on place names, their meanings and to clarify if any of the oral history supported the archaeology of Mapungubwe, as well as investigated any linkages of traditional knowledge from the Venda or Sotho. Ralushai was fully aware of political posturing and the accrued climate of land claims, but sought as objectively as possible to record any historical oral affiliations. See, N.M.N. Ralushai, Preliminary report on the oral history of the Mapungubwe area, unpublished report for the Department of Environmental Affairs and Tourism, Pretoria, 2002, pp. 7–10; N.M.N. Ralushai, Additional information on the oral history of Mapungubwe, unpublished addendum to the World Heritage Nomination Dossier for Mapungubwe, Department of Environmental Affairs and Tourism, Pretoria, 2003.

Returning to Fouché, it is apparent that he failed to interpret any of the oral findings of Lestrade in further detail or in a meaningful way. However, it is not unexpected that he also failed to provide a comprehensive historical overview of the region's white or settler history before Mapungubwe was discovered. It appears that Fouché was driving an archaeological agenda, rather than a historical one, and perhaps even viewed the *bywoners*, i.e. the impoverished whites (tenant farmers) who could have supported historical accounts of Mapungubwe on the same discriminated level as his local Bantu-speaking informants. Oral history is nonetheless an important point of historical evidence that was previously under-represented, and it was this very local knowledge in fact that pointed to Mapungubwe's later gold discovery. Until more research interest in the vernacular interviews and early oral records about Mapungubwe prior to 1933 are considered to be reliable, they remain untapped historical sources of valuable information to local knowledge about Mapungubwe's early history. This neglect of the role of oral records, whether by black people or the Boers, as well as the omission of the early ethnological findings in the twentieth century, played a crucial role in negating Mapungubwe as an African discovery and perpetuated "the empty land myth".[291]

3.4. Legendary Lotrie: Francois Bernard Lotrie (1825–1917)

Before the 1890s little in general was known by outsiders about African prehistory. Yet during the mid-nineteenth century, the northern region of the Transvaal was a wild "hunting frontier" and a largely unexplored region for Western prospectors that sought and mapped rich mineral resources such as gold and diamond deposits.[292] The nearest white settlement was a remote Boer republic known as the *Zuid-Afrikaansche Republiek* (1852–1902) in the Zoutpansberg, surrounded by black communities.[293] This northern frontier was home not only to the local black populations who were forced into militarization, subjugation, servitude and other means of forced labour, but also to agrarian inhabitants such as the first white settlers, both the Afrikaner Boers, pro-British Boers, as well as the impoverished *bywoners* or the poor white tenants who served as manual labourers.[294]

The second half of the nineteenth century was also the era of gold discoveries. It brought with it immense economic repercussions that eventually led to the development of the South African gold mining industry at the end of the nineteenth century. Geographically, southern Africa

Figure 3.4. Francois Bernard Lotrie (1825–1917).

became a magnet for prospectors and fortune-seekers that followed the discovery of the vast gold deposits which had been mapped out in the Transvaal, and also found at Pilgrims Rest in 1873, Barberton in 1880 and later the Witwatersrand in 1886.[295]

The farm *Greefswald No.615*, where Mapungubwe was located, did not exist then because the area had not yet been apportioned into farms, and the region was arid and still very sparsely populated by white settlers. Early maps of the Transvaal or the South African Republic (ZAR) by Fred Jeppe indicated that this northern frontier was only inspected in the late 1860s for the purposes of dividing the land into farms, and by the 1890s a grid pattern of cadastral (square) plots covered the entire region.[296] The delineation of the property on which Mapungubwe

---

[291] See for example, S. Marks, "South Africa: the myth of the empty land". *History Today* 30(1), 1980, pp. 7–12.

[292] See for example, J.S. Bergh (ed.), *Geskiedenisatlas van Suid-Afrika: die vier Noordelike Provinsies*. Pretoria: Van Schaik, 1999.

[293] R. Wagner, "Zoutpansberg: the dynamics of a hunting frontier 1848–67". In S. Marks and A. Atmore (eds.), *Economy and society in pre-industrial South Africa*. London: Longman, 1980, pp. 313–349.

[294] See for example, L. Kriel, "The scramble for the Soutpansberg? The Boers and partition of Africa in the 1890s". *Scientia Militaria South African Journal of Military Studies* 31(2), 2003, pp. 74–91.

[295] See for example, L. Stiebel, "A treasure story: Thomas Baines's map to the gold fields of south eastern Africa 1877'". *English Studies in Africa* 45(1), 2002, pp. 1–17; F. Jeppe also produced a map in 1896 of the gold fields.

[296] The early maps by F. Jeppe, "Map of the South-African Republic (Transvaal) and surrounding territories" (1877) and "Jeppe's map of the Transvaal or S.A. Republic". London: Edward Stanford, 1898. Jeppe compiled his maps directly from the Surveyor-General's Office and Registrar of Deeds, as well as material published in other geographical European journals. He combined these with his own observations during his fifteen years of residence in the country, including information from A. Merensky, as well as directly from travellers, route explorations and surveys made by C. Mauch, E. Mohr, A. Hubner, T. Baines and many others. See also, L.F. Braun, *Colonial survey and native landscapes in rural South Africa 1850–1913: the politics of divided space in the Cape and Transvaal*. Leiden: Brill, 2015.

was situated, *Greefswald No. 615* (which later became *Greefswald No. 37 MS*) was first recorded in 1871 when the Surveyor General's Office allocated the farm as a Deed to Grant to a Dutch settler named Frederik Willem Claus.[297]

This dynamic regional historical and economic backdrop served as a crucial geographical nexus to the first European discovery of Mapungubwe. Despite Fouché being a respected historian, throughout his 1937 *Mapungubwe Volume I,* he did not provide a critical historical background to this bourgeoning northern region, and thus pretty much neglected any earlier histories. Instead, he painted a picture of Mapungubwe's discovery as a remote, solitary and isolated site, shrouded in mystery. Fouché indicated that although the local Africans knew of Mapungubwe Hill, he partially dismissed the verity of oral traditions as merely fearing ancestral agency. He did however acknowledge in his *Mapungubwe Volume I,* that it was this local oral tradition that eventually led to the discovery of Mapungubwe by Europeans.

According to Fouché, the "first white man" to have claimed the discovery of Mapungubwe was a hermit known as Frans Lotrie or Lottering, who allegedly lived in a cave on the banks of the Limpopo in the late nineteenth century.[298] The historical account of Lotrie's association with Mapungubwe was largely distilled by Fouché as taken from the 1912 German publication entitled, *Der Wilde Lotrie* (The Wild Lotrie) by Carl Moerschell.[299] Lotrie was recorded to have lived temporarily as a guest on Moerschell's farm, *Bergfontein,* which was situated on the western edge of the Zoutpansberg.

Furthermore, Lotrie supposedly found an alluvial deposit of gold somewhere, the only evidence being a single gold bangle which he apparently wore until his death.[300] Fouché ascribed Mapungubwe's major discovery to a solitary figure and described its discovery as follows:

> … [H]eard from a very old Native the strange story of a white man gone wild, who had lived a hermit's life in a cave on the banks of the Limpopo. This was a well-known character, Lottering (or Lotrie), who in the last decades of the nineteenth century had established himself in that remote wilderness, half a mile from Mapungubwe Hill. He had apparently climbed the sacred hill and found things there, because he presented to Van Graan's informant a big earthenware

pot, beautifully made, and quite unlike modern Native ware, which he (Lotrie) had brought down from the hill.[301]

There is a scarcity of historical records that pertain to Francois Bernard Lotrie and his direct association with Mapungubwe remains cautionary. Nonetheless, it is only more recently that diverse archival threads traced and pulled together over a decade now serve as some form of evidential and reliable primary record. These provided a sketchy and patchy outline of an obscure historical figure critical to Mapungubwe's early history which can now be examined in finer detail.[302] Much of what was known about this elusive figure had been anecdotally and historically repeated, revisited and reinterpreted by several authors throughout the past century.[303] Nonetheless, all shared a similar view that Lotrie was largely viewed as the discoverer of Mapungubwe and was confirmed as the "eremite on the Limpopo".[304]

Shortly after the South African War (1899–1902), Carl Moerschell, a German immigrant and farm settler in the hinterland of the Transvaal, first encountered Lotrie while he waited for his repatriation money at the Mara Mission Station, a major trading route near the western end of the Zoutpansberg.[305] Around the year 1905, Moerschell invited Lotrie, who was then in his eighties, to stay as his guest on the farm *Bergfontein*. For a number of years Lotrie lived in a small rondawel a short distance from the house. The evenings over dinner were spent listening to Lotrie relate his life story, and the subject of Mapungubwe often arose. According to Moerschell, Lotrie was adamant that Mapungubwe Hill was a "king's treasure chest", but admits he "placed no value" on his story and thought much of it was part of his wild imagination, and instead paid more attention to his adventurous hunting stories.[306]

---

[297] Mapungubwe Archive, UP/AGL/D/808, Surveyor General's Office, true copy of the General Deed of Transfer of *Greefswald Nos. 615*, 17 April 1871.

[298] L. Fouché, (ed.), *Mapungubwe: ancient Bantu civilization on the Limpopo: Reports on excavations at Mapungubwe (Northern Transvaal) from February 1933 to June 1935,* Cambridge: Cambridge University Press, 1937, p. 1.

[299] C.J. Moerschell, *Der Wilde Lotrie.* Würzburg: Begleiter Livingstones Voortrekker, 1912.

[300] Mapungubwe Archive, copy of E. Rosenthal, *The hinges creaked: true stories of South African treasure, lost and found.* Cape: Town H. Timmins, 1951, p. 184.

[301] L. Fouché, (ed.), *Mapungubwe: ancient Bantu civilization on the Limpopo: reports on excavations at Mapungubwe (Northern Transvaal) from February 1933 to June 1935.* Cambridge: Cambridge University Press, 1937, p.1

[302] J. Wintjes and S. Tiley-Nel, "The Lottering connection, *South African Archaeological Bulletin,* No. (210), 2019, pp. 101–110.

[303] See for example other references to Lotrie's life by, D.J. Kotzé, *Dapper kinders van Suid-Afrika.* Bloemfontein: Die Sondagskool-Boekhandel, 1962; J.B. de Vaal, "Lotrie: François Bernard Rudolph" In D.W. Kruger and C.J. Beyers (eds.) *Dictionary of South African Biography,* Part 3. Cape Town: Nasionale Boekhandel, 1977, p. 239; E. Rosenthal, *The hinges creaked: true stories of South African treasure, lost and found.* Cape Town: H. Timmins, 1951, pp. 182–193; K. Anderson, *Heroes of South Africa.* Johannesburg: AD Donker, 1983.

[304] C.J. Moerschell, "The eremite on the Limpopo", *Sunday Times,* 10 March 1933; Mapungubwe Archive, UP/AGL/D/127, C.J. Moerschell, "The hermit of the Limpopo", *Sunday Times,* 7 May 1933.

[305] The National Archives and Records Services of South Africa (NARSSA) list several German references and other types of correspondence between the Governor of the Transvaal Colony (1901–1910), the State Secretary and the Transvaal Agriculture Department (1900–1919) to Carl Josef Moerschell on several issues ranging from crown grants, land sales, supply of cattle statistics and the purchase of farms named: *Lucern* No.182; *Uitzicht* No. 221; *Louisville* No. 180; *Hoogland* No. 181. Including, mention of compensation of goods (six oxen and £90) for a plundered store in Zanderivierpoort and reference to "Becker and Moerschell" in Mara, Zoutpansberg.

[306] J.B. de Vaal, "Lotrie: baas olifantjagter". *Die Volkstem,* October, 1948.

Moerschell was obviously impressed by Lotrie and described him as the "last of the Voortrekkers" with a distinct, but strange "Boer dialect" (similar to Afrikaans but more like a High Dutch speaker). In 1912 he wrote a comprehensive monograph on the biographical life of Lotrie entitled, *Der Wilde Lotrie*.[307] Lotrie was considered to be the epitome of a nineteenth century colonial Boer adventurer and an enigmatic character who served once as a companion guide to Dr Livingstone. Moerschell extensively detailed Lotrie's life, travels, observations and adventures. Chapters were devoted to the *Dorslandtrekkers* (Thirstland Trekkers), how game such as elephants, crocodiles, lions and buffalo were hunted, as well as Lotrie's participation in the second Great Trek and his expectations as a diamond prospector, but no mention was made of Mapungubwe. The frontispiece of the book included the only known portrait sketch (a scrawled signature is included) of F.B. Lotrie drawn by an unnamed English officer. Moerschell also produced two other publications entitled, *Und de Grenze der Zivilisation: Sudafrikanische Skizzen* (On the border of civilisation: South African sketches) (1910) and *Afrikanische fahrten und abenteuer und beobachtungen des buren Bernard Francois Lotrie* (African travel: adventures and observations of the Boer Bernard Francois Lotrie) (1911).[308]

Moerschell first referred to Lotrie as *"Die Wilder Lottering"* and this nickname "Wild Lotrie" was attributed to his unwillingness to tolerate association even with the rough and ready Voortrekkers, and as such he lived much of a sedentary life that expected him to be moved around, never settled and joined several treks and military expeditions. His reputation and identity were considered eccentric as he trekked and criss-crossed the southern continent, like a recluse through uncharted territory. Lotrie constantly travelled and sometimes kept up with the waxing and waning of seasonal hunting. He made wagons and moved with his grazing cattle to avoid disease-ridden areas.[309]

Francois Bernard Rudolph Lotrie was born on 11 February 1825 in the embryonic English settler town of Grahamstown, a small military outpost in close proximity to the Cape frontier which became the largest settlement of the Eastern Cape.[310] In February 1836, while still an adolescent, young Lotrie and his parents joined the Andries Potgieter trek party that included about two hundred trekkers with sixty wagons. They crossed the Orange River and by July had reached the western end

of the Zoutpansberg. Lotrie further served on commando and is reported to have taken part in several expeditions and battles that included the fight against the Matabele at Vegkop in 1836; the punitive attack on the Ndebele at Mosega in 1837; as well as other military defeats such as the Battle of Boomplaats near Bloemfontein led by Andries W. Pretorius, which eventually drove and forced the Voortrekkers further northwards. Lotrie was also involved in the Boer and Griqua skirmishes at Zwartkoppies in 1845, the later Siege of Makapansgat and the historic month-long standoff between the Kekana Ndebele and the Voortrekkers in 1854.[311]

It is estimated that around 1848, Lotrie formed part of the number of white settlers that arrived in the Zoutpansberg region under the leadership of Potgieter. Lotrie settled in the northern-most Voortrekker town of Schoemansdal and earned a living as a big game hunter as most of the Zoutpansberg economy was generated from elephant hunting. Lotrie had a reputation as "one of the main elephant hunters" as he hunted almost daily and dealt in the trade of masses of ivory that was a lucrative industry with good market value. This contributed to the extensive decimation of wildlife and natural game that was so characteristic of the Zoutpansberg region. During the 1850s the annual average shipment of ivory from the small town of Schoemansdal amounted to an astonishing 45, 000kg, with no less than 1 000 elephant hunted within a single year.[312] Lotrie was therefore considered a highly-prized elephant hunter, *"Die Olifantjager van Schoemansdal"* which earned him the nickname *Dali* that meant "The Thunderer", given by the local black ivory carriers that laboured for the extensive ivory trade for Schoemansdal.[313]

Lotrie's five children appear to have taken on variations of the surname, "Lotrie", "Lottering" or "Lottrie".[314] In 1874, his family joined the Thirstland Trek to Angola, a major exodus of *trekboers* (migrating farmers) under the leadership of Gert Alberts who traversed Bechuanaland (Botswana) and crossed the Cunene River into Angola in 1875 in search of better living conditions. Lotrie's wife died the following year. He then joined a western-southern move to Walvis Bay (Namibia) where he undertook minor

[307] C.J. Moerschell, *Der Wilde Lotrie*. Würzburg: Begleiter Livingstones Voortrekker, 1912.

[308] See other titles by C.J. Moerschell, *Und de Grenze der Zivilisation: Sudafrikanische Skizzen*. Würzburg: Stürtz 1910; C.J. Moerschell, *Afrikanische Fahrten Und Abenteuer Und Beobachtungen des Buren Bernard Francois Lotrie*. Würzburg: Stürtz, 1912. It is not yet determined if the latter title is somehow the same title as *Der Wilde Lotrie* (1912).

[309] D.J. Kotzé, *Dapper kinders van Suid-Afrika*, Die Sondagskoolboekhandel, Bloemfontein, 1962, pp. 90–98.

[310] S. Tiley-Nel, "François Bernard Rudolph Lotrie". In S. Tiley-Nel (ed.) *Mapungubwe remembered: contributions to Mapungubwe by the University of Pretoria*. Johannesburg: Chris van Rensburg Publications (Pty) Ltd, 2011, pp.10–11.

[311] C.J. Moerschell, *Der Wilde Lotrie*. Würzburg: Begleiter Livingstones Voortrekker, 1912, pp.19–33.

[312] J.W.N. Tempelhoff, *Die okkupasiestelsel in die distrik Soutpansberg, 1886–1899*, Archives yearbook for South African History 60. Pretoria: Government Printers, 1997, p. 8.

[313] J.B. de Vaal, "Lotrie: baas olifantjager", *Die Volkstem*, n.d. October 1948.

[314] In 1861, at the age of 36, Lotrie married Helena Beatrix Botha who was from the district of Lydenburg. Their firstborn was a son named Willem Frederick Lotrie (12 April 1862) and they also had a daughter, Helena Catherina Beatrix Lottering (20 July 1864). Following the evacuation of Schoemansdal in July 1867, due to precarious tensions and wider political deterioration between the Voortrekkers, the Ndebele to the West, the Ngoni to the East, and the Venda inhabitants, the Lotrie family migrated south. A further three siblings were born later: Cornelius Stephanus Lotrie (Lottrie) was born in Newcastle in Natal (7 March 1869); Barend Christoffel Johannes was born in the Bloemfontein area (20 July 1874) and a fifth child that was adopted named Nella or Nellie Talietha, was born in Natal (19 January 1887). See, J. de Villiers Roos's account of Lotrie's brief biography and list of children in, "'n Romantiese figure verdwene". *Die Volkstem*, 13 March 1917.

transport labour between Angra Pequena (now Lüderitz) and the interior of the country.[315] Sometime before the South African War, Lotrie was reported to have returned to the Limpopo region and supposedly lived with his family for fifteen years on the southern portion of the farm *Greefswald*. He established himself as a wagon-maker along the Limpopo River on the north-western border of the Transvaal.

In 1888 Piet Grobler, the Consul of the Transvaal Republic, was sent on a treaty mission by President Kruger to represent the Republic to the Matabele, as much of the northern region of the Transvaal was governed by Chief Lobengula from his capital in Bulawayo, Rhodesia (now Zimbabwe). On Piet Grobler's return expedition along the Limpopo River he came across the Lotrie family and they were involved in a skirmish with Kgama's Ngwato subjects in which Lotrie and his son sustained injuries, whilst Grobler was fatally wounded. Apparently Lotrie's eldest daughter, Helena Catherina Beatrix, was elevated to Voortrekker history as a heroine, as according to legend, she, "saved the life of her wounded father by spreading her skirt to catch the deadly spears of the fierce black hoarders", whilst other accounts of the Grobler skirmish say Helene in fact attempted to protect Grobler. [316]

In his late eighties, Lotrie reportedly lived, either as a "hermit in a cave along the banks of the Limpopo" or in a rock-shelter at the foot of Mapungubwe Hill where, as the story goes, he frequently climbed it to "potter round among the many sherds and pieces of slag littered upon its summit".[317] Lotrie apparently removed a "very handsome earthenware pot" and offered this as a gesture to his friend named Mowena, also elderly and an African labourer who lived in a nearby kraal a distance from his cave. Historical evidence of the life of Lotrie and his "discovery" of Mapungubwe remains based on patchy, scant, disjointed and circumstantial evidence, but he was nevertheless an odd character from a bygone era and one of the last of the nimrod Voortrekker pioneers of the nineteenth century.[318]

Lotrie lived in a makeshift *hartebeeshuisie* (a traditional reed house), and tended a small vegetable garden, had a handful of cattle and reportedly ate meat only as an exception. He died at age ninety-two in the south-western Zoutpansberg region of Kalkbank in 1917. From those that met him, encountered him and knew of him in the last decade of his life, the following can be loosely translated and extracted about a remarkable and certainly forgotten historical figure in Mapungubwe's early history. Lotrie was said to have done more than enough in "one lifetime that would fill a dozen men's lives" and those that came into contact with him in his last years were inevitably struck by the "internal burning fire of his being", notwithstanding his physical external deterioration that came unfortunately with a great age. His manners were at all time's cordial, his speech peculiar, but dignified, "more Dutch than Afrikaans". Lotrie was considered the last link of his current generation to the "romantic past of the land", and considered once "almost a rebel against the Republic", was acknowledged as a "forgotten romantic figure" that is said to have discovered Mapungubwe.[319]

Nonetheless, the only direct link of Lotrie to Mapungubwe lies archivally remote within a hand-written letter in 1933 by B.C. Lottering (presumably Barend Christoffel, Lotrie's son) who lamented the fact that his father, Lotrie, was the "actual discoverer" of Mapungubwe. He further claimed that he (Barend) assisted the Van Graans to locate Mapungubwe and that he was also responsible for taking Frobenius to its location while the Van Graans used his knowledge to locate the Mapungubwe gold. Lottering stated that he tried to inform people of the site, but did not know how to formally report it, and as a consequence the "actual" discovery of Mapungubwe gold was formerly attributed to the Van Graan family.[320]

Following the First World War (1914–1918) there is then a silence in the archival records with no mention or link to Mapungubwe between the periods that followed Lotrie's death until the farm name, *Greefswald*, resurfaced later in 1922 but this time from "botanical" interest due to the floral diversity of the region.

3.5. Back to the Battle of Dongola: 1922

In 1922, a decade before the discovery of gold on Mapungubwe Hill, a significant portion of the northern reaches of the Transvaal north of the Zoutpansberg territory became the experimental focus of botanical and agricultural research, largely through the efforts of the prominent Welsh botanist, Dr Illtyd B. Pole Evans (1879–1968).[321] Pole Evans was Chief of the Division of Botany in the Department of Agriculture at the Royal Botanic Gardens, Kew in London.[322] In 1918, "at the request of Smuts", the national government had initially already set aside a block of nine farms to form what became part of

---

[315] C.J. Moerschell, *Der Wilde Lotrie*. Würzburg: Begleiter Livingstones Voortrekker, 1912.

[316] D.J. Kotzé, *Dapper kinders van Suid-Afrika*. Bloemfontein: Die Sondagskool-boekhandel, 1962, p. 98.

[317] E. Rosenthal, *The hinges creaked: true stories of South African treasure, lost and found*. Cape Town: H. Timmins, 1951, p. 183.

[318] Mapungubwe Archive, UP/AGL/D/895, "Mapoengoebwe [sic]: 'n Oorblyfsel van die ryk van Monomotapa", *Die Brandwag*, 17 September 1937.

[319] See newspaper article that appears as an obituary to Lotrie by J. de Villiers Roos, "'n Romantiese figure verdwene", *Die Volkstem*. 13 March 1917.

[320] Mapungubwe Archive, UP/AGL/D/3465, B.C. Lottering wrote to Mr H. Visser (farm owner of *Grootdraai*) asking for his assistance in reporting the fact his late father was actually the discoverer of the site, 10 April 1933.

[321] For further detail about the political and contested history of the Dongola Wild Life Sanctuary, see J. Carruthers, "Trouble in the garden: South African botanical politics ca. 1870–1950". *South African Journal of Botany* 77(2), 2011, pp. 258–267.

[322] The Archives of the Royal Botanic Gardens at Kew have in their possession (Ref: ROS Collection catalogued) ten black and white photographs of the area of Mapungubwe taken by Reginald-Rose Innes (1915–2012), a South African Grassland Ecologist, copies of these were lodged in the Mapungubwe Archive in May 2014.

Figure 3.5. Portrait of John Mhlope, first resident warden of the Dongola Botanical Reserve in 1934.

the Dongola Botanical Reserve where wildlife and natural vegetation could be preserved.[323] Pole Evans headed the South African Botanical Survey, and established a botanical research station in the Mapungubwe area, which was the first protected area or ecological park in South Africa to be delimited for the sole purposes of its ecological value and scientific research.[324]

This vision of creating a national park for "science" formed part of Smut's idea of the "South Africanisation of science" and Dongola was greatly supported by Smuts, who as a "dynamic botanist"[325] was also responsible for conducting the National Botanical Survey and for the establishment of what later became known as the Dongola Botanical Reserve along the Limpopo River. The Archive mentions John Mhlope as the first resident warden and caretaker of the Dongola Botanical Reserve as early as 1934. Dongola was named after a volcano-shaped mountain situated on the north-east corner of the farm *Goree 728 MS* and is historically relevant due to its very close proximity to

Mapungubwe situated on the farm *Greefswald* 37 MS.[326] Between 1936 and 1948, Dongola had been placed under the curation of Pole Evans as warden, who controlled and issued access permits not only to Dongola, but sometimes for access to Mapungubwe from the Department of Agriculture and Forestry.[327]

Throughout the 1930s and 1940s, Pole Evans hosted many visitors, dignitaries and notably members of the media at Dongola, in the hope of gaining support and adding government interest to the idea of establishing a national park, particularly after Smuts was back in government. Smuts frequently visited Pole Evans at Dongola to "botanise" and even built a modest simple thatched two-roomed stone cottage situated high on a sandstone ridge overlooking the Limpopo River with a nearby seat built and walled in. Known commonly as, "Smuts House", this now historical structure lies to the east of Mapungubwe Hill on the border of the farms, *Greefswald* and *Schroda*.[328]

Later by the 1940s, the Dongola Botanical Reserve would be expanded and grow to twenty seven farms owing to the support of Andrew Conroy, Minister of Lands and Irrigation in the Department of Agriculture.[329] This redefinition and extension of the botanical reserve included *Greefswald*, on which Mapungubwe Hill is situated and thus any plans for scientific research at Dongola would have included the core area of Mapungubwe. The initial aim for the Dongola area was to establish a nature reserve for the preservation of fauna and flora, however this development benefited the first aerial survey of Mapungubwe in August 1933.[330] Col. F.R.G. Hoare was one of Conroy's Board members in the Department of Agriculture and formed part of the flight crew for two military planes Dh-9s (British WWI bombers) provided by Smuts's fledgling air force together with photographic equipment to conduct the aerial survey.[331] This survey proved to be the first of its kind in South Africa, where aircraft were used for archaeological reconnaissance.[332]

---

[323] The nine farms names were *Goeree* 728 MS; *Sharlee* 729 MS; *Rossynlee* 730 MS; *Giesdendam* 731 MS; *Dunsappie* 732 MS; *Brunsfield* 733 MS; *Moerdyk* 736 MS; *Vernon* 737 MS and *Shelton Hall* 738 MS.

[324] See, J. Carruthers, *National Park Science: a century of research in South Africa*. Cambridge: Cambridge University Press, 2017, pp. 108–116.

[325] T. Cameron, *Jan Smuts: an illustrated biography*. Pretoria: Human & Rousseau (Pty) Ltd, 2004, pp. 102–105.

[326] J. Carruthers, Jan Smuts and the Dongola Wild Life Sanctuary. Talk to the Friends of Smuts Foundation, Irene (Pretoria), 21 May 2003.

[327] Mapungubwe Archive, UP/AGL/D/649, I. Pole Evans, Department of Agriculture and Forestry Division of Plan Industry, Pretoria - Van Riet Lowe correspondence and enclosed permit to camp at Dongola; thank-you note for issuance of permit, 6 March 1936.

[328] A. Meyer, "Mapungubwe: the Smuts connection". *South African Archaeological Society Newsletter* 3(2), 1980, pp. 8–10.

[329] J. Carruthers, "The Dongola Wild Life Sanctuary: 'psychological blunder, economic folly and political monstrosity' or more valuable than rubies and gold?" *Kleio* XXIV 1992 pp. 82–100.

[330] L. Fouché, *Mapungubwe: ancient Bantu civilization on the Limpopo, reports on excavations at Mapungubwe (Northern Transvaal) from February 1933 to June 1935*. Cambridge: Cambridge University Press, 1937, p. 8.

[331] S Tiley-Nel, The reconnection: on Smuts and Mapungubwe's early history. Paper presented to the Friends of the Smuts Foundation, Irene, 24 April 2014; see also Mapungubwe Archive, UP/AGL/D/206, "Akin with Zimbabwe? Discoveries at Mapungubwe: aerial survey in progress". *The Star*, 29 August 1933.

[332] Mapungubwe Archive, 254 aerial photographs reproduced on glass negatives were taken of *Greefswald* and the Limpopo region. The strip of land photographed was about 10 miles (± 16km) broad and about 30 miles (±48km) long. It was an experimental flight that aimed at photographing Mapungubwe hill and the surrounding environment in the hope of identifying archaeological settlements and related features,

Figure 3.6. First aerial views of the Shashe and Limpopo Rivers and aerial surveys of the landscape in August 1933.

Andrew Conroy, the Minister of Lands and Irrigation (1939–1948) together with Pole Evans advocated for a Dongola National Park, which he planned to re-name after Smuts as "The Smuts National Park".[333] These early beginnings of the Dongola Botanical Reserve became the creation and core of what was called the Dongola Wildlife Sanctuary.[334] The jointly proposed idea by Pole Evans and Smuts served as a blueprint for Mapungubwe as a national park, as well as the region's prospects for a future Transfrontier cross-border conservation area.[335] When Minister Conroy announced his intention of including a further 124 farms to the plans, this was met with unexpected opposition from the National Parks Board of Trustees, as well as many private landowners and the Zoutpansberg Farmers Union.[336]

The Dongola proposals received an immense amount of criticism and it became such a controversial debate among farmers in the region that it was named the "Battle of Dongola".[337] This battle generated some of the longest and most bitter debates in parliament up to then and one of the largest Select Committee Reports in South Africa on record.[338] Dongola became such a political battle between the Smuts government and the new opposition National Party that was coming into power in 1948, that the new government gave priority to the abolition of the Dongola Wild Life Sanctuary.[339]

Dongola was evidently an election issue in 1948, which provided the Nationalists with a good platform to put an end to Smuts's vision and as such the Dongola Wild Life Sanctuary Act, No. 6 of 1947 was deproclaimed in 1949.[340] On the other hand, had this Act not been politically and foolishly overturned, Dongola would have provided: "[a] sanctuary... for the protection and preservation, in the national interest, of the land comprised therein, of its natural vegetation, wildlife and of objects of geological,

---

saving months of tedious ground work and surveys. The aircraft provided by the Union Air Force were equipped with long-range cameras and flew from Pretoria to Messina to conduct the aerial survey of the Mapungubwe region over a period of a week. The aircraft were piloted under Major C.J. Venter with Lieutenants King and Fourie and Staff-Sergeant Photographer named Ireland. Prof. L. Fouché and Col. F.R.G. Hoare was also part of the flight crew.

[333] J. Carruthers, 2015, "The 'Battle of Dongola' and the Mapungubwe National Park", Royal Society of South Africa, see online article, <http://www.royalsocietysa.org.za>, *s.a.* access: 2015.01.28.

[334] The Dongola Wildlife Sanctuary Act, No. 9 of 1947, the Dongola Wildlife Sanctuary Repeal Act, No. 29 of 1949.

[335] On 22 June 2006, the Transfrontier Limpopo-Shashe Memorandum of Understanding (MOU) was signed by Ministerial dignitaries from South Africa, Botswana and Zimbabwe which made the cross-border park a reality and a multi-national approach first mooted by Jan Smuts.

[336] "Dongola Reserve controversy: Zoutpansberg Farmers state their case". *Primary Producer*, February 1946.

[337] M. Berry and M. Cadman, *Dongola to Mapungubwe: the 80-year battle to conserve the Limpopo valley.* Swartwater: Mmabolela Press, 2007, pp. 14–15.

[338] Union of South Africa, Report of the Select Committee on the Dongola Wild Life Sanctuary Bill (Hybrid Bill), Vol. 1, section 12, Cape Town, 1945; Union of South Africa, Report of the Select Committee on the Dongola Wild Life Sanctuary Bill (Hybrid Bill), Vol. 2, section 6–46, Cape Town, 1946.

[339] J. Carruthers, "The Dongola Wild Life Sanctuary: 'psychological blunder, economic folly and political monstrosity' or more valuable than rubies and gold?" *Kleio* XXIV, 1992, pp. 82–100.

[340] The Dongola Wildlife Sanctuary Repeal Act 29 of 1949.

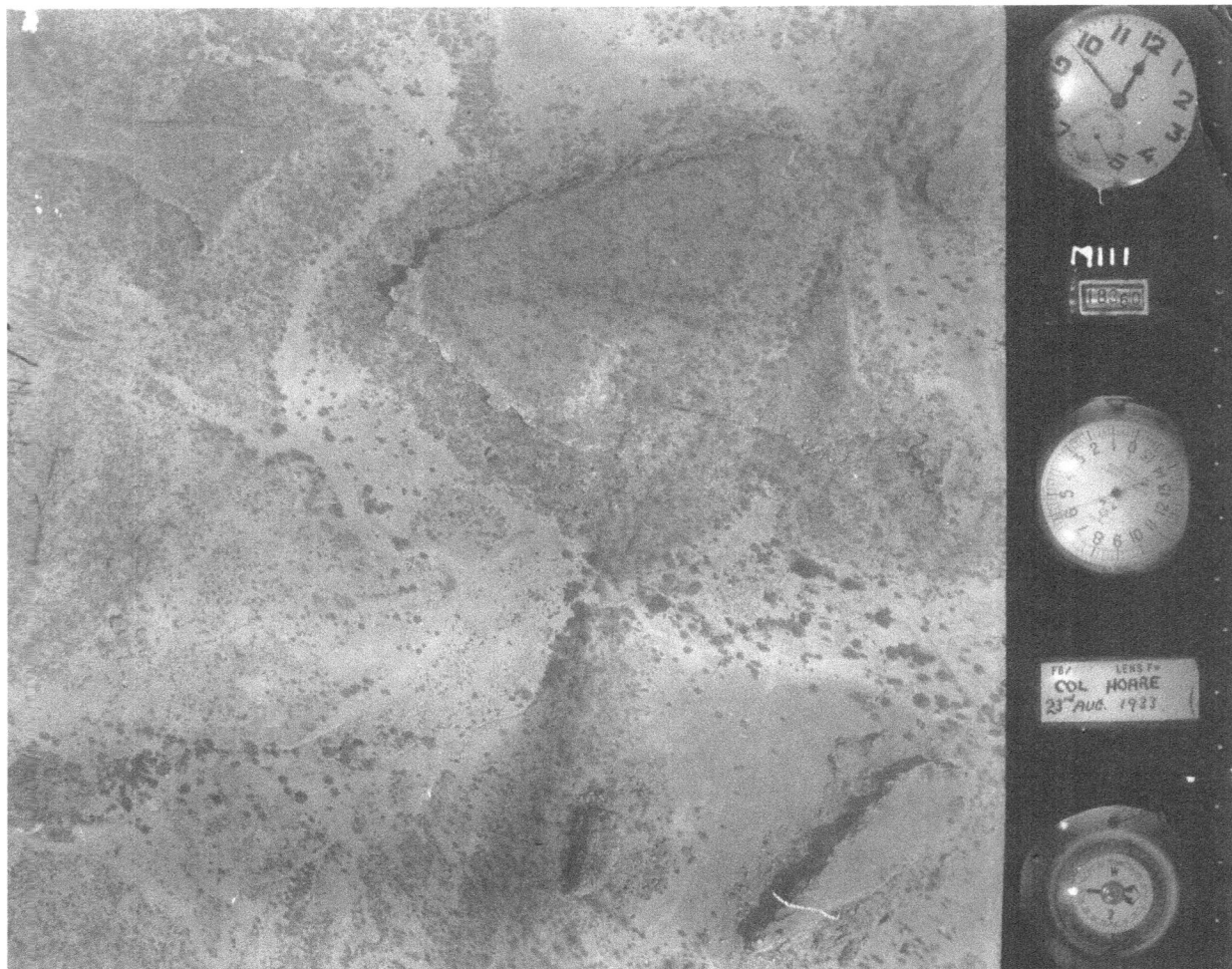

Figure 3.7. Earliest aerial photograph of Mapungubwe Hill and surrounds, 23 August 1933.

ethnological, historical, or other scientific interest therein".[341] In Smuts's House of Assembly address in 1949, he had stressed again the importance of the potential of the region:

> I am thinking of what would happen if this Dongola reserve were functioning fully on both sides of the Limpopo... You would have a stream of tourists here in the winter months, first passing through Kruger Park, then going north to the Limpopo Park and then going further to other parks, leaving behind a wealth of dollars and other good things which will help this country.[342]

The Dongola Wild Life Sanctuary Act, No.29 of 1949 was repealed by the National Party, funding was returned to donors, properties and farms that comprised the Dongola Botanical Reserve were re-allocated, hunting of wild life proliferated as a result any efforts for a national park "faded from public memory".[343]

3.6. 'Forgetting Frobenius'[344]: 1928–1929

Scholars have long been aware that the rise to fame of Mapungubwe was much earlier than previously thought, but unfortunately little of this pre-1933 history has been reflected in the literature. Scholars who had previously published on the discovery of Mapungubwe all alluded to the "work of Frobenius who was in the neighbourhood in 1929", but outwardly "forgot" about this German's so-called scientific discovery.[345] Beyond Mapungubwe, the observations of the German ethnologist, Leo Frobenius, in southern African history in particular, has commonly been ignored by South African academics, with the exception of earlier research in the field of rock art and some much

---

[341] Dongola Wildlife Sanctuary Act, No. 6 of 1947.
[342] Union of South Africa, 1949, pp. 3775–3776.
[343] See, J. Carruthers, *National Park Science: a century of research in South Africa*. Cambridge: Cambridge University Press, 2017, p. 115.

[344] Title kindly borrowed from a previous article with mention of "Forgetting Frobenius" by M. Schoeman, "Co-operation, conflict and the University of Pretoria Archaeological committee". In S. Tiley-Nel (ed.) *Mapungubwe remembered: contributions to Mapungubwe by the University of Pretoria*. Johannesburg: Chris van Rensburg Publications (Pty) Ltd, 2011, p. 90.
[345] See L. Fouché, *Mapungubwe: ancient Bantu civilization on the Limpopo: Reports on excavations at Mapungubwe (Northern Transvaal) from February 1933 to June 1935*, Volume I. Cambridge: Cambridge University Press, 1937, p. 4; A. Meyer, *The Iron Age sites of Greefswald: stratigraphy and chronology of the sites and a history of investigations*. Pretoria: University of Pretoria, 1998, p. 17.

more recent work.[346] The Frobenius material should be considered of immense value, and whilst it can be argued that the reason for neglect is because all the accounts are in German, the Frobenius Institute in Frankfurt, Germany remains an untapped source to the historian of early twentieth century South Africa.[347]

Frobenius who devoted his life's work to Africa was obsessed with "culture" in all its forms, including rock art, the southern Rhodesian ruins (now known as Great Zimbabwe), and also material culture. This all intrigued his ethnographic mind as did the rest of Africa. Frobenius endeavoured to develop a total synthesis of African cultures and even began a monumental work titled, *Atlas Africanus*, which aimed to cartographically combine all the elements of African cultures into a single map or series of maps.[348] This map was consequently never finished, but he published twice on his ethnographic expedition to southern Africa, but no specific mention of his "discovery" of Mapungubwe.[349] According to the Frobenius Institute he was credited with the establishment of the *Africa Archive* and subsequently travelled from the period 1904 to 1933, extensively "doing" ethnography, undertaking a total of thirteen expeditions and accrued over 6 000 artefacts and objects for the Frobenius Art Collection from all over the African continent.[350]

His African expedition to the south, formed part of his ninth trip to the continent, and it was to be his last in southern Africa. This twenty-month, southwards expedition took place from August 1928 to March 1930, with a route that passed through the Mapungubwe region, over the Limpopo River along the northern border of the Transvaal and into southern Rhodesia (today Zimbabwe). It was no coincidence that the Frobenius expedition overlapped with the ninety-ninth year meeting of the British Association for the Advancement of Science held in Johannesburg and Cape Town from 22 July to 2 August 1929.[351] General Smuts was

Vice-President of the Association, and in the following year of 1931 he became its President, although just previously in June 1929, he had lost his position to J.B.M. Hertzog as Prime Minister. The connection of Smuts to Frobenius and the archaeologists that attended the meeting would have long-term implications for Mapungubwe research later. After the "formal" gold discovery in 1933, Smuts had even considered Frobenius to possibly take on the archaeological excavations at Mapungubwe.[352]

The 1929 British Association for the Advancement of Science meeting was particularly significant as Dr Percy Wagner, a reputed geologist, had just exhibited and presented the first map that showed the distribution of pre-European metal mining in Transvaal and Southern Rhodesia.[353] This same map was published for the first time in Fouché's *Mapungubwe Vol. I*[354] Masses of worked gold had already been exclusively processed by the Rhodesia Ancient Ruins Ltd. of Cecil John Rhodes by the late nineteenth-century from sites north of the Limpopo.[355] In addition, British archaeologists such as D. Randall-MacIver and G. Caton-Thompson, along with J. Schofield, a South African engineer, had already called greater attention to these sites which were also reported on in the British Association for the Advancement of Science Meeting.[356]

Within this historical context, the southern African goldfields, an immense and vast area between the Zambezi Valley and the Witwatersrand, included the Limpopo River and thus awaited further discovery based on the international and local interest of stone-walled structures and their

[346] See example of recent article by J. Wintjes, "The Frobenius expedition to Natal and the Cinyati archive". *Southern African Humanities* 25, 2013, pp. 167–205.

[347] The Frobenius Institute is associated with the Goethe University in Frankfurt, Germany and retains records and materials by Leo Frobenius (1873–1938) and expeditions in Africa. Considered a "legacy collection" in the archive, it contains around 250 boxes of diaries, draft manuscripts, lectures, notebooks and letters. Frobenius was the founder of the Africa Archive (1889) and he later became the Director of the Research Institute of Cultural Morphology in Munich (1926–1938), see further detail at <https://frobenius-institut.de/en/collections-and-archives/legacies>, access: 2018.07.10.

[348] For a synthesis of Frobenius' work in Africa, see for example, J. Zwernemann, "Leo Frobenius and cultural research in Africa". *Institute of African Studies Research Review* 3(2), 1967, pp. 2–20; see also E. Haberland (ed.), *Leo Frobenius on African history, art, and culture: an anthropology*. Princeton: Markus Wiener Publishers, 2007.

[349] L. Frobenius, *Madsimu Dsangara Südafrikanische Felsbilderchronik*. Berlin: Atlantis, 1931; L. Frobenius, *Erythräa Länder und Zeiten des heiligen Königsmordes*. Berlin: Atlantis, 1931.

[350] See more about the Frobenius Collection, <https://frobenius-institut.de/en/collections-and-archives/ethnographic-collection>, access: 2018.07.13.

[351] This gathering was a highly influential meeting and was attended by Smuts, government administrators and other top scholars in the field of anthropology, archaeology and palaeontology, botany and many other disciplines. The contingent included: L. Leaky; R. Broom; H. Balfour; C. van Riet Lowe; R. Dart; N. Jones; L. Fouché; W.V. Eiselen; G. Caton-Thompson

and L. Frobenius to name just a few. See Report on the British Association for the Advancement of Science, (sectional transactions 368), Office of the British Association. London: Burlington House, 1930.

[352] See S. Tiley-Nel, "The reconnection: Smuts and Mapungubwe early history". Paper and lecture presented to the Friends of the General Smuts Foundation, 24 April 2014; See also correspondence, July 1. Frobenius, Leo. *Forschungsinstitut für Kulturmorphologie*, Frankfurt – J.C. Smuts, Irene. Recalls his stay in South Africa; sends Smuts a newly compiled work by Jensen of his Institute on the peoples of Abyssinia in appreciation of the help and hospitality he enjoyed. Letter is written in German. (Inventory Nos. 233), Letters to J.C. Smuts 1902–1950. Historical Papers: University of Witwatersrand.

[353] See, Report on the British Association for the Advancement of Science, (sectional transactions, H-369), Office of the British Association, Burlington House, London, 1930; as well as P.A. Wagner, "Map showing some of the more important Pre-European mine workings of Southern Africa", 1929.

[354] See L. Fouché, *Mapungubwe: ancient Bantu civilization on the Limpopo, reports on excavations at Mapungubwe (Northern Transvaal) from February 1933 to June 1935*, Volume I. Cambridge: Cambridge University Press, 1937, facing p. 4.

[355] Mapungubwe Archive, UP/AGL/D/286/2, Letter from W.G. Neal to T. Peachy, 23 September 1895. The British South Africa Company granted exclusive rights to the Rhodesia Ancient Ruins Ltd (1897–1900) to explore and work for "treasure". The first shareholders were M. Gifford; J. Clark; T. Peachy; W.G. Neal; G. Johnson and F. Leech with Rhodes offered the first right of purchasing any discoveries. It was estimated that in 1897, over 21, 000,000 ounces of gold had been mined from ancient ruins by treasure seekers. See, P. Hubbard, "The Ancient ruins Company". *Prehistory Society of Zimbabwe Newsletter* Issue 144, May 2010, p. 2.

[356] See D, Randall-MacIver, *Medieval Rhodesia*. London: MacMillan, 1905; G. Caton-Thompson, *The Zimbabwe Culture*. Oxford: Clarendon Press, 1931.

association with "ancient workings".[357] It was believed that the ancient mines were not only used mainly for the exploitation of copper and tin sources, but also pointed to rich gold deposits. Frobenius collected several items of metal such as iron, bronze and brass as ethnographic samples, but unfortunately no record was kept of their provenance or origin. He did however briefly describe the examination of these finds in his report on the expedition.[358]

Dr E.H. Schultz, a German metallurgist, produced the earliest metallographic and chemical analysis of the metal artefacts from southern Africa collected by Frobenius. In 1950, he published a report, *Zuzammensetzung und Aufbau einiger Metallfunde der Afrika Expedition von Leo Frobenius 1928/30* (Composition and structure of some metal finds of the Africa Expedition of Leo Frobenius 1928/30).[359] It is not unlikely that some of these metal samples may have derived from his expedition to Mapungubwe, but there is no record of gold artefacts. This report was later translated and re-examined in 1992 with technical comments by Duncan Miller from the University of Cape Town.[360] In May 1928, just a few months earlier than Frobenius's expedition another prospecting party ascended Mapungubwe Hill and illegally disturbed what was called the "chief's grave". They removed "large upright, monolith-like stones" in order to get to "metal items", pottery and agate stones.[361] In Fouché's version of the discovery of Mapungubwe, he stated that whilst there were visible disturbances on the hill, this evidence "may have been the work of Frobenius", but reported that Frobenius' trial excavation on Mapungubwe Hill revealed nothing of importance.[362] This was later confirmed by J.C.O. van Graan.[363]

Frobenius only went to Mapungubwe later in October 1928 The Frobenius expedition prospecting party comprised Baron Von Leesen, an electrical supplier from Winchester House in Johannesburg, Barend Lottering, son of F.B. Lotrie and A. Parpendorf from the Van Ryn Deep Mine (Benoni), accompanied by Leo Frobenius (1873–1938), the leader of the expedition and his colleagues, Adolf Jensen (1899–1965) and Heinz Wieschhoff on 6 October 1928. This expedition was aimed at the explicit

search for ancient metals and prehistoric mines, and they headed further north towards the ruins of Great Zimbabwe. Lottering had been approached a month prior to their intended departure by the Johannesburg-based businessman, Mr H. von Leesen to serve as their guide and to indicate the locality of the Hill as he had been party to the earlier prospectors that had disturbed the grave site on Mapungubwe Hill in May 1928.[364]

In 2017, Wintjes published an article which presented fine detail on the Frobenius expedition to Mapungubwe that referred to the locality as "*Manopi*" on the property called *Greefswald*. It was established that *Manopi* in fact referred to the wider Mapungubwe valley according to Wintjes's research. Frobenius and his team explored the site for seven days and two trenches were dug in search of sample material. Several photographs and field sketches were taken of pottery, the natural landscape and some stone structures that were uncovered, but it remains unknown how many and what samples were removed. This recent research, with the aid of a combination of correspondence and historical records from the Mapungubwe Archive, complemented by the maps, diary entries, photographs, sketches and manuscripts from the Frobenius Institute confirm that Mapungubwe Hill was in fact discovered before 1933 by the Germans.[365]

In a 1972 article by J. Ita on Frobenius in West Africa, general observations of the Frobenius "scientific" approach are said to point to common knowledge that, despite his vigour for excavation, he "lacked archaeological method" and was unscrupulous in "forcing the sale of artefacts". Frobenius was known to keep inadequate site records and in the process "destroyed a considerable amount of archaeological evidence".[366] Nonetheless, Frobenius did make some valuable contributions to African history that at the time represented a landmark in ethnography, which in the context of its time, science was chiefly in a sense considered historical. To current knowledge, Frobenius failed to uncover any gold on Mapungubwe Hill. If Frobenius was touted as the "discoverer of Mapungubwe" there is no doubt that the site may have been further raided and pillaged to fill the grand ethnographic museums made by the German Empire that were so typical of the first decade of the twentieth century.

3.7. The famous five discoverers: 1932 and J.C.O. van Graan (1908–1987)

In W.P. Taylor's book on *African Treasures* in 1902 he identified different "types of treasure-seekers" and grouped them as the pioneers, the raiders, "trekkers" and concession-hunters, the surveyor and engineer,

---

[357] Mapungubwe Archive, UP/AGL/D/1, J.F. Schofield, "The case against the Ancients". *Sunday Times*, 3 January 1926.

[358] L. Frobenius, *Erythräa Länder und Zeiten des heiligen Königsmordes*. Berlin Atlantis, 1931, pp. 288–293.

[359] E.H. Schultz, "Zuzammensetzung und Aufbau einiger Metallfunde der Afrika-Expedition von Leo Frobenius 1928/30". *Paideuma* 5, 1950, pp. 13–134.

[360] D. Miller, "Pioneering metallographic analyses of indigenous metal artefacts from southern Africa: collected by the Frobenius expedition 1929–1930". *South African Archaeological Bulletin* 4(156), 1992, pp. 108–115.

[361] Mapungubwe Archive, UP/AGL/D/34, Unsigned sworn affidavit by Richard Glen Rorke, 2 March 1933.

[362] L. Fouché, *Mapungubwe: ancient Bantu civilization on the Limpopo, report on excavations at Mapungubwe (Northern Transvaal) from February 1933 to June 1935*. Cambridge: Cambridge University Press, 1937, p. 4.

[363] Mapungubwe Archive, UP/AGL/D/89, J.C.O van Graan letter to L. Fouché informing him that he met the man who helped Frobenius dig the trial holes, 24 March 1933.

[364] Mapungubwe Archive, UP/AGL/D/3464, Letter from H. van Leesen to B.C. Lottering, 27 September 1928.

[365] J. Wintjes, "Frobenius discovered before crossing Limpopo ruins: ancient fortificated settlements, beautiful pottery mountains stop". *De Arte* 52(1), 2017, pp. 31–67.

[366] J. Ita, "Frobenius in West African History". *Journal of Africa History* 13(4), 1972, p. 673.

Figure 3.8. Jeremiah Cornelius Olivier Van Graan (1908–1987).

his first temporary teaching position in the "northern bushveld", soon after he graduated from the Transvaal University College (TUC). The family moved to the farm, *Barend 1089* (near Musina) in the Mopani district of the northern Zoutpansberg (North Transvaal) when J.C.O. van Graan took up his position at Brombeek, a single-teacher primary school near Alldays in the Transvaal.[371]

The most common narrative of the discovery of gold on Mapungubwe Hill began in earnest on 29 December 1932, when E.S.J. (Ernst) van Graan and J.C.O van Graan (Jerry) first met with H.P (Hendrik) van der Walt on the farm, *Congo*. They appeared to be living as *bywoners* on the farm as they resided in a dilapidated three-sided thatched house built or rather supported by a large baobab tree. Their intended black guide, Mowena, lived on or nearby the farm as a labourer.[372] Initially, Mowena "'flatly refused" to go with the party of men and issued a stern warning that if they found the secret path to the top, the "*Modimo* (God) would speak" and if they did not listen, they would be "killed".[373]

According to J.C.O. van Graan, Mowena, who was apparently then about in his eighties and had served as a policeman under President Paul Kruger during the period of the Zuid-Afrikaansche Republiek (ZAR), admitted to them of his local knowledge of Mapungubwe Hill as the secret burial place of his ancestors. After a long argument, Mowena suggested that his son who lived in a nearby village on the way to the hill would point them in the right direction.[374]

Late in December 1932 the men tracked down Mowena's son in the nearby Musina village, but he also refused to take them to the secret location. Yet, with some coercion and payment in "copper and silver' coins", the young man reluctantly served as their guide. They travelled through the rough bushveld, sometimes along a path no wider than a metre, where detours had to be taken and trees chopped down along the winding and difficult route. Their "guide" was forced to cut open a path through the dense mopane bush, while the men followed in a car until after an hour they came to an escarpment that looked down on the Limpopo Valley, with the Shashe River in the distance.

financiers and directors, and lastly, the mines and mine workers.[367] The often romanticised and sentimental view of the Transvaal veld and its wild interior frontier was not immune to the effects of the South African economic depression of the early 1930s. The beckoning of gold between the Zoutpansberg and Limpopo had already been set by the late nineteenth century that spilled over into the twentieth century tall-tales of gold treasure. The lost trails and neglected spaces of the northern Transvaal were rapidly filled with mystery and E.S.J. van Graan, a well-educated farmer and a prospector in the Limpopo Lowveld was determined to investigate the rumours of a "mystery of the Hill of the ancient dead".[368] His father had shared stories with him and his son about an old blind African man who talked of "how the kings of his ancestors and all their treasures were buried on a certain inaccessible hill" with "pots that were filled with gold, diamonds and green stones" and was regarded as a graveyard to his ancestors.[369]

In about 1928, the Van Graan family pursued this legend rather seriously or from desperation, as their discovery apparently took "five years" to plan in an attempt to locate the secret hill.[370] An ideal opportunity arose, as well as the impetus for the search when J.C.O. van Graan received

[367] W.P. Taylor, *African* treasures: sixty years among diamonds and gold. London: John Long Limited, 1912, pp. 177–216.
[368] Mapungubwe Archive, UP/AGL/D1114, C. Birkby, "Mystery of the hill of the ancient dead", *Cape Argus*, 18 March 1939.
[369] Mapungubwe Archive, van Graan Collection, unappraised records.
[370] Mapungubwe Archive, UP/AGL/D/4, Letter from J.C.O to Prof. Fouché, 13 February 1933.

[371] Mapungubwe Archive, UP/AGL/D/12, Letter from J.C.O. van Graan titled, "Die ontdekking van Mapungubwe" (The discovery of Mapungubwe), n.d. (possibly 1933). J.C.O. van Graan stated that he first met Mr van de Walt whose children attended Brombeek School near Alldays.
[372] Van Warmelo's oral sources refer to Mowena as the half-brother of Tshiwana, the so-called "legendary chief" and a descendant from the communities of the Machete or Mmathsete. Mowena (Mabina/Mavhina) is of the Bakwena communities originating from the Protectorate, see footnote 4, In N.J. van Warmelo (ed.), *Copper miners of Messina and the early history of the Zoutpansberg*. Pretoria: Department of Native Affairs Union of South Africa, 1940.
[373] Mapungubwe Archive, see the verbatim account (transcribed from Afrikaans to English) of the Mapungubwe discovery by J.C.O. van Graan published for the first time, "The discovery of Mapungubwe". In S. Tiley-Nel (ed.) *Mapungubwe remembered: contributions to Mapungubwe by the University of Pretoria*. Johannesburg: Chris van Rensburg Publications (Pty) Ltd, 2011, pp. 44–45.
[374] Mapungubwe Archive, Van Graan Collection, unappraised.

Figure 3.9. Only existing historical photograph of the other discoverers, H.P van der Walt flanked by his two sons-in-law, D. J du Plessis and M Venter. © E. V. Adams Archive.

Eventually they arrived at a large tree at the foot of "an imposing hill with a sheer rock face" and Van Graan claimed to have "instinctively" known that this was the hill. and the search for the secret entrance commenced but proved difficult.[375] By this time, their guide refused to go any further: "You will not only get wet from the rain, but you will also not return alive". Mowena, "shivering with fright", turned his back and reluctantly "pointed out the secret stairway to the top".[376] According to Fouché's version of the discovery:

> Our hill is known to these Natives as "Mapungubwe" – the hill of the jackals. To them it had always been taboo – a place of dread. They would not so much as point at it, and when it was discussed with them they kept their backs turned carefully towards it. To climb it meant certain death. It was sacred to the Great Ones among their ancestors, who had buried secret treasures there.[377]

The sun had already set so the men searched the summit very briefly on 29 December 1932, and recovered some metal such as iron and copper fragments, some gold foil, glass and gold beads. As predicted by Mowena it began to rain and so they vowed to return the next day and resume their search.[378] The five discoverers returned the following New Year's day, 1 January 1933, this time in a party of five consisting of: E.S.J. (Ernst) van Graan, his son J.C.O. van Graan, H.P. (Hendrik) van der Walt and his two sons-in-law, D.J. (Dawid) du Plessis and M. (Marthinus) Venter. All were considered as "local" farmers and "not educated people", except for the Van Graans who came from a middle working-class educated background.[379] The others were regarded as "uneducated" men as they were impoverished as the Van der Walt's were *bywoners* on the farm named *Congo*.[380]

The big find of clearly ancient, wrought gold and beads was apparently discovered on 2 January 1933 and included masses of gold bangles, gold beads and fragments of gold foil of what appeared to be portions of the now famous, gold rhinoceros figurine. The five discoverers filled their hats to the brim. Among themselves, they came to an arrangement to divide the finds into five parts and drew

---

[375] Mapungubwe Archive, J.C.O. van Graan, "The discovery of Mapungubwe". In S. Tiley-Nel (ed.) *Mapungubwe remembered: contributions to Mapungubwe by the University of Pretoria.* Johannesburg: Chris van Rensburg Publications (Pty) Ltd, 2011, pp. 45–46.

[376] L. Fouché, *Mapungubwe: ancient Bantu civilization on the Limpopo, reports on excavations at Mapungubwe (Northern Transvaal) from February 1933 to June 1935,* Volume I. Cambridge: Cambridge University Press, 1937, p. 1.

[377] See further L. Fouché, *Mapungubwe: ancient Bantu civilization on the Limpopo, reports on excavations at Mapungubwe (Northern Transvaal) from February 1933 to June 1935,* Volume I. Cambridge: Cambridge University Press, 1937, p. 1.

[378] J. van Graan, "The discovery of Mapungubwe". In S. Tiley-Nel (ed.) *Mapungubwe remembered: contributions to Mapungubwe by the University of Pretoria.* Johannesburg: Chris van Rensburg Publications (Pty) Ltd, 2011, p. 46.

[379] Mapungubwe Archive, Roos unappraised documents, letter from Rooth and Coxwell to Registrar, 4 November 1938.

[380] Mapungubwe Archive, unappraised tape recording in Afrikaans by Martie van Staden, daughter to Hendrik van der Walt in a transcription of the Van Der Walt account of the Mapungubwe discovery. According to her, their family was extremely poor and her father was a very ill man. The Van der Walt's and the Van Graan did not trust each other and apparently a gun-fight and serious threats ensued on the day of the discovery. This feud between the two families remained ongoing for over eight decades. Recording originally in Afrikaans, transcribed and translated into English.

lots for the first, second, third, fourth and fifth which was duly appropriated and each removed their share of the gold. Oddly, the Van Graans were under the impression they had committed a crime, as they stated "the prison doors are waiting for us".[381] According to an interview in the *Flying Springbok* in 1984, the Van Graans claimed they did not want their discovery kept quiet, in the hope that they could make arrangements with some authorities at that time, in order to protect them in case of prosecution and perhaps that they could further obtain a "fair price for their share" as some sort of financial compensation.[382]

There are several versions of this original gold discovery. The first reports of their discovery in 1933 are in the form of hand-written accounts, letters by both Van Graan Senior (E.S.J. van Graan) and Junior (J.C.O. van Graan) to L. Fouché at the University of Pretoria. Then later his recollections at the age of seventy-five in several media interviews held in 1984, J.C.O van Graan recounts the discovery narrative, each differs somewhat in detail.[383] Perhaps one of the most poignant recollections of the discovery of Mapungubwe is related in a verbatim, oral account recorded on cassette tape by B. (Bennie) van Graan, J.C.O. van Graan's brother. His version of the discovery is very telling as it distinctly showed that the 1933 discovery to Mapungubwe Hill was led to some extent under duress.[384] Given the pivotal role of the Van Graans in this gold discovery, the information garnered together from a range of sources is provided and further emphasises that the Van Graan family were well-educated and their intentions about Mapungubwe were honourable at the time by reporting the discovery to his *alma mater*.

Jeremiah (Jerry) Cornelius Olivier van Graan was born on 23 January 1908 on a farm near Frederikstad, north of Potchefstroom in the north-west Transvaal, just after the 1907 election and the progressive period towards a Union of South Africa. Van Graan's father, Ernst Stephanus Johannes van Graan (ca. 1847) was the son of a prominent wagon-maker originally from Robertson in the Western Cape. E.S.J. van Graan served as dispatch rider under the Boer military leader, Commander/Captain D.S.J. (Danie) Theron and then moved to the Transvaal in 1897.[385] From 1903, E.S.J. van Graan worked as a reduction worker for a gold mine in Roodepoort on the Witwatersrand where he

met Gertie, a teacher formerly from Bethlehem and they had six children, and Jerry was their second born son.[386] In 1912 in pursuit of cattle farming prospects, the Van Graan family moved to the Northern Transvaal to a farm named *Barend*, an isolated outpost between Musina and Louis Trichardt north of the Zoutpansberg region. Young J.C.O. van Graan received his first tuition directly from his mother as he was home schooled in Dutch due to a lack of formal schools in the remote northern bushveld.[387]

In 1918, at the age of about ten, Van Graan as the second eldest son, together with his two brothers were sent to a boarding school in Eestegoud near Pietersburg. In that year both his brothers died at a young age of the Spanish influenza epidemic which tragically struck South Africa. Van Graan as one of the youngest had survived and was left behind to sweep the sick rooms, serve meals and perform other menial chores. Instinctively, his mother Gertie van Graan, arrived in a horse-drawn cart on the day of his brothers' burial as there was no communication to parents, and the school was closed within a week.[388] The years 1918 to 1919 were referred to as "Black October" and were considered a landmark in South African social, medical and administrative history. This epidemic left its mark and was the catalyst for the Public Health Act of 1919.[389]

By 1919, as one of the fortunate few to have survived the national epidemic, Van Graan's mother immediately placed him nearer to home in a private school in Louis Trichardt, the new capital of the Zoutpansberg. In the early 1920s Van Graan returned to the northwest Transvaal. Here he completed the remainder of his formal schooling at the Potchefstroom Gimnasium, a boarding school that was once under the authority of the Dutch Reformed Church but was then under government control, but nevertheless firmly rooted in the traditions of Christian reformation and Afrikanerdom. Potchefstroom Gimnasium was regarded as an exponent of the Christian National Educational principles.[390] Heavily influenced and protected by his mother, Van Graan thus chose an obvious career in teaching and went to the Pretoria Teachers College from 1927 to 1931. He completed his academic training at the Transvaal University College and graduated in 1932 with a BA-degree in the year the College became the University of Pretoria. It was during his tertiary education at the University of Pretoria that Van Graan was introduced to

[381] Mapungubwe Archive, UP/AGL/D/27, Agreement between the discoverers, landowner and the University of Pretoria, including affidavits and copies of enclosed documents, 1 March 1933.

[382] "The face of South Africa: Mapungubwe". *Flying Springbok*, June 1984.

[383] Mapungubwe Archive, UP/AGL/D3777, C. van der Merwe, "The face of South Africa: Mapungubwe", *Flying Springbok*, June 1984; see also, "Na 52 jaar is die glans nog nie daar", *Die Vaderland*, 27 October 1984.

[384] Discussion with Bennie van Graan, son of E.S.J van Graan and brother to J.C.O. van Graan about the discovery of Mapungubwe, 18 August 2000. This tape cassette recording has since been duplicated, transcribed and translated. S. Tiley-Nel, the Curator of the Mapungubwe Collection met Mr B. van Graan in 1999 and thereafter was fortunate to have stayed in contact with his brother, Ernst van Graan, the last surviving member of the immediate family who generously donated family photographs and documents detailing the Van Graan family history which now forms part of the Van Graan Collection in the Mapungubwe Archive.

[385] Mapungubwe Archive, Van Graan Collection, unappraised.

[386] The first born son was named Hermanus Johan (b. 1906); Jeremiah Cornelius (b. 1908); Ernst Stephanus (b. 1911); Johan Christoffel (b. 1917); Sebastian Jan or Bennie (b. 1920), and one daughter named Zacharia Gertruida (b. 1914).

[387] S. Tiley-Nel, "Jeremias Cornelius Olivier van Graan 1908–1987". In S. Tiley-Nel (ed.) *Mapungubwe remembered: contributions to Mapungubwe by the University of Pretoria*. Johannesburg: Chris van Rensburg Publications (Pty) Ltd, 2011, pp. 12–14.

[388] Mapungubwe Archive, Van Graan Collection, tape recorded interview with B. van Graan made in 2000.

[389] For a studied account of the national impact of the outbreak see, H. Phillips, 'Black October': the impact of the Spanish Influenza Epidemic of 1918 in South Africa, PhD, University of Cape Town, 1984.

[390] See P.P. de Bruyn, Die Geskiedenis van Potchefstroom Gimnasium 1907–1982. Unpublished Master's Degree, North West University, 1988.

the subject of history under Fouché which consolidated and combined his hobbies of hunting, minerals and archaeology, but set his intellectual interest squarely in prehistory.[391]

During the depression of the 1930s teachers had been subject to severe wage cuts, despite a surplus of over eight hundred urban teachers in the Transvaal. Van Graan was unemployed, and there was a greater demand for schoolmasters at single-teacher schools in the remote rural settlements across the Transvaal. Driven by the requirements of the Transvaal Education Department (TED) for more rural teachers, between 1927 and 1934 Van Graan served as a temporary teacher across the northern regions of the Transvaal. Within twelve months he was moved from one rural primary school to the next, from Brombeek School near Alldays, then from Slangskool near Potgietersrus to Brooklands Primary School in Sabie in the eastern Transvaal where in 1934 he received his first permanent appointment. On 18 December 1935 he married Machtil Johanna (Tillie) Broodryk (1915–1976) whom he knew from Potchefstroom Gimnasium and they had six children. He joined the Defence Force at the outbreak of World War II in 1939.[392]

After the end of the Second World War hostilities in 1945, Van Graan resumed teaching again in the eastern Transvaal at Pilgrim's Rest Primary School, and from there was relocated once more by the Transvaal Education Department to establish a small school at Bushbuckridge. He was then requested to move south to Komatiepoort to begin another new school there. In 1950 Van Graan contracted malaria and together with his ailing wife who suffered from asthma and under the doctor's advice they moved to a larger city with better medical care. The Van Graans then relocated to the East Rand where he served as Principal of the Roodstein Primary School in Vereeniging.[393]

Van Graan yet once again was transferred by the Transvaal Education Department, this time to Vaalrivier Primary School in 1965. He took up his final appointment as the Principal of Verkenner Primary School in Benoni from 1966 until his retirement in 1973.[394] Following the death of his wife on 16 June 1976, Van Graan at age seventy-two underwent a back operation in 1979 which affected his health.[395] J.C.O. van Graan remained in Farramere, Benoni where he died on 18 August 1987. After this chequered teaching career that criss-crossed the northern region of South Africa, Van Graan was laid to rest with a headstone on his grave which carries the Mapungubwe symbol of the gold rhino and the inscription, *"Die Ontdekker van*

Mapungubwe" (The discoverer of Mapungubwe).[396] This testifies to his and his family's belief of the pivotal role they played in the discovery.

3.8. The Transvaal Treasure: 1933

As previously mentioned in Fouché's version of the history of Mapungubwe, published in 1937, the so-called "accidental" discovery of gold by "five fossickers" was said to have taken place on Mapungubwe Hill in December 1932.[397] The formal reported discovery of a gold treasure personally reached Fouché, on 6 February 1933.[398] This connection was made solely on the basis that Van Graan as a former student of Fouché, had recalled his history lessons and lectures that piqued his interest in antiquity and prehistoric treasures.[399] In immediate response, "in order to avoid the possibility of the total loss of valuable archaeological material", the Van Graans were informed about the University of Pretoria's acute interest to enter into negotiations taking the matter further and a meeting was requested as soon as possible with his father, E.S.J van Graan in Pretoria.[400] The Van Graans were warned by Fouché not to "talk to others" about the discovery as this would compromise their discoverer's gold rights as laid down by the Department of Interior and since they had trespassed on private property.[401]

Later, in February 1933 and soon after the discovery was reported to the University, the Van Graans directed accusations towards the Van der Walts for allegedly and illegally selling gold in Musina.[402] The Van Graans further pointed to F.B. Lotrie as an "outlaw from justice", and claimed that Lotrie stole as "the hunters kept the gold treasure for themselves, instead of reporting it to the

---

[391] Mapungubwe Archive, Van Graan Collection, J.C.O. van Graan personal account of his life and interests.

[392] Mapungubwe Archive, Van Graan Collection, unpublished account of life history by J.C.O. van Graan, undated.

[393] Mapungubwe Archive, Van Graan Collection.

[394] Mapungubwe Archive, Van Graan Collection.

[395] Mapungubwe Archive, UP/AGL/D/1848, "Hy's nog nie klaar met die heuwel en goue skate". *Die Vaderland*, 3 November 1979.

[396] In researching the Van Graan family history in 2000, the author tracked down the family still living in Farramere, Benoni and investigated the Benoni Cemetery in search of Van Graan's place of burial and unbeknown to many J.C.O. van Graan's headstone has "Die Ontdekker Van Mapungubwe" engraved into the granite slab together with an engraved image of the gold rhino, he is buried alongside his wife Tillie Brooderyk. See photograph of horizontal headstone in S. Tiley-Nel, "Jeremias Cornelius Olivier Van Graan 1908–1987". In S. Tiley-Nel (ed.) *Mapungubwe remembered: contributions to Mapungubwe by the University of Pretoria*. Johannesburg: Chris van Rensburg Publications (Pty) Ltd, 2011, p. 14.

[397] L. Fouché, *Mapungubwe: ancient Bantu civilization on the Limpopo, reports on excavations at Mapungubwe (Northern Transvaal) from February 1933 to June 1935.* Cambridge: Cambridge University Press, 1937, p. 2.

[398] Mapungubwe Archive, UP/AGL/D/2, Letter to Prof L. Fouché from J.C.O. van Graan from the farm Mopani informing the University of Pretoria of the discovery of gold ornaments in the northern reaches of the Transvaal, 6 February 1933.

[399] Mapungubwe Archive, Van Graan Collection, J.C.O. van Graan personal account of his life and interests.

[400] This contract which was signed on 28 February 1933, in hindsight was considered an "emergency measure taken at the time when the University was not in possession of the full facts or of an accurate statement of the local position". See Mapungubwe Archive, Roos unappraised legal opinion documents and notes. Annexure to opinion, University of Pretoria, 29 March 1938.

[401] Mapungubwe Archive, UP/AGL/D/3, Letter from Prof. L Fouché to J.C.O. van Graan, 10 February 1933.

[402] Mapungubwe Archive, UP/AGL/D/22, Letter from E.S.J van Graan to Prof. L. Fouché with accusations that H. van der Walt sold Mapungubwe gold to a Mr P. Franklin and Mr Osmer in Messina, 29 February 1933.

Figure 3.10. Transvaal Treasure ownership puzzle, *The Star Newspaper* **26 March 1933.**

the part of J.C.O. van Graan who claimed that was "if not for my interest in the archaeology of our land, then surely Mapungubwe would today be completely unknown".[404] In 1938, the van Graans approached their lawyers, Rooth and Coxwell to act on their behalf to commence litigation procedures against the University.[405]

Acting on their behalf, Roos in response did not take this legal threat lightly and responded that the "Committee resents your unjustifiable imputation of *mala fides*" and "if you must have litigation, however while regretting it, we can only say proceed".[406] According to Roos, the University had "accounted to the client for every particle of gold" during the contract 1933–1938 and they have "neither a legal nor a moral claim" to the continuation of a "bonus out of funds" contributed by government or the University.[407] Lawsuits never followed, but the Van Graans went on to expect that the University should "now and then send them a short report on the work at Mapungubwe" and keep them "informed of developments of the archaeological work".[408]

This ensuing bitterness and resentment again became evident in several negative media reports almost fifty years later. Van Graan is quoted as claiming, "I do not expect anything". Yet they had expected the University of Pretoria to consider placing a bronze plaque at the site in order to "say thank you to a young teacher for his honesty and interest in science", yet this never happened.[409] Over and above the generous treatment that was accorded, they received in the form of financial compensation, a total of over £670[410] between 1933 and 1936, the Van Graans presumed further praise.[411] Furthermore, they were invited to the Department of Archaeology as "honoured guests" to view the gold collection display, they were also personally thanked for their contribution and received "a small gold rhino tie pin" as a gift of appreciation.[412]

By February 1933 several gold samples were submitted to Dr Roger Pearson at the Royal Mint in Pretoria to be authenticated for their purity.[413] In March 1933, the *Rand*

authorities".[403] From the outset of the reported discovery, there was a sullenness towards the University of Pretoria on

---

[403] In the Van Graan transcription of the discovery, he hints at larceny among the discoverers, and claimed that Lotrie was in fact on the run from the police and as a result hid in the mountains near the Limpopo River. The Van Graans claimed they "researched Lotrie" at the State Library and found evidence to suggest he was a "fugitive from the law and went into hiding up north". This spurred the Van Graan's excitement of a similar discovery and they sought to find his son, Barend in the hope of leading them to the sacred hill, see also N. Oosthuizen, "Afrika se skatte is dalk deur jagter weggedra". *Die Vaderland*, 21 April 1983.

[404] Mapungubwe Archive, UP/AGL/D/ 388, Letter from J.C.O. Van Graan to the University, 14 October 1934.
[405] Mapungubwe Archive, Roos unappraised documents, 4 November 1938.
[406] Mapungubwe Archive, Roos unappraised documents, 1938.
[407] Mapungubwe Archive, Roos unappraised documents, 1938.
[408] Mapungubwe Archive, UP/AGL/D/388, Letter from J.C.O. van Graan to University of Pretoria, 14 October 1934.
[409] "Na 52 jaar is die glans nog nie daar". *Die Vaderland*, 27 October 1984, "Hy's nog nie klaar met die heuwel en goue skate". *Die Vaderland*, 3 November 1979.
[410] Mapungubwe Archive, Roos unappraised hand-written notes.
[411] Mapungubwe Archive, Roos unappraised documents. This document drafted by the Government Law Advisors from the Department of Justice advises the University and refer to "the burdensome obligation of the payment to the discoverers of half the gold value" of over £670s and recommend the termination of the contract as the discoverers are "obsessed with the idea that Mapungubwe is an inexhaustible Golconda", 10 March 1938.
[412] Mapungubwe Archive, UP/AGL/D/ 1848, 30 October 1984.
[413] Mapungubwe Archive, UP/AGL/D/7, Report by Dr Roger Pearson from the Royal Mint in Pretoria to Fouché on the analysis of the gold samples that were submitted in February 1933 by the University of

Daily Mail headlined, "The discovery of gold ornaments: claimed by Pretoria University". The article further stated that the value of the metal had been exaggerated, but issued stern warning "that as all discoveries are the sole property of the University, selling any of the articles or even harbouring any, may incur serious penalties".[414] The University of Pretoria was said to have put the pressure on Fouché who conducted and handled:

> The entire affair of the Mapungubwe discovery… with great urgency owing to the fear that the discoverers might melt down their metallic articles or dispose of them and so irretrievably destroy articles of great archaeological value.[415]

This discovery in the Transvaal turned out to be one of South Africa's most significant archaeological finds and generated a wide interest in scientific and research interest on Mapungubwe by the University of Pretoria. The discovery came at a critical time during the South African general election, when Hertzog served as Prime Minister and Smuts as Deputy Prime Minister, after they had formed a coalition government in May 1933 with the assistance of J.S. Smit, the Administrator of the Transvaal. A few years earlier information about another major discovery, known as the Taung fossil of the specimen *Australopithecus africanus,* had been published by the anatomist, Raymond Dart (1893–1988) from the University of the Witwatersrand. This discovery was to "transform conceptions of South African prehistory" and one which Smuts too had openly backed.[416] With this discovery at the time, Smuts openly stated that the Taung fossil was "an epoch-making discovery, not only of far-reaching importance from an anthropological point of view but also well calculated to concentrate attention on South Africa as the great field for scientific discovery which it undoubtedly is".[417]

News of the discovery on Mapungubwe Hill of gold and other "finds of utmost importance"[418] spread rapidly, with extensive media coverage and monthly public updates on excavation discoveries in several newspapers such as the *Sunday Times*, *Rand Daily Mail* and *The Star*. This also included an international platform when the discoveries of gold treasures were reported in April 1933

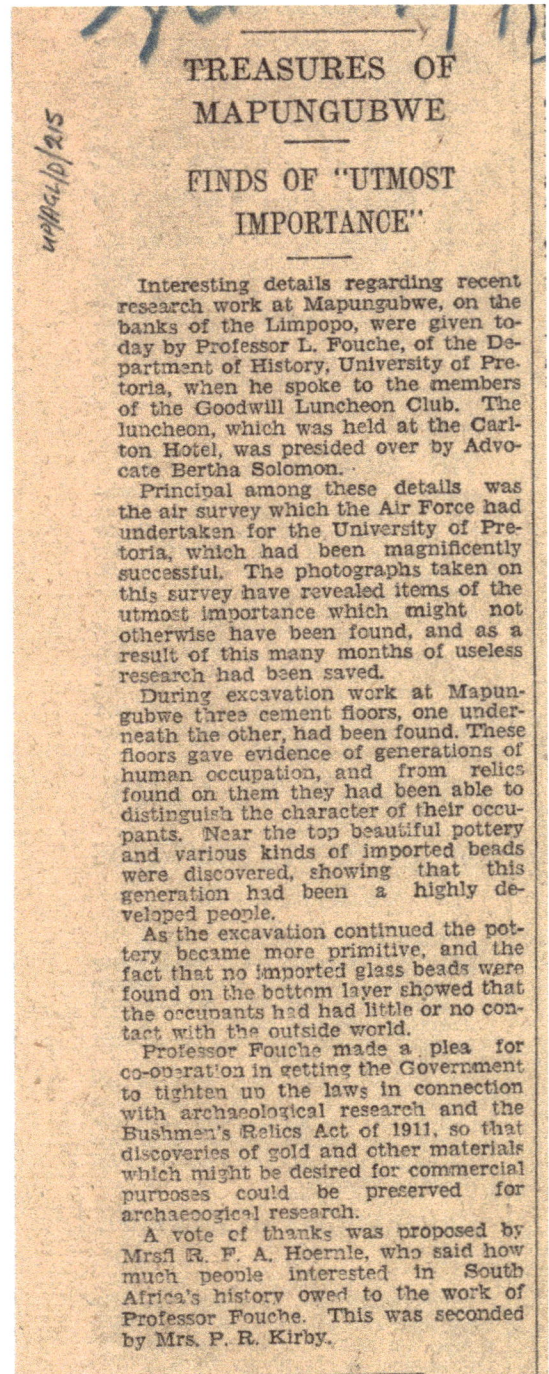

TREASURES OF MAPUNGUBWE

FINDS OF "UTMOST IMPORTANCE"

Interesting details regarding recent research work at Mapungubwe, on the banks of the Limpopo, were given to-day by Professor L. Fouche, of the Department of History, University of Pretoria, when he spoke to the members of the Goodwill Luncheon Club. The luncheon, which was held at the Carlton Hotel, was presided over by Advocate Bertha Solomon.

Principal among these details was the air survey which the Air Force had undertaken for the University of Pretoria, which had been magnificently successful. The photographs taken on this survey have revealed items of the utmost importance which might not otherwise have been found, and as a result of this many months of useless research had been saved.

During excavation work at Mapungubwe three cement floors, one underneath the other, had been found. These floors gave evidence of generations of human occupation, and from relics found on them they had been able to distinguish the character of their occupants. Near the top beautiful pottery and various kinds of imported beads were discovered, showing that this generation had been a highly developed people.

As the excavation continued the pottery became more primitive, and the fact that no imported glass beads were found on the bottom layer showed that the occupants had had little or no contact with the outside world.

Professor Fouche made a plea for co-operation in getting the Government to tighten up the laws in connection with archaeological research and the Bushmen's Relics Act of 1911, so that discoveries of gold and other materials which might be desired for commercial purposes could be preserved for archaeological research.

A vote of thanks was proposed by Mrs. R. F. A. Hoernle, who said how much people interested in South Africa's history owed to the work of Professor Fouche. This was seconded by Mrs. P. R. Kirby.

Figure 3.11. Treasures of Mapungubwe: Finds of "Utmost importance", *The Star* 11 September 1933.

in *The Illustrated London News*.[419] This indicated that this discovery of a treasure trove was not merely an academic pursuit kept exclusively for the vestiges of science, but was also an attempt to elicit and generate as much public interest in this new exciting discovery in South Africa.[420]

Pretoria for examination, authentication and evaluation. See also, M. Wel er, "Notes on some ancient gold ornaments". In L. Fouché, (ed.), *Mapungubwe: ancient Bantu civilization on the Limpopo: Reports on excavations at Mapungubwe (Northern Transvaal) from February 1933 to June 1935,* Volume I. Cambridge: Cambridge University Press, 1937, p. 114.

[414] Mapungubwe Archive, UP/AGL/D/61, "Discovery of gold ornaments: claimed by the Pretoria University". *Rand Daily Mail*, 11 March 1933.

[415] Mapungubwe Archive, UP/AGL/D/30, Adams & Adams statement of case for Council's opinion, ex parte the University of Pretoria opinion, 20 April 1933.

[416] M. Shepherd, "Disciplining archaeology: the invention of South African prehistory 1923–1953". *Kronos* 28, (November 2002), p. 132.

[417] "Human origins". *The Star*, 6 February 1925.

[418] "Treasures of Mapungubwe: finds of utmost importance". *The Star,* 11 September 1933.

[419] Mapungubwe Archive, UP/AGL/D/61, F.R. Paver, "The mystery grave of Mapungubwe: a remarkable discovery in the Transvaal: a grave of unknown origin containing much gold-work, found on the summit of a natural stronghold in a wild region". *The Illustrated London News*, 8 April 1933.

[420] See article by N. Haw, "Mapungubwe and the media: refuting the myth". In S. Tiley-Nel, (ed.), *Mapungubwe remembered: contributions*

TREASURE FROM A MYSTERIOUS GRAVE IN SOUTH AFRICA: RELICS OF GOLD.

PHOTOGRAPHS SUPPLIED BY MR. F. R. PAVER. (SEE HIS ARTICLE ON THE OPPOSITE PAGE.)

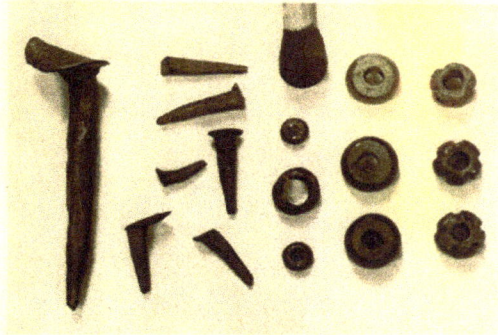

FIG. 4. SMALL OBJECTS FROM THE GRAVE SHOWN WITH AN ORDINARY MATCH-HEAD (TOP CENTRE) TO INDICATE THEIR SIZE: (LEFT TO RIGHT) A GOLD NAIL, GOLD TACKS, AND VARIOUS BEADS, PLAIN AND LOBED.

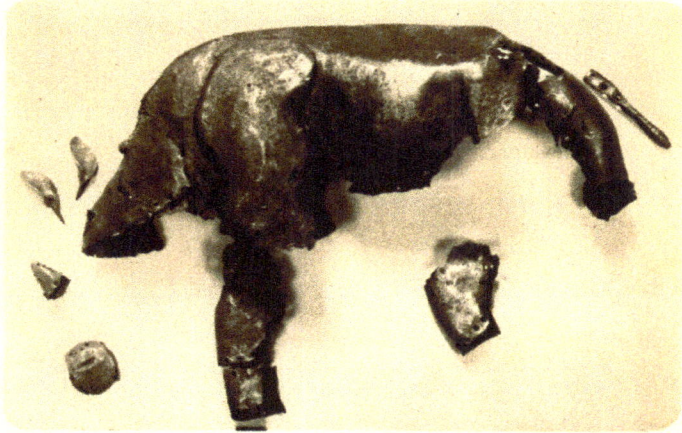

FIG. 5. THIN GOLD PLATING OF A FIGURE OF A RHINOCEROS, MADE IN SECTIONS FASTENED BY GOLD TACKS TO WOOD OR OTHER SHAPED MATERIAL, AND HAVING SOLID EARS AND TAIL. (TWO-THIRDS OF ACTUAL SIZE.)

Figure 3.12. Treasure from a mysterious grave in South Africa, *Illustrated London News,* 8 April 1933.

The University of Pretoria, as a tertiary education institution, had never dealt with major scientific discoveries of this magnitude before, and therefore sought legal advice from their solicitors, Adams & Adams Attorneys. The lawyers questioned the possibility of criminal liability of opening ancient graves and questioned the ownership of the finds, whether accidentally or deliberately. Considered an "accidental" find in 1933, the opening or illegal exhumation of ancient graves or any other types of grave would therefore not constitute a criminal offence.

Advocates J.M. Murray, A.A. Roberts and C. Niemeyer advised the University of Pretoria that the Mapungubwe discovery did in fact fall within the legal definition of a "treasure trove".[421] However, it did not necessarily fall under the ambit of the Bushman Relics Act No 22 of 1911, since this legislation only dealt with the removal of relics from the Union itself.[422] This line of legal enquiry suggested that the University of Pretoria held the view that the discovery of gold at Mapungubwe was deemed "accidental", despite the suggestion in the discoverers' affidavits that there was in fact a "deliberate" search for the legendary hill of gold by the five discoverers earlier in December 1932.[423]

On 28 February 1933, the University of Pretoria signed a Notarial Deed of Agreement with Mr Ernst Ewen Collins from the Johannesburg-based landowner of the farm *Greefswald* on which Mapungubwe was situated, in order to exercise the benefits of ownership of the treasure trove.[424] After lengthy negotiations, the five discoverers, J.C.O van Graan and his father E.S.J. van Graan, M. Venter, D. du Plessis and H. van der Walt as well as the land owner, consented to sign affidavits and entered into a reasonable agreement with the University of Pretoria.

The legal statements, prepared together with the Notarial Deed of Agreement, entitled each discover, as well as the landowner to half the metallic value of the gold in exchange for sole excavation rights for the University to legally take over possession of the gold handed over by them, and to keep the property *Greefswald* for future archaeological investigation.[425]

This payment in terms of treasure trove was regarded not as compensation, but as a simple reward or finder's fee, a practice which completely ignored the question of ownership. The University paid half the metallic value to the five discoverers.[426] In 1933, each received £239 for 69.16 ounces of gold and the landowner, Mr E. Collins, received £203 for his share of the gold.[427]

The legal agreement ceded all rights to the University of Pretoria to investigate, explore and excavate on the farm *Greefswald* for scientific purposes.[428] In addition, the University, together with government's assistance

to Mapungubwe by the University of Pretoria. Johannesburg: Chris van Rensburg Publications (Pty) Ltd, 2011, pp: 242–253.

[421] Note that Advocate Adrian Roberts was the first President of the Convocation of the Transvaal University College, and served from April 1919 as Registrar and later also on the University Council from 1931 to 1932.

[422] Mapungubwe Archive, UP/AGL/D/30, Legal document by Adams & Adams Attorneys to Murray and Roberts & Niemeyer Attorneys, 23 February 1933.

[423] Mapungubwe Archive, UP/AGL/D/24 and UP/AGL/D/27, Adams & Adams agreement between the discoverers, affidavits and the University of Pretoria, 23 February 1933.

[424] Mapungubwe Archive, UP/AGL/D/27 and UP/AGL/D/30, Legal document by Adams & Adams Agreement between the University of Pretoria and Prof. L. Fouché, and R. Howden, acting under Power of Attorney for Mr E.E. Collins, 1 March 1933.

[425] Mapungubwe Archive, UP/AGL/D/26, Legal binding agreement in which E. Collins grants sole excavation rights on his farm to the University of Pretoria, 28 February 1933.

[426] Mapungubwe Archive, Roos unappraised documents, financial receipts and hand-written notes, 1933.

[427] Mapungubwe Archive, UP/AGL/D/24, Adams & Adams Attorneys agreement between the University of Pretoria, Fouché and Collins, 1 March 1933.

[428] Mapungubwe Archive, UP/AGL/D/29, Agreement between the discoverers and the University of Pretoria, rights and privileges accorded to them, 23 February 1933.

took additional measures to protect Mapungubwe Hill, which ceased any prospecting and mining activity by the Transvaal Exploring Land & Minerals Company Ltd. who had mineral rights on *Greefswald* and to avoid any potential or further pillage of the site.[429]

In 1933, the University of Pretoria Council had also sought advice and permission from the Administrator of the Transvaal to back the legal contract drafted by Adams & Adams Attorneys, and to seek government support for funding Mapungubwe research and excavations. In April 1933, Adams & Adams queried whether the gold articles found by the five discoverers and handed over to the University of Pretoria constituted a treasure trove. Secondly, who would the lawful owner be, and if any gold was withheld by the discoverers, what would the implications be, particularly in light of whether the University had any right to recover such articles despite having a signed agreement in place.[430]

The University of Pretoria Council were advised that the legal agreement dated 23 February 1933 between them, the land owner and the discoverers was valid and that any articles of value would fall within the legal definition of a treasure trove, yet there was some doubt about legal position and possession.[431] They further advised the University that an agreement with the owner of the land would be more beneficial to ensure rights to any further discoveries as well as bound compensation to all parties, and to avoid any further difficulty they should obtain permission from the Administrator of the Transvaal.[432]

To approach the government was a significant move in this regard, since no statute law or legislation reinforced treasure trove discoveries and therefore they instead borrowed from English common law regulations. The treasure trove at Mapungubwe had piqued the Union's interest and the government purchased the farm *Greefswald* "for the nation" in June 1933.[433]

This strategic move was no doubt influenced by Smuts as Deputy Minister and Minister of Justice, also a close confidant and advisor to the Minister of the Interior, Jan Hofmeyr. The University of Pretoria was awarded legal and research privileges to excavate, as after viewing the archaeological finds in July 1933, the Prime Minister,

General J.B.M. Hertzog, declared the undertaking as a national concern:

> The view of the government is that while the University of Pretoria has secured a treasure for the nation, a national treasure is a national responsibility. Therefore the citizens of the Union, and more especially those resident in the Transvaal, should be given the opportunity to contribute towards the cost of an undertaking, which promises so notable an enrichment of their historical heritage. [434]

The gold discovery of Mapungubwe was legally declared a treasure trove and a formal deputation was requested by the Minister of the Interior to take steps to legally protect and preserve Mapungubwe Hill and its archaeological finds from the onset as a matter of priority in October 1933.[435] By late October 1933, the University of Pretoria entered into an agreement with the Transvaal Museum who were willing to provide the storage facility and exhibition space for the Mapungubwe Collection as well as any additional findings.[436]

The government agreed to provide funds for research on the basis of £2 for every £1 raised by the University of Pretoria, with a minimum contribution of £500 per year. With the support of the Minister of the Interior, the Archaeological Committee of the University of Pretoria was formally constituted on 17 November 1933. The Committee was magnanimously supported by the government, the Municipality of Pretoria and included a handful of private donors, among them mostly ardent Smuts supporters who contributed to a University of Pretoria Excavation Fund.[437]

Few historical archaeological discoveries in South Africa are deemed as "treasures" since the discovery of worked gold is rare. As a consequence such precious findings do not only have important historical repercussions, but also legal implications despite the widely recognised value that to:

> … [t]he historian or archaeologist, the objects themselves are the prime concern. What really matters is that these objects, within their context of discovery, have the potential to tell us a good deal about the people who made them, and how they lived and died. That is what archaeological excavation and research are about.[438]

[429] Mapungubwe Archive, UP/AGL/D/21, Legal instruction by Adams & Adams to the Transvaal Exploring Land & Minerals Co. Ltd. to refrain from prospecting, mining and other operations over mineral rights on the farm *Greefswald* for a period of six months for the purposes of continuing archaeological investigations, 28 February 1933.

[430] Mapungubwe Archive, UP/AGL/D/30, E.V Adams letter to Advocates, J. Murray, A.A. Roberts and E.C. Niemeyer, Acting Solicitors on behalf of the University of Pretoria, 1 April 1933.

[431] Mapungubwe Archive, UP/AGL/D/37, points to be put to Council, 28 March 1933.

[432] Mapungubwe Archive, UP/AGL/D/30, Adams & Adams statement of case for Council's opinion, ex parte the University of Pretoria opinion, 20 April 1933.

[433] Mapungubwe Archive, UP/AGL/D/132, Letter from P.I. Hoogenhout, Secretary of the Interior to A.E. du Toit, Rector of the University of Pretoria, 8 May 1933.

[434] Mapungubwe Archive, UP/AGL/D/38, "Archaeological treasure trove on the Limpopo", un-authored manuscript possibly dated to July 1933.

[435] "Historic spots in Union: deputation asks for preservation". *The Star*, 26 October 1933.

[436] E. Grobler, Collections management practices at the Transvaal Museum, 1934–1964. PhD thesis, University of Pretoria, 2005, pp. 270–271.

[437] L. Fouché, (ed.), *Mapungubwe: ancient Bantu civilization on the Limpopo: Reports on excavations at Mapungubwe (Northern Transvaal) from February 1933 to June 1935*, Volume I. Cambridge: Cambridge University Press, 1937, p. 6.

[438] C. Renfrew, "Art fraud: raiders of the lost past". *Journal of Financial Crime* 3(1), 2007, p. 8.

4

The University of Pretoria Archaeological Committee

A meeting of the Archaeological Committee dealing with the exploration of the terrain on and around Mapungubwe Hill on the Limpopo River near Messina, where the remains of the ancient king, wrapped in gold, now to be seen in the Pretoria Museum, were found, was held on Saturday in the University Buildings, Pretoria.[439]

4.1. Institutional control

This chapter provides a historical overview of the University of Pretoria Archaeological Committee that was established when the discovery of gold on Mapungubwe was first reported in February 1933 to Fouché at the University of Pretoria as outlined. In 1933 and 1934, during its maiden years, the Committee set guidelines for excavations, scientific research and served as a formal forum since they acted on behalf of the University of Pretoria Council on all matters that pertained to Mapungubwe. As indicated, the Committee was established soon after the newly founded University of Pretoria (formerly the Transvaal University College) came into being.[440]

The early 1930s was a key moment when the institution expressed conciliation both officially and to the public in an effort to foster a broader South Africanism within the higher education landscape. However, this soon became a "graveyard of hopes" as underlying forces put Afrikaner nationalism into full practice via decree by the University Council in 1932.[441] During this period, the public manifestations of the discovery of a "treasure trove" of Mapungubwe as a "natural fortress of the Limpopo" had already spread conspicuously into the newspapers and brought greater public attention to the "Pretoria party's research experiences" which called for immediate action from the University of Pretoria.[442]

The aims of this chapter are twofold. The first focus is on a relatively unknown, but critical historical figure, the "man of the moment", that controlled the early history of Mapungubwe: Jacob de Villiers Roos (1869–1940). Roos served on the Archaeological Committee from its inception, and became the Chairman in 1934 until the end of his association with the University of Pretoria in 1938. In 1908 he had also been a founding member of the Transvaal University College together with his long-time

friend, Smuts.[443] Roos is researched in-depth for this book for the sole purpose that literature on Mapungubwe has omitted this historical and highly influential character from any narrative or history and secondly, Fouché is lauded with praise on this first 1937 volume on Mapungubwe- while actually accomplishing very little during his tenure at the University of Pretoria.

The second focus of this chapter will be on the early years of the founding and purpose of the University of Pretoria Archaeological Committee. Its constitution, mandate and institutional actions and its close alliance with the Transvaal Museum are considered.[444] Whilst Roos is primarily the dominant focus, the chapter also includes a sketch of the other members of the Committee, their influence, efficacy and decisions. It also considers the internal and external mechanisms that controlled Mapungubwe via the Committee until its dissolution around the time of the Second World War. Apart from the archaeological records, more primary sources such as minutes of the meetings and original newspaper articles from the Mapungubwe Archive elucidate the nature of the early years of the Committee's activities from 1933 until its termination in 1947. A recent discovery in January 2017 in the Special Collections of the University Library suggests that Roos, not Fouché, was truly at the helm of authority.[445] Roos, who is certainly the lesser known of the two figures in early Mapungubwe history, is by far the most influential and unsung hero during his tenure at the controls of the University's Archaeological Committee for at least six years.

---

[439] "Exploration at the Limpopo". *Pretoria News*, 18 June 1934.
[440] See C.H. Rautenbach, (ed.) et al., *Ad Destinatum. Gedenkboek van die Universiteit van Pretoria*. Johannesburg: Voortrekkerpers Beperk, 1960.
[441] B.L. Strydom, Broad South Africanism and Higher Education: The Transvaal University College (1909–1919), PhD History, University of Pretoria, 2013, p. 194.
[442] "Mapungubwe natural fortress of the Limpopo: an impregnable hill Pretoria party's research experiences". *The Star*. 15 March 1933.

[443] "Men of the moment: Mr J. de V. Roos". Newspaper unknown, 3 January 1925.
[444] Mapungubwe Archive, the link between the Transvaal Museum and Mapungubwe is not well-known and over 100 valuable archival records reflecting correspondence between the Museum and the University of Pretoria were traced in the Transvaal Museum Archive as recently as 2018. The Ditsong Museums of South Africa were generous to provide copies of all related archival material to the Mapungubwe Archive in exchange for preservation services, 2018.03.12.
[445] The J. de Villiers Roos Collection held under Special (Africana) Collections in the Department of Library Services at the University of Pretoria contains private correspondence, and other documentation pertaining to his numismatic collection, other historical manuscripts and reports, newspaper clippings and telegrams from the South African War, law statutes and related legal papers, photo albums (1894–1930), maps as well as his extensive collection of Africana books. In 2017 the Roos archivalia relating to the Archaeological Committee was formally transferred to the Mapungubwe Archive. The donation to the University of Pretoria was handled by his daughter, D.C. (Ellaline) Malan in 1958.

Figure 4.1. Professor Leo Fouché (1880–1949).

Characteristic of the public enthusiasm around the major gold discovery at Mapungubwe in 1933, Fouché adopted a public persona which featured prominently in the newspapers.[446] In contrast, behind the scenes there was Roos, not only a studious and cloistered intellectual, but an established journalist as well as a prodigious advocate that held major positions of power in government. He was a conservative and progressive thinker for his time, with an inordinate wide influence, moving in extensive circles with notable individuals and forged friendships that extended to prominent members of State.[447]

In this chapter, therefore the private, political and academic life of Roos is examined and provides insight into the conceptual and partisan roles he played while on the Archaeological Committee. In addition, there was also the way in which he mediated the legal concerns and

power of the University of Pretoria over Mapungubwe during a crucial period in both the University's own history as well as in the broader context of South African history. Although equally prominent scholars, Fouché and Roos, both of whom in very different ways made substantial contributions to Mapungubwe's early history, were nonetheless contesting personalities that set apart those who partake and those who make history. This chapter briefly considers Fouché but, while not intended on downplaying his role, its main focus is on the contributions made by Roos. Fouché is nonetheless greatly eclipsed by the fact that Roos cemented the authorizations, agreements and affluence of the Archaeological Committee as an institutional instrument of power, which profoundly shaped and directed the early history of Mapungubwe during his tenure at the University of Pretoria.

4.2. Formidable Fouché: a frontier of 'his' history

The South African historian F.A. Mouton has already published extensively on Professor Leo Fouché (1880–1949), the first professionally trained South African Afrikaner historian, the pioneer teacher of university history and his role within history at the University of Pretoria.[448] Mouton has also covered Fouché's biographical

---

[446] Mapungubwe Archive, UP/AGL/D/216, "Discoveries of ancient civilisation: Professor Leo Fouché speaks on Mapungubwe". *Rand Daily Mail*, 11 September 1933; Mapungubwe Archive, UP/AGL/D/554, "First Transvaal Bantu? "Bronze Age site" New development in Limpopo Valley. *The Star*, 12 October 1935; Mapungubwe Archive, UP/AGL/D/555, "Archaeology on the Limpopo: results of excavations at Mapungubwe". *The Star* 17 October 1935; Mapungubwe Archive, UP/AGL/D/895, "Mapoegoebwe: 'n oorblyfsel van die ryk van Monomotapa". *Die Brandwag*, 17 September 1937.

[447] See for example, W.J. de Kock, *Jacob de Villiers Roos, 1869–1940, Lewenskets van 'n veelsydige Afrikaner.* Cape Town: A.A. Balkema, 1953; L.C. Chisholm, "Crime, class and nationalism: the criminology of Jacob de Villiers Roos, 1869–1918". *Social Dynamics: Journal of African Studies* 13(2), 1987 pp. 46–59.

[448] See, F.A. Mouton (ed.), *History, historians and Afrikaner nationalism: essays on the History Department of the University of Pretoria, 1909–1985.* Vanderbijlpark: Kleio, 2007, pp. 13–43.

history and his association with the Transvaal University College (TUC) that dates back to 1909, when he was one of the founding fathers of the College and appointed as Professor of History and Philosophy.[449] In the light of this, what follows is a discussion of Fouché and his relevance to Mapungubwe.

During the First World War (1914–1918) Fouché served at the headquarters on the personal staff of J.C. Smuts, whom he worshipped and remained a loyal friend, as well as a life-long supporter.[450] Smuts undoubtedly influenced Fouché's professional career, first with his position in the TUC in 1908, then his appointment in 1934 as the Chair of History at the University of the Witwatersrand.[451] Smuts also supported Fouché's later post in 1942 as the Chairman of the South African Broadcasting Company (SABC) Board of Governors, as well as when he served as the South African Minister Plenipotentiary at The Hague in the Netherlands in 1947.[452]

Within the University of Pretoria he also laid the first foundations for the Department of History and served as Chairman of the Senate in 1915, and from 1924 to 1929 as Chairman of the Library Committee, in total twenty-five years of service.[453] Mouton's biographical essay also states that during this period in particular, Fouché increasingly struggled to identify with the bourgeoning Afrikaans movement as it moved towards transforming the institution's identity to that of a *volksuniversiteit* and away from the bilingual 50-50 policy, thus giving way to Afrikaner loyalists and rising nationalism.[454]

Other contestations plagued Fouché as well including his altercations with the University Rector, A.E. du Toit, a steadfast Nationalist that eventually led to Fouché's dismissal in 1932, by the very same Council which had previously elected him. Fouché heard of his intended notice, rescinded and the Council changed their tone just as a motion of no confidence in the Rector arose at the same time.[455] Fouché continued to be marginalised and toiled

within an increasingly hostile Afrikaner Nationalist and separatist environment at the University, but the discovery of Mapungubwe gold in 1933 brought about a new frontier to his history.[456] Ostensibly, Fouché reassessed his position when he wrote to the Chairperson of the Council and implored the following:

> The archaeological discoveries on "Greefswald", with all the consequences thereof have wholly been left in my hands by the discoverers. It was immediately obvious that this matter is of national interest and a choice stands before me… Either this national matter is left for government and museums are approached or the University of Pretoria is provided the opportunity to be given the honour of the discovery and to further explore the site… Against strong opposition from friends… I have decided to give the University another chance. What led me to this decision is a feeling of loyalty to an institution that I have dedicated my life to from its inception.[457]

As previously detailed in the literature review, even though Fouché dominated the main thread of the historical Mapungubwe narrative, his influence on South African history was impressive. In March 1949, at Fouché's funeral a tribute by Smuts acknowledged that, "he made an important contribution to South Africa, he was a man who could see beyond the details and of outstanding intellectual gifts" and he has "left us the fruits of his labour and the example of his life".[458] Likewise, the pioneer South African historian, Phyllis Lewsen (1916–2001) recalled that Fouché was an "addicted and dedicated scholar, who worshipped history but could not write it", yet he taught historians the importance of primary records, in which he "included artefacts and buildings" and how to analyse and evaluate documents with his "contributions to the new science of archaeology extending the frontiers of history".[459]

The wide-ranging opinion that the first platform for Mapungubwe at the University of Pretoria was largely indebted to the historian Fouché has also been well-grounded in archaeological literature as detailed in previous chapters and therefore will not be expanded upon any further. However, Fouché's contributions were relatively short-lived. Having served for only two years organizing Mapungubwe research in 1933, his *magnum opus* was his editorial of the 1937 *Mapungubwe Vol. I*. In September 1934 under the guidance of Smuts, Fouché moved on to a more liberal history as Chair of the History Department at

[449] See, F.A. Mouton, "Professor Leo Fouché, the History Department and the Afrikanerization of the University of Pretoria". *Historia* 38(1), 1993, pp. 92–101; F.A. Mouton (ed.), *History, historians and Afrikaner nationalism: essays on the History Department of the University of Pretoria, 1909–1985*. Vanderbijlpark: Kleio, 2007, pp. 13–43

[450] One of Fouché's military duties whilst working as personal secretary to J.C. Smuts was the writing of his "Report on the Rebellion of 1915", known as the Blue Book U.G. 10 of 1915. This was not well-received by a majority of the Afrikaners and Fouché was lambasted for his subjectivity and apologetic tone for the Botha regime leading to his further estrangement.

[451] See for example, B. Murray, "Leo Fouché and history at Wits University 1934–1942". *African Historical Review* 48 (1), 2016, pp. 83–99.

[452] "Funeral of Prof. Fouché: tribute by Smuts". *Rand Daily Mail*, 21 March 1949.

[453] See, F. A. Mouton, "Professor Leo Fouché, the History Department and the Afrikanerization of the University of Pretoria". *Historia* 38 (1), 1993, pp. 95–98.

[454] F.A. Mouton (ed.), *History, historians and Afrikaner nationalism; essays on the history department of the University of Pretoria, 1909–1985*. Vanderbijlpark: Kleio, 2007, p. 23.

[455] University of Pretoria Archives (UPA), B-4-1-2, Minutes of Council, 26 May 1932.

[456] See for example, S. Tiley-Nel, "Leo Fouché (1880–1949)". In S. Tiley-Nel (ed.) *Mapungubwe remembered: contributions to Mapungubwe by the University of Pretoria*. Johannesburg: Chris van Rensburg Publications (Pty) Ltd, 2011, pp. 15–19.

[457] Mapungubwe Archive, UP/AGL/D/55, Letter from L. Fouché to Chairperson of Council, 5 March 1933.

[458] "Funeral of Prof. Fouché: tribute by Smuts". *Rand Daily Mail*, 21 March 1949.

[459] P. Lewsen, "What history means to me". *South African Historical Journal* 28, 1993, pp. 8–9.

J. de Villiers Roos

Londen, 1913

Figure 4.2. Jacob de Villiers Roos (1869–1940).

the University of the Witwatersrand.[460] Nonetheless, Fouché did play a crucial role in the Mapungubwe saga as the University Council reappointed him in 1933 as an agent for the Archaeological Committee in order to pursue Mapungubwe's scientific research on behalf of the University of Pretoria.[461]

4.3. Renaissance man and reformer: J. de Villiers Roos (1869–1940)

Considered a twentieth century "renaissance man" and a fearless critic who gave a lifetime of loyal service to South Africa, Roos has not been given the attention by historians that he deserves.[462] Jacob de Villiers Roos (also known as "Jimmie Roos") was born on 24 November 1869 at Helderberg near Stellenbosch in the Cape. After school, he entered the Normal College in Cape Town where he

qualified as a teacher, but never took to a teaching career. He then completed his BA in Literature at the South African College, which later became the University of Cape Town.[463]

De Villiers Roos first entered journalism when he was appointed as sub-editor of *De Zuid Afrikaan*, the anti-liberal newspaper for progressive Dutch speakers of the Cape Colony which was subsequently amalgamated into J.H. Hofmeyr's paper, *Volksvriend* in 1871. This period was a seminal episode in Roos' early writing career as his meeting with "The Historiographer of the Cape Colony" and first archivist of the Cape, George McCall Theal stimulated his lifelong interest in history. Roos had a "small share" with Theal in the preparation for the press of the first edition in 1894 of C.C. de Villiers' work on the genealogical history of the Old Cape Family.[464]

Roos then joined the editorial staff of the Argus Printing and Publishing Co., Ltd. and worked as a reporter where he published primarily on the proceedings of the Dutch Reformed Church's Cape Republican *Volksraad*. Roos continued working as a journalist and upon his permanent appointment, he worked under the Company's Managing Director, Francis J. Dormer on *The Cape Argus* and then *The Star* in Johannesburg from 1889. In August 1890, he relocated to Pretoria writing a column titled, "Pretoria Day by Day" for *The Star* newspaper. In July 1891, Roos entered into a partnership with Eugène N. Marais (1871–1936) as young co-owner and editor of the iconic controversial publication, *Land en Volk*, which they collectively purchased for £500 that aimed to strengthen the growing anti-Kruger sentiments.[465]

In October 1892, Roos sold half his share in *Land en Volk* to E. Marais, and returned to Cape Town to pursue a legal calling in the Cape Legislative Assembly. From 1893, Roos spent five years in the Cape as a civil servant at the House of Assembly for Parliament where he worked as a committee clerk and shorthand scribe. The old Cape Parliament only sat for quarterly meetings, so for eight months of the year for a "young man of restless energy" these prolonged spells of unwanted time were intolerable. As a result, during the parliamentary recesses Roos volunteered his leisure time to the Cape Archives, under the direction of the official archivist, Rev. H.C.V. Leibbrandt, custodian of the Archives of the Colony of the Cape of Good Hope.[466]

---

[460] See further, F.A. Mouton (ed.), *History, historians and Afrikaner nationalism: essays on the history department of the University of Pretoria, 1909–1985*. Vanderbijlpark: Kleio, 2007, p. 38; B. Murray, "Leo Fouché and history at Wits University 1934–1942. *African Historical Review* 48(1), 2016, pp. 83–99.

[461] L. Fouché, (ed.), *Mapungubwe: ancient Bantu civilization on the Limpopo: reports on excavations at Mapungubwe (Northern Transvaal) from February 1933 to June 1935*, Volume I. Cambridge: Cambridge University Press, 1937.

[462] The idea of a "Renaissance Man" is borrowed from the philosophical ideal that embodied the basic tenets of Renaissance humanism, which considered man the centre of the universe, limitless in his capacities for development, and led to the notion that men should try to embrace all knowledge and develop their own capacities as fully as possible.

[463] See, W.J. de Kock, *Jacob de Villiers Roos, 1869–1940, Lewensskets van 'n veelsydige Afrikaner*: Cape Town: A.A. Balkema, 1958, pp. 7–8.

[464] See further, C.C. de Villiers, *Die Geslacht Registers de Oude Kaapsche Familien*. Kaapstad: Van de Sandt de Villiers & Co. Beperkt, Drukkers, 1894.

[465] S.S. Scott, "A 'Ware Afrikaner' – an examination of the role of Eugene Marais (1871–1936) in the making of Afrikaner identity", PhD Modern History, University of Oxford, 2001, pp. 5–6.

[466] Hendrik Carel Von Leibbrandt was the Keeper of the Archives and Acting Librarian of the Parliamentary Library, see his seminal publication, H.C. Von Leibbrandt, *Rambles through the archives of the*

During this time, Roos took up additional post graduate studies at the University of Cape Town and won the prestigious J.B. Ebden Prize for his essay on national banks in 1896.[467] During this period, Roos crossed paths with John X. Merriman, who later became the last Prime Minister of the Cape Colony, but was the former Treasurer General of the British Financier, Cecil John Rhodes' government. Merriman took a father-like interest in Roos when he served as the Chairperson of the Cape Commission. On an occasion when Roos refused to carry out an order set by the parliamentary committee, Merriman sternly advised him:

> I think your way of conveying an evasive answer was rather bold. But I am to some extent to blame for that. I can excuse anything for I know how pressed with work you are, but take a word of advice and cultivate the true, flowery private secretary style, the world exists on humbug.[468]

The following year in 1895, probably recommended by Merriman, Roos was approached by Cecil John Rhodes to complete several translations from his valuable Africana book collection in Groote Schuur. Rhodes, via his secretary Gordon Le Sueur, issued a cheque for £10 for his services. Roos promptly rejected it and openly stated, "It was only natural that Rhodes should come to look upon a gift of money, as in all cases an acceptable reward for services rendered, and the means or recompense to be his cheque-book. He never expected anyone to do anything for nothing".[469] Taken aback by Roos's response, Rhodes then personally wrote to Roos:

> I have to thank you for the translation you made for me, and I find its answers what I was desiring. You must allow me to send you what I think is a fair return for the work or else I should not like to bother you with further work, though please understand that I fully appreciate that it was voluntary work on your part and you were glad to help me.[470]

Whilst Roos was in the Cape he dabbled in many intellectual ventures, but his studies were interrupted by his appointment as Secretary for the Labour Commission in order to draft a "convenient and exhaustive arrangement" of the index to a three-volume report for which he received a special commendation from the House of Assembly. Employed for five years from 1893 until 1897 in the Cape Parliament, Roos studied law in the last two years and in 1895 he passed his LL.B. He was admitted to the Cape Bar in 1896 and developed his legal expertise and reputation alongside his friend Smuts. It was during this time too that "Jimmie" Roos got to know "Jannie" Smuts better, both were young aspiring attorneys and highly intellectual academics who in their spare time frequently wrote controversial articles for the newspaper *Ons Land*.[471] Under the editorship of F.S. Malan, a barrister and fellow Cambridge scholar of Smuts, *Ons Land* was an influential Dutch newspaper in the Cape Colony that served as the mouthpiece for the Afrikaner Bond and encouraged pan-Afrikaner unity.[472]

In 1897, Roos moved back to Johannesburg in the Transvaal where he was admitted as an attorney, notary and conveyancer of the Transvaal High Court as a sworn translator in Dutch and Portuguese. Roos then worked as an attorney for a prominent legal firm in Johannesburg, Tredgold, Steytier & Beyers and then later joined in partnership with another attorney, I.E. Stegman in Pretoria, as the firm of Stegman & Roos. In December 1899 he married Elizabeth Krog Scheepers (1874–1933) in Alexandria, the daughter of J.C. Scheepers and sister-in-law of Justice N.J. de Wet. Roos fathered five children, four daughters and their last born was a son.[473] Mrs J.E. Roos, like her philanthropic husband, was a great charity worker within the church as she was a member of the Women's Missionary Association. She was devoted to relief and community work among the poor and was responsible for the financial reduction of debt of the Pretoria East Dutch Reformed Church.[474]

Before the end of the Zuid-Afrikaansche Republiek (ZAR), Roos had formed part of the group of the Anglo-Afrikaner elite intellectuals who, from a young age, sought the reform of the Kruger State by extending their sympathy towards an alliance and compromise with British Imperialism. Together with his confidant Smuts, Roos continued to produce Afrikaner opposition articles against the Kruger government, first for *Land en Volk* and then *The Star* between 1889 and 1893. Roos and Smuts frequently corresponded on political, social and private matters. Their positions later intertwined in government and their

Colony of the Cape of Good Hope 1688–1700, Cape Town: J.C. Juta and Co, 1887.

[467] Refer to Cape of Good Hope 1896 Report of the Council of the University of the Cape of Good Hope, Colonial Secretary's Ministerial Division, 1897, p. 1. John Bardwell Ebden (1787–1873) was a politician of the Cape Colony and a member of the Cape Legislative Council who established the Cape Commercial Exchange. He also founded the Cape of Good Hope Bank and was President of the Chamber of Commerce. The Ebden Prize or Scholarship became "famous" in institutions in the Cape and J.H. Hofmeyr was awarded the prize in 1916. Its scholarship enabled J.C. Smuts to graduate from Cambridge. In 1890, Smuts wrote an essay entitled, *South African Customs Union*, it did not win, but was highly commended by the J. B. Ebden Prize.

[468] W.J. de Kock, *Jacob de Villiers Roos, 1869–1940, Lewenskets van 'n veelsydige Afrikaner*. Cape Town: A.A. Balkema, 1958, p. 26; see also, J de V. Roos Collection, Special (Africana) Collections, letters from John X. Merriman to J. Roos dating 1894 to 1923.

[469] W.J. de Kock, *Jacob de Villiers Roos, 1869–1940, Lewenskets van 'n veelsydige Afrikaner*. Cape Town: A.A. Balkema, 1958, p. 27.

[470] J. de V. Roos Collection, Special (Africana) Collection, JVR29, Letter from C. John Rhodes to J. Roos, 8 March 1895.

[471] W.J. de Kock, *Jacob de Villiers Roos, 1869–1940, Lewenskets van 'n veelsydige Afrikaner*. Cape Town: A.A. Balkema, 1958, pp. 24–35; see also National Archives of South Africa (NASA), file A9, Adv. J. de V. Roos.

[472] F.A. Mouton, "A free, united South Africa under the Union Jack": F.S. Malan, South Africanism and the British Empire, 1895–1924". *Historia* 51(1) 2006, pp. 32–33.

[473] The youngest daughter was Ellaline born in 1903 who married Pierre Louw, but he died two years after their marriage, she later remarried Daniel Cillie Malan; Rita (1904–1925); Margaretha Jacoba (1906–1930); Beatrix (1908–1919) and their last born was a son named Jimmy Roos (1910–1970).

[474] "Death of Mrs J. E. Roos". *Rand Daily Mail*, 4 August 1933.

friendship was thus cemented throughout their lives.[475] Largely written by Roos and co-authored with Smuts, they wrote the classic, *Een Eeuw van Onrecht*, "A Century of Wrong" written in High Dutch, a propaganda text that reflected on the metaphorical injustices perpetrated by the British on the Boers.[476]

During the South African War from 1899 to 1902, Roos frequently wrote as a Boer War correspondent for Reuters, a British press organization that used local South African correspondents. Reuters employed over one hundred "stringers" or freelance journalists during the two-and-a-half-year conflict, as they had an international reputation for fairness that contributed to its accessibility to both sides of the War.[477]

During his years as an attorney and solicitor, he was appointed as Executor to the Estate of Emily Hobhouse (1850–1926), the British welfare campaigner.[478] Roos also became a partner of the Transvaal-based Dutch-Afrikaner progressives and formed bonds within the influential circles of the *Het Volk* party of Louis Botha in 1907, which undoubtedly led to his government career that was supported by his comrade Smuts. With the outbreak of World War One in 1914, Roos continued as a Reuter's freelance correspondent in Natal and later the Free State, reporting on the state of War. Roos was also a member of the Archive Committee that made recommendations concerning the preservation and improvement of archival records, which later resulted in the promulgation of the Union's first Archives Act of 1922.[479]

Perhaps Roos' major contribution to South African history was in his position as the First Secretary of Justice and Director of Prisons. On 1 December 1908, at the age of 39 and at the invitation of Smuts, Roos became the Secretary of the Department of Law (Justice) and one month later the Director, a position he held until 1918. Just before the granting of self-governance to the Transvaal, Roos played a prominent role in the drafting of important Transvaal legislation, including the Prescriptions Act of 1908; the Indeterminate Sentence Act of 1909; the Companies Act of 1909; the Prisons Act of 1911; the Bushmen Relics Protection Act of 1911.[480]

In 1910, upon Smut's recommendation, the Minister of Justice, J.B.M. Hertzog invited Roos to become Administrative Secretary for Justice and Director of Prisons for the entire Union. Government appointed a new commission that comprised only three honoured members:

Roos as Secretary of Justice, Sir H. George, Secretary of the Interior and J.R. Liesk, the Secretary for Finance. This delicate and epic task discharged by the new Union government aimed to reorganise the four colonial civil services and bring them into line with one service for the whole of South Africa. It was during this eight-year tenure that Roos single-handedly created a centralised Department of Prisons for the new Union of South Africa, and introduced the Prisons and Reformatories Act of 1911, followed by The Children's Protection Act of 1913. Undoubtedly still discriminatory, the social reforms of 1911 were nevertheless a watershed as this was the first legislation to establish the principle that juveniles should not be imprisoned.[481]

Moreover Roos also drove the first wedge into the harsh and often very cruel colonial penal system. He "abolished the treadmill, the stocks and breaking of stones by African women" by ardently pursuing his reforms to humanise prison treatment.[482] Roos's national prison system laid the basis for the current criminal justice and penal system in South Africa, a practical albeit less than ideal system, he justified using the "considerable use of the concepts of science and modernity".[483]

Nationwide, Roos was held in very high esteem and regarded as a humanitarian leader, who in his new justice position was sympathetic and aspired to bring South Africa in line with international developments in the penal system. For Roos, unlike his nineteenth century predecessors, rehabilitation was a critical factor and he was emphatic that clemency be extended to certain long term prisoners such as inmates serving life sentences that were reduced to time with hard labour.[484]

Between the formative years of the Union between 1908 and 1918, Roos effected fundamental changes in South African criminology and penology. These ten years in his dual position as Secretary of Justice as well as Director

[475] See letters of correspondence between Smuts and Roos, J de V. Roos historical manuscript collection, Special Collections (Africana), Department of Library Services, University of Pretoria.
[476] H. Giliomee, *The Afrikaners: biography of a people*. London: Hurst & Company, 2012, p. 249.
[477] M.P. Roth, *Historical dictionary of war journalism*. London: Greenwood Press, 1953, p. 33; see also Reuters Archive, LN542/1/910125, H.A. Gwynne letter to J. de V. Roos dated 25 August 1899.
[478] See J. de V. Roos Collection, Special (Africana) Collection, letters of correspondence between Emily Hobhouse to J. de Villiers Roos from the period 1915 until 1926.
[479] W.J. de Kock, *Jacob de Villiers Roos, 1869–1940, Lewenskets van 'n veesydige Afrikaner*. Cape Town: A.A. Balkema, 1958, pp. 67–68.
[480] L.C. Chisholm, "Crime, class and nationalism: The criminology of Jacob de Villiers Roos, 1869–1918". *Social Dynamics: Journal of African Studies* 13(2), 1987 pp. 53–54.

[481] L.C. Chisholm, Reformatories and industrial schools in South Africa: a study of class, colour and gender, 1882–1939. PhD thesis, University of the Witwatersrand, 1989, pp. 89–91.
[482] L.C. Chisholm, "Crime, class and nationalism: the criminology of Jacob de Villiers Roos, 1869–1918". *Social Dynamics: Journal of African Studies* 13(2), 1987, p. 53.
[483] See, D. van Zyl Smit, "A legitimate prison system in a future South Africa?" *Legal Studies* 16(2), 1992, pp. 168–171.
[484] Refer to article about a pioneering study of a particular inmate name "Nongoloza", a founder of a major prison gang and reference to Roos who favoured replacing "prisoner isolation with enquiry, deprivation with dialogue and lashings with listening", see for example, C. van Onselen, "Crime and total institutions in the making of modern South Africa: the Life of 'Nongoloza' Mathebula, 1867–1948. *History Workshop* 19 (Spring 1985), p. 71.

of Prisons, was nonetheless a heavy burden on Roos as his health began to deteriorate at age 44. By mid-1913, he took recuperative trips to Europe and travelled to the East, Singapore, India, and China all entirely at his own expense.[485]

In 1918, General Louis Botha persuaded Roos to accept a position as Controller and Auditor-General for the Union of South Africa from 1918 to 1929.[486] Reluctant to move away from his humanitarian and civic duties, Roos nonetheless accepted the position as a challenge that involved a new study of the profession of accounting:

> He threw himself into his new duties with enthusiasm that amounted almost to fervour, and succeeded in gaining for himself an ever higher reputation in his new post than he had won in that which he had previously held. He was a fearless critic and a most effective guardian of the national expenditure.[487]

Historically the office of the Auditor-General in South Africa became a leading proponent of several reforms in relation to public finance. In the archives of the Auditor-General South Africa (AGSA) the acknowledgement of the office held by Roos from 1918 to 1929 is one that was "clearly well-known and respected in academic circles", often evidenced by his brilliant lectures he delivered to the Accounting Student's Society. According to author G. Woods, one of Roos' many influences was his "firm views about the role of money, whether public or private, and its proper use". His often draconian approach and stance to audits and public accountability was pursued with unbending rigour.[488] This would be a significant trait in his dealing with the Archaeological Committee and Mapungubwe.

In addition, in 1931 Roos as Chairperson of the Pretoria Thrift Committee published, *Outlines of Thrift: for the use of teachers*, making him one of the country's leading advocates of the thrift movement. Roos fiercely proposed that thrift was the way to success in life and emphasised the importance of savings and cutting out luxuries. During his last year just before the Great Depression of the 1930s, he knew full well that the solution would hopefully be one in which, "a State emerges from a cycle of depression by the aggregate savings of its citizens".[489] He supported the

views of J.H. Hofmeyr, the Administrator of the Transvaal, believed that "the public economy could never be expected to be fully effected until it was the desire of the people as a whole".[490]

Roos viewed his role as the Auditor-General as partisan and without prejudice, and with no political influence. He regarded the Auditor as, "the establisher of truth, order, and the way to success in business, the man who hears both sides of a question before deciding, the only reliable factfinder". He laid his draconian rule with principles and guidelines as the Auditor-General, but like his close colleague Smuts, he was a visionary. According to Woods, Roos ended one of his lectures as follows: "Although I am no prophet, it seems to me that the future of Government audit will tend more and more to test the merits of expenditure, to see that the State gets value for it".[491]

The historical association of Roos with the University began with the founding of the Transvaal University College (TUC) from 1908 to 1910. Roos was one of seven Council members and under his "conservative and careful hands" he was also the institution's financial advisor from 1908 to 1913.[492] It was during this time that Roos, together with Dr Veale, were hand-selected by the Council to present a report and ground plans for a new building in Brooklyn. It was considered to be "the finest in South Africa" at a cost of £50 000 for the Transvaal University College for the purposes of Higher Education in perpetuity.[493] The Transvaal Government had pledged these funds, but Roos beseeched Smuts for a further £5000 with the aim of building the Old Arts Building which by 1911 originally housed the entire TUC.[494]

In June 1911, Roos was called upon again as one of the Council's most energetic members and together with the Department of Public Works volunteered his time and planned the first planting of trees in the avenues on the new grounds of the Transvaal University College. The holes for planting large Plane and Eucalyptus trees required the use of dynamite as well as hard labour, and under Roos's personal supervision prison labourers

www.businessdictionary.com/definition/paradox-of-thrift.html> access: 2018.07.31.

[490] See, G. Woods, *The legacy book: the Auditor General's 100 year publication*. Johannesburg: Auditor General of South Africa, (AGSA), 2014, p. 18, see, <https://www.agsa.co.za/Portals/0/AG/AGSA%20 Legacy%20Book.pdf> access: 2018.07.25.

[491] G. Woods, *The legacy book: the Auditor General's 100 year publication*. Johannesburg: Auditor General of South Africa 2014, p. 21, <https://www.agsa.co.za/Portals/0/AG/AGSA%20Legacy%20Book. pdf> *s.a.* access: 2018.07.25.

[492] C.H. Rautenbach, (ed.) et al, *Ad Destinatum. Gedenkboek van die Universiteit van Pretoria*. Johannesburg: Voortrekkerpers Beperk, 1960, p. 15.

[493] C.H. Rautenbach, (ed.) et al, *Ad Destinatum. Gedenkboek van die Universiteit van Pretoria*. Johannesburg: Voortrekkerpers Beperk, 1960, pp. 21–22.

[494] C.H. Rautenbach, (ed.) et al, *Ad Destinatum. Gedenkboek van die Universiteit van Pretoria*. Johannesburg: Voortrekkerpers Beperk, 1960, p. 275.

[485] W.J. de Kock, *Jacob de Villiers Roos, 1869–1940, Lewenskets van 'n veelsydige Afrikaner*. Cape Town: A.A. Balkema, 1958, p. 60.

[486] D.W. Kruger (ed.), *Dictionary of South African Biography*. Cape Town: Human Sciences Research Council, 1972, p. 721.

[487] "Funeral of Mr J. de Villiers Roos". *Rand Daily Mail*, 5 August 1940.

[488] G. Woods, *The legacy book: the Auditor General's 100 year publication*. Johannesburg: Auditor General of South Africa, 2014, pp. 21–22, <https://www.agsa.co.za/Portals/0/AG/AGSA%20Legacy%20 Book.pdf> access: 2018. 07.25.

[489] The term "thrift" is an economic concept popularised as the "paradox of thrift" by the renowned economist Maynard Keynes. It states that by increasing savings during an economic recession, essentially leads to a diminishing circular flow of income, and as a result the economy slows down from a reduction in demand. Thus, citizens eventually become poorer when saving, instead of richer, Read more about thrift, <https://

planted the beautiful tree-lined avenues characteristic of the TUC in 1912.[495]

Roos always held a close connection with the TUC throughout his life, but resigned formally as a Council member in 1913. He followed the growth of the College with great interest and made some financial contributions towards the establishment of the men's residences. In 1924 Fouché, as a member of the Council and Senate, insisted that Roos should stand for the position of Rector at the general elections. He guaranteed Roos the full backing of the Senate, but on 9 August 1924. Roos declined the offer. Again in 1928, just before his retirement, Roos was approached to take up the Rectorship of the Transvaal University College. Had Roos availed himself for the position, he would have been supported once again by the Senate and Council. In writing to the Acting Rector, Prof A.E. du Toit, Roos declined this position once again primarily due to health reasons.[496] As a result, Roos also formally retired from public service in 1929.

Roos was a deeply cultured man and in 1929 formed part of a twenty-four man Committee at the Afrikaans Language and Cultural Conference of the Union held in Bloemfontein. Here Afrikaners were rallied towards unified cultural action, with the aim of establishing a dedicated Afrikaans culture professorship at the TUC.[497] It was at this conference that the *Federasie van Afrikaanse Kultuurvereniginge* (FAK) (Federation of Afrikaans Cultural Associations) was founded by the *Afrikaner-Broederbond* (Afrikaner Brotherhood). Although they were primarily concerned with economic and political power, cultural concerns were never absent from their agenda as the Association "virtually controlled organised Afrikaner culture".[498]

Following the Adamson Commission of 1933 that investigated institutional financial subsidies and the effects of the "skraal jare" (lean years) of the Great Depression within the University of Pretoria, the Council appointed the Roos Commission on 19 May 1933 to inspect the financial and economic conditions at the University. Roos was appointed Chairman together with S.P.E. Boshoff, Council member and Director of Education in the Transvaal and Prof. P.J du Toit, Dean of the Faculty of Veterinary Sciences. The Roos Report of 1934 intended, as a commission of enquiry, to investigate and determine the feasibility of staff appointments, organization and lecturing timetables, their efficacy and economic viability.

The Roos Report was at first perceived as a "wonderful document", from outlining the need for more mining equipment to how to address the problem of "indifferent, short-sighted, myopic lecturers" who did not fulfil their teaching responsibilities.[499] Yet, the Report was overall very critical and concluded amongst other issues that there was a surplus of lecturers to the ratio of students, and he recommended that certain departments fall away, students should not be lobbied and the library be reorganised. It was hoped that the Roos Report would find financial solutions, outline norms for lecturers and set practical guidelines for financial policy, but the report was perceived as "too negative", "draconian" and "uninspirational".[500]

Among others, the Roos Report also recommended the extension of the Rector's term of office and on 20 April 1934, the Council requested A.E. du Toit to remain in his position for another term. In opposition, however, the Senate decided that, "it was against the interests of the University for the service of Prof. A.E du Toit to be extended" and recommended in the interim that the Chairperson of the Senate be appointed until such time a new Rector took up the position. Negotiations between the Council and Senate proved unfruitful and the Rector, Prof. A.E. du Toit resigned on 28 May 1934 with immediate effect. In the history of the University of Pretoria, Du Toit was contentious, a brilliant academic and an astute diplomat, yet was considered tactless, having no social filter system in his relationships with colleagues and other people. Du Toit's successor as the University Rector (1935–1940) was none other than C.F. Schmidt (1875–1948), the Controller and Auditor-General of the Union, Roos' successor from 1929 to 1935.[501]

Among other institutional issues, the Roos Commission of 1934 also determined the responsibilities of the Registrar of the University of Pretoria. In the capable hands of Roos, with his vast experience as the former Auditor-General, this crucial position had no prior status under the Laws and Statutes of the University. Under the Roos Commission and his recommendation on 19 September 1940, the Council accepted without doubt or deliberation the definition, responsibilities and status of the Registrar as applied *de facto*, whether by right or not, as well as *de jure* although not officially sanctioned.[502]

Owing to the astute mind of Roos, the Registrar's position was essentially a Chief Executive and Administrative

[495] C H. Rautenbach, (ed.) et al, *Ad Destinatum. Gedenkboek van die Universiteit van Pretoria.* Johannesburg: Voortrekkerpers Beperk, 1960, p. 265.
[496] W.J. de Kock, *Jacob de Villiers Roos, 1869–1940, Lewensskets van 'n veelsydige Afrikaner.* Cape Town: A.A. Balkema, 1958, p 16.
[497] C H. Rautenbach, (ed.) et al, *Ad Destinatum. Gedenkboek van die Universiteit van Pretoria.* Johannesburg: Voortrekkerpers Beperk, 1960, p.127.
[498] M. Kriel, "Culture and power: the rise of Afrikaner nationalism revisited". *Journal of the Association for the Study of Ethnicity and Nationalism* (ASEN) 16(3), 2010, p. 411.

[499] C.H. Rautenbach, (ed.) et al, *Ad Destinatum. Gedenkboek van die Universiteit van Pretoria.* Johannesburg: Voortrekkerpers Beperk, 1960, p. 82.
[500] C.H. Rautenbach, (ed.) et al, *Ad Destinatum. Gedenkboek van die Universiteit van Pretoria.* Johannesburg: Voortrekkerpers Beperk, 1960, p. 82.
[501] C.H. Rautenbach, (ed.) et al, *Ad Destinatum. Gedenkboek van die Universiteit van Pretoria.* Johannesburg: Voortrekkerpers Beperk, 1960, p. 82.
[502] C.H. Rautenbach, (ed.) et al, *Ad Destinatum. Gedenkboek van die Universiteit van Pretoria.* Johannesburg: Voortrekkerpers Beperk, 1960, p. 301.

Officer to act as Secretary to the University Council and Senate, including academic administration, legal and financial responsibilities, and a distinguished position much similar to today. Later in 1934, Roos was called on once again by the government to act as Chairman of the Provincial Finance Commission to investigate the transfer of education from the Union Education Department to the Provinces.[503]

Nonetheless, within family circles Roos secretly admitted that he would have been ideally placed in politics, but decided against this calling following his illness in the 1920s, which left his speech greatly affected while his overall health had further deteriorated from his stressful years in civil service. Instead, he privately focused on the documentation of his immense numismatic collection, antique coins from all over the world, and wrote his own manuscript in 1931 entitled, *some notes on new coinage proposals*.[504] In April 1930, after tragically losing one of his daughters, Roos decided to have no further major responsibilities. In May 1933, due to his wife's declining health, they travelled to Mauritius to warmer tropical climates.

On 3 August 1933 Roos' wife also passed away and he spent the next five years sorting out his personal affairs. In late 1933, during these dark grieving months, and after decades in prestigious and distinguished positions, Roos was approached by the University of Pretoria to serve on the Archaeological Committee.[505] Roos generously gave a seed donation of £100 to contribute to the initial costs adherent to the archaeological discovery and later agreed to serve as Chairperson of the Archaeological Committee from April 1934 until November 1938.[506]

This was only after Roos' retirement from government that he was elected Chairperson of the University of Pretoria Archaeological Committee but, nearing the age of seventy, he stepped down citing health reasons, although he once again delved into an array of other committee work. He was approached by J.H. Hofmeyr to serve as Chairperson of the provincial committee for Hospital Studies and in the following year he became a member of the Transvaal Museum Council of Curators, a committee member of Diamond Control and continued his membership at the *SA Akademie vir Wetenskap en Kuns* (South African Academy for Science and Art). In 1939, Roos meticulously prepared his last will and testament, and bequeathed his valuable and ancient numismatic coin and medallion collection to the

Transvaal Museum.[507] He donated his extensive library and valuable Africana book collection to the Merensky Library at the University of Pretoria and included a further £500 for preservation purposes.[508] Roos also donated £1000 to his *Pretoria-Oos* (Pretoria East) Church.[509] Jacob de Villiers Roos died from a cerebral thrombosis in Pretoria on 2 August 1940.

4.4. Contesting personalities: Fouché vs Roos

A brief review of Fouché and detailed account of Roos as historical personages is necessary to support the concept that as individuals they had a direct bearing and impact not only on the Archaeological Committee, which was historically important, but also on the University of Pretoria. This is important particularly in the context of this book which demonstrates that the early history of Mapungubwe can be moved away from an archaeological perspective towards a revival of the archival and biographical narrative. Therefore, the contesting personalities of Fouché and Roos are briefly explored here as a conceptual and comparative tool for a better understanding of the experiences and actions of their individual personalities and elucidating the historical consequences.[510]

Additionally it is suggested that the early history of Mapungubwe is not as linear as traditionally outlined and that Roos deserved the recognition accorded to him, although the important role that Fouché played must still be recognised. This further demonstrates that the University of Pretoria certainly did not act alone. Without the personalities involved, as well as the external influences from other individuals and their positions within government that set the scene for political influence, Mapungubwe would certainly not have been possible within the University of Pretoria. It is therefore telling to briefly reflect upon these two personalities as a means of historical enquiry for purely comparative purposes.

In defence of Roos who was ahead by leagues, he was more politically influential and astutely connected than Fouché. His private and direct networks included the likes of L. Botha; J.H. Hofmeyr; N.J. de Wet; C.F. Beyers; A.J. de Villiers and J.C. Smuts, among others. This enabled him to have several private one-on-one discussions with them on almost any matter, to the extent that in 1908 Roos highlighted several major shortcomings

[503] See for example study by, J.L. Gibson, A critical study of the report of the de Villiers Commission on technical and vocational education. Unpublished Masters of Education degree, University of Natal, 1968.
[504] W.J. de Kock, *Jacob de Villiers Roos, 1869–1940, Lewenskets van 'n veelsydige Afrikaner*. Cape Town: A.A. Balkema, 1958, p. 73.
[505] W.J. de Kock, *Jacob de Villiers Roos, 1869–1940, Lewenskets van 'n veelsydige Afrikaner*. Cape Town: A.A. Balkema, 1958, pp. 73–74
[506] Mapungubwe Archive, UP/AGL/D/64, Letter from Roos to Fouché financial contribution of £100 towards the Archaeology Fund, 12 March 1933.

[507] Refer to Transvaal Museum, 1939, file9/39.
[508] The Roos Collection was donated in 1958 to the University of Pretoria, see C.H. Rautenbach, (ed.) et al, *Ad Destinatum. Gedenkboek van die Universiteit van Pretoria*. Johannesburg: Voortrekkerpers Beperk, 1960, p. 319.
[509] Special Collections, Department of Library Services, see A.M. van Ryneveld, "Die Adv. J de V. Roos Versameling in die Staatsargief 1884–1940", 1969; E. Klopper & J. Coetzee, "Gids op aanwinste in die Merensky Biblioteek". Pretoria: Universiteit van Pretoria; Jacob de Villiers Boekery, 13 Junie 1979.
[510] See article by K.H. Craik, "Assessing the personalities of historical figures". In W.M. Runyan (ed.), *Psychology and historical interpretation*. Oxford: Oxford University Press, 1988. pp. 196–215.

in the Transvaal legislation ranging from the Minister's office, mining rights, marriage laws to the amendment to the Transvaal Precious and Base Metals Act, No. 35 of 1908. As stated above, as a founding father of the TUC, Roos was actually responsible for Fouché's appointment. As a Council member of the TUC, Roos made contact with Fouché's father, a well-known historian and school Principal from Robertson in the Boland. On 17 December 1908, Roos wrote to Fouché, who was in Berlin, and offered him the position as first professor in history at the TUC.[511]

Fouché was unquestionably comparatively speaking less persuasive and uninfluential, and considered more of a libertarian and a person of acquiescent character. He perhaps lacked a meaningful sway and stature among his contemporaries during what was considered a volatile period in the University of Pretoria's history in the midst of pro-Afrikaner Nationalism. Whilst Fouché was eventually marginalised and pushed aside within the institutions, he remained somewhat loyal to both the universities of Pretoria and the Witwatersrand, which clearly were not faithful in return. Fouché left the University of Pretoria under the epithet of "traitor" and *persona non grata* among Afrikaner circles, and when he resigned from the University of the Witwatersrand upon his retirement in 1942, they even refused to contribute to his pension.[512]

At the University of the Witwatersrand, Fouché filled the shoes of the revisionist historian, W.M. Macmillan in the Department of History, but he was regarded as "a distinct let-down" and, owing to the paucity of his publication record, was blamed for the eventual loss of the department's reputation.[513] In his defence, historian Bruce Murray remarked however that Fouché's overall tenure at the University of the Witwatersrand was generally "a more positive one for the Department of History" in comparison to his time in the same Department at the University of Pretoria. Those that personally remembered and came into contact with Fouché described him as "conservative, a major disappointment both as a researcher and as a teacher", but he was a "perfectionist not easily satisfied" yet "charming" and "distinguished".[514]

In contrast, Roos, ten-years or so Fouché's elder, was a more malleable character, considerably shaped by the time and place as set by the pro-state capitalist, political and economic idealism environment in which he operated. This is evidenced by the upbringing by

his father, a respected barrister, and his erudite private life and political career. These included his internal connections between his work, those he supported (and did not support), and those who supported him throughout his lifetime. Roos's professional and social history equipped him for the integral role he played within the founding of the TUC, later to become the University of Pretoria, and his notable position on several major committees, along with the positions of power he previously occupied in government. Roos's journalist career also enabled him to draft and write endless reports on Mapungubwe. With his legal aptitude he reported favourably to the government, and captured the public's attention to this major South African discovery on behalf of the institution which remained eternally loyal towards him.

His naturally inventive intellect and calm temperament allowed him to handle the negotiations with the five discoverers with equal fairness as far as their compensation was concerned, without focusing on their criminality. This in retrospect from his years as Director of Prisons, was certainly not viewed in his eyes as a "crime worth punishing against".[515] On the Archaeological Committee, Roos was solely responsible for most of the writing and submission of the reports, annual reports as well as the financial reports for the University Council. Fouché in contrast was known to be a very unproductive and unpublished historian, despite his high standards and strict lecturing style.[516]

Roos dealt with Mapungubwe in an authoritative, yet draconian manner, which was clearly influenced by his career as a journalist, as a financial administrator, attorney, conveyancer, translator and notary. He was a prolific writer and his meticulous, almost perfectionist and purist personality is very much reflected in his correspondence with a multitude of notes, side notes and summaries always attached.[517] Even his personal letters and replies focused on accuracy, "true" reporting of facts and always within ethical parameters, and on his dire need to find a practical, financial or legal solution. This is perhaps why Roos, unlike his father, pursued a life in civil service and not as a politician. According to the author, W.J. de Kock, Roos was considered energetic, an exceptional and a transitional figure, a contentious worker within whatever sphere he worked in, self-sufficient and independent. Those that remembered Roos, considered him to be, "highly respected, competent, and dedicated" and a man of "integrity and dedication" who was "trustworthy" and open-hearted.[518]

---

[511] W.J. de Kock, *Jacob de Villiers Roos, 1869–1940, Lewenskets van 'n veelsydige Afrikaner*. Cape Town: A.A. Balkema, 1958, pp. 47–48.

[512] See for example, F.A. Mouton, "Professor Leo Fouché, the History Department and the Afrikanerization of the University of Pretoria". *Historia* 38(1), 1993, pp. 92–101.

[513] E.K. Murray, *Wits: The early years: a history of the University of the Witwatersrand, Johannesburg, and its precursors 1896–1939*. Johannesburg: Wits University Press, 1982.

[514] See further, B. Murray, "Leo Fouché and history at Wits University 1934–1942". *African Historical Review* 48(1), 2016, pp. 83–99.

[515] Mapungubwe Archive, Roos unappraised documents and personal notes.

[516] See P. Lewsen, "What history means to me". *South African Historical Journal* 28, 1993, pp. 8–9.

[517] Mapungubwe Archive, Roos unappraised documents, notes and scribbles.

[518] W.J. de Kock, *Jacob de Villiers Roos, 1869–1940, Lewenskets van 'n veelsydige Afrikaner*. Cape Town: A.A. Balkema 1958, p. 76.

Roos was a polymathic character whose optimism, impartiality and greater world-vision was supported by his litany of contributions ingrained in him as the architect of the Union Government's penal system and other notable legislative and economic contributions already mentioned. However, Roos was not a political activist, but rather sympathetic as a founder of the South African Prisoners' Association and the forerunner of the National Institute for Crime and Rehabilitation of Offenders. Roos's political knowledge and connections were advanced and consolidated by influential friendships with other advocates, reformist politicians and Afrikaner intellectual elites who were also considered the progressive thinkers and "renaissance men" of their time who embodied South African history.[519]

Perhaps as a generalist, Fouché had a more cynical disposition, maybe as part of his defensive posture he "saw history not as a means of praising heroes or besmirching opponents, but of placing the past in the right perspective".[520] Yet, many complained about him within the wider academic fraternity. Fouché pursued archaeology as a frontier of history and as a result formed his own expectations of Mapungubwe as "an ancient civilisation" and the gold discovery as largely plunder, possession and treasure-seeking. In contrast, Roos, an altruistic personality influenced the University's legal chartering of Mapungubwe's discovery to be scientific and that of protection, preservation and patriation.

4.5. Scientific endeavours: the Archaeological Committee's maiden years

As indicated, very little has been previously published on the Archaeological Committee. Fouché's *Mapungubwe Volume I* first introduced it by referring to it as the "special committee". Also, as outlined above, in the literature review other archaeological scholars have focused on the functionality of the Archaeological Committee for its supervisory capacity to oversee the excavations from 1933 to 1947.[521] Pelzer's *Ad Destinatum* written almost fifty years later,

degenerated the Committee's role to a single sentence stating that, "under the leadership of the Archaeological Committee of the University and with government's support, a beautiful collection of artefacts were found and important discoveries were made on site".[522] This was in line with the political stance of the institution at the time with not much fuss being made of the Mapungubwe gold discovery within the University of Pretoria's own written history.

The first ad-hoc meeting of the Archaeological Committee initially appointed by the University Council comprised the Chairperson, J.S. Smit, Prof. L. Fouché and Prof. D.E. Malan and took place on 23 March 1933. At that time it was also decided that the "new government" would only be approached for assistance after the South African general elections which were to be held on 17 May 1933.[523] Within a month of the gold discovery reported to the University in February 1933, Fouché, from the UP Department of History and Prof. D.E. Malan, from the Department of Zoology, accompanied by Mr Eustace V. Adams, the University's Attorney from Adams & Adams, as well as Dr L.J. Krige (brother-in law to Smuts) from the Geological Survey, conducted a site visit to Mapungubwe.[524]

They included in their visit a personal meeting with both the Van Graans and Van der Walts (the *trekboer* or migrant farmer discoverers), in order to further negotiate and propose future scientific expeditions for the University of Pretoria. According to a report in *The Star*, the University representatives, "armed with the authority from the owner of the land... and the ambassadors of learning were able to assume possession... of what should be called in scientific meaning of the term - "the treasure".[525] This initial physical site inspection was crucial for consultations with the five discoverers and laid the basis for the requirements and prerequisites for the workings of the Archaeological Committee in its first year of operation in 1933.

On 28 March 1933, in a letter to A.E du Toit, Rector of the University of Pretoria, the Minister of the Interior, D.F. Malan,[526] undertook to support the archaeological and scientific work at Mapungubwe for a period of five years that commenced from 25 April 1933. This correspondence

[519] Roos received support and was backed by many other theoretical and creative intellectuals, he maintained close ties with N.J. de Wet, J.C. Smuts and E. Marais.
[520] Although Fouché was described by his colleagues as objective, courteous, tolerant and good humoured, he remained a renegade, a type-of historical activist frequently unpopular in his views and actions and even complained about petty issues such as the University postal system. He was continually hounded even earlier in his career for his role in the Afrikaner rebellion of 1914, an apologetic plea for Louis Botha and throughout his scholarly life was disapproved by staunch Afrikaner Nationalists. See more detail by F.A. Mouton, "Professor Leo Fouché, the History Department and the Afrikanerization of the University of Pretoria". *Historia* 38(1), 1993, pp. 92–101.
[521] See L. Fouché, (ed.), *Mapungubwe: ancient Bantu civilization on the Limpopo: reports on excavations at Mapungubwe (Northern Transvaal) from February 1933 to June 1935*, Volume I. Cambridge: Cambridge University Press, 1937, p. xiii; A. Meyer, *The Iron Age sites of Greefswald: stratigraphy and chronology of the sites and a history of investigations*. Pretoria: University of Pretoria, 1998, p. 20; See also, M. Schoeman, "Co-operation, conflict and the University of Pretoria Archaeological committee". In S. Tiley-Nel (ed.) *Mapungubwe remembered: contributions to Mapungubwe by the University of*

Pretoria. Johannesburg: Chris van Rensburg Publications (Pty) Ltd, 2011, pp. 89–101.
[522] See, C.H. Rautenbach, (ed.) et al, *Ad Destinatum. Gedenkboek van die Universiteit van Pretoria*. Johannesburg: Voortrekkerpers Beperk, 1960, p. 123.
[523] Mapungubwe Archive, UP/AGL/D/88, Minutes of the Meeting of the Archaeological Committee, 23 March 1933.
[524] See L.J. Krige, "Geological report on Mapungubwe". In L. Fouché (ed.), *Mapungubwe: ancient Bantu civilization on the Limpopo: reports on excavations at Mapungubwe (Northern Transvaal) from February 1933 to June 1935*, Vol. I. Cambridge: Cambridge University Press, 1937, pp. 3–4.
[525] "Mapungubwe natural fortress of the Limpopo: an impregnable hill Pretoria party's research experiences". *The Star*, 15 March 1933.
[526] D.F. Malan served as Minister of Interior Affairs from 19 June 1924 until 17 May 1933, he was a member of the National Party and later became Prime Minister of South Africa from 1948 to 1954.

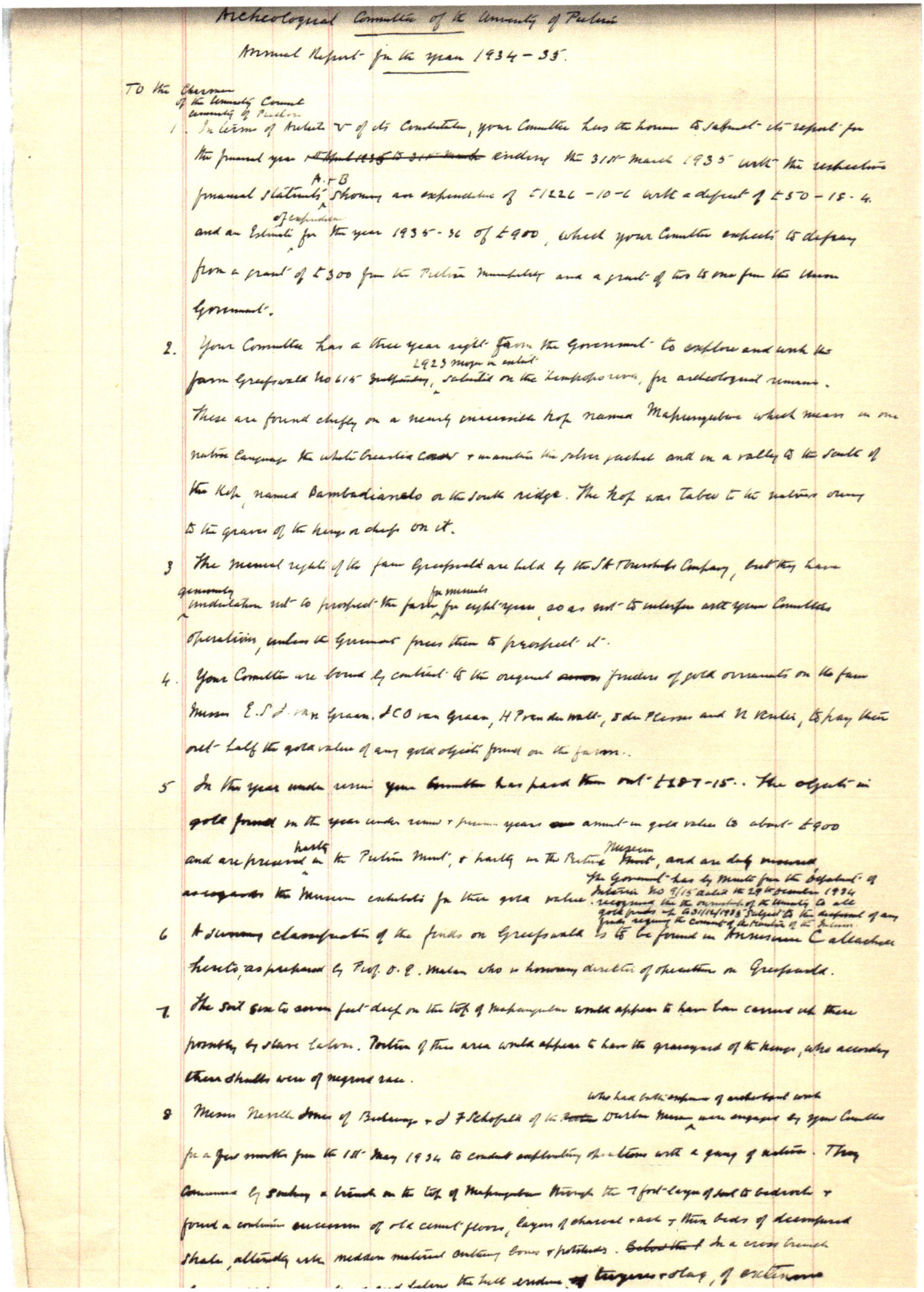

Figure 4.3. Hand-written notes of the Archaeological Committee of the University of Pretoria's Annual Report 1934–1935 by J. de Villiers Roos.

immediately asserted government control of the finds, as all "artefacts of historical and archaeological value" were under "the charge and responsibility" of the Minister of the Interior's Office.[527]

The ad hoc Archaeological Committee then met again on 28 April 1933. They reported that the contract between the University of Pretoria and the farm owner, E.E. Collins, had been settled and the government would purchase the farm *Greefswald* in order to secure the University of Pretoria research rights for scientific interest. Furthermore, the Minister of the Interior wanted to ensure that all finds were made publicly accessible and treasury provisionally made £500 available for this purpose.[528] Under the insistence of the Minister of the Interior, public interest in research and any new finds were to be garnered. Public support would serve as a line of possible future funding and in the form of endorsed subscriptions, and so the public were invited to contribute to the "University of Pretoria Excavation Fund".[529] Government had only promised some assistance on the condition that the University appealed to the public and therefore:

> The citizens of the Union, and more especially those of the Transvaal, should be given the opportunity to contribute towards the cost of an undertaking which promises so notable an enrichment of their historical heritage.[530]

For the Union, the Mapungubwe discovery was considered "unique" and it was predicted that "the complete scientific exploitation of the site will take some years and cost thousands of pounds" and as a result the exploration fund was proposed.[531] As mentioned, the government had undertaken to contribute two pounds for every pound raised by the University as the government was of the opinion that the treasure secured by the University was "a national responsibility". After personally viewing the treasures, the Prime Minister, Hertzog actually declared the undertaking "a national matter".[532]

It is important to note that the Rector's role should not be underestimated as Du Toit served as the intermediary between the University and Hertzog's cabinet. He secured the University "exclusive rights" as a simple cession without conditions and was instrumental in ensuring that these rights would be "unhampered" and thus secured the continued undertaking from one government transition to the next.[533]

In May 1933, the archaeological investigations then fell under the charge of the new Minister of the Interior, J.H. Hofmeyr, and it was intended that the Committee would be responsible for all the work in connection with the proposed excavations at Mapungubwe.[534] This Committee would have to raise funds for the purpose of excavations, they had to direct operations in the field, arrange for publication (both public and scholarly) and would be assessed by annual reports and financial accounts submitted via the University Council directly to the Minister of the Interior.[535]

In June 1933, under the directive of the Minister of the Interior, the Secretary of the Interior, P.I. Hoogenhout, instructed the Rector, Du Toit, that the University Council may now formulate a Committee, yet it "should not be viewed as a separate body" and must be comprised of nine members.[536] The government approved five representatives from the University of Pretoria, complemented by four government administrators, with at least two representing the public. In addition the state pledged further financial support of £1500 for the first year.[537]

In August 1933, at the behest of Fouché, the University Council was requested to determine the powers and responsibilities of the Archaeological Committee.[538] A constitution of the Committee was regarded as necessary as it affected the rules about how the Committee would function on matters at hand, its responsibilities, decision-making powers and dealing with other issues such as representation, administration and financial support. The Council decided that the Committee shall act on its behalf, supervise and arrange all excavations and otherwise consult with the Council. They had to submit monthly as well as annual reports, including financial and inventory listings. The Rector was liable for the responsibility, preservation, housing and handover of all the excavated finds, which meant that as inventories were created, these would be sent to the Rector's Office, thus the Rector would be informed at all times of any new discoveries.[539]

Concerning financial matters, the Archaeological Committee would have to submit budgets and keep scrupulous audits of income and related expenses for the Financial Committee of the Council. It was further made abundantly clear that the Archaeological Committee would not have any financial responsibilities without prior

---

[527] University of Pretoria Archives, Ref/1672. No 80/73, Letter from P. I. Hoogenhout to A.E. du Toit, 8 May 1933.
[528] University of Pretoria Archives, Ref/1671, Minutes of the Meeting of the ad hoc Committee, 28 April 1933.
[529] Mapungubwe Archive, UP/AGL/D/38, "Archaeological treasure trove on the Limpopo", undated.
[530] Mapungubwe Archive, UP/AGL/ D/246.
[531] Mapungubwe Archive, UP/AGL/D/39.
[532] Mapungubwe Archive, UP/AGL/D/128, 8 May 1933.
[533] Mapungubwe Archive, UP/AGL/D/111, Notes on interview between Minister of Interior, Secretaries of Interior and Lands, Prof. A.E. du Toit and Mr E.V. Adams held at the Minister's office, 21 April 1933.

[534] J.H. Hofmeyr took up the position of Minister of the Interior from 17 May 1933 to 1936, under Hertzog's Third Cabinet.
[535] L. Fouché, (ed.), *Mapungubwe: ancient Bantu civilization on the Limpopo: Reports on excavations at Mapungubwe (Northern Transvaal) from February 1933 to June 1935*, Volume I. Cambridge: Cambridge University Press, 1937, p. xiii.
[536] University of Pretoria Archives, Ref. 1694, Letter from P.I. Hoogenhout to Prof. A.E du Toit, Rector, 12 June 1933.
[537] Mapungubwe Archive, J. de Villiers Roos Collection, Minutes of Archaeological Committee, 26 August 1933.
[538] Mapungubwe Archive, J. de Villiers Roos Collection, Minutes of Archaeological Committee, 26 August 1933.
[539] Mapungubwe Archive, UP/AGL/D/248, Constitution of the Archaeological Committee, 17 November 1933.

approval of the Council.[540] The above outlined more than eleven responsibilities contained in the Archaeological Committee's constitution, which clearly indicated that the Committee had a much more complex role to play within the University than merely the task of excavation at Mapungubwe.

The Committee consisted of the Chairperson of the Council (ex-officio), the Rector (ex-officio), three persons appointed by the Council and four members appointed by the Minister of the Interior. The Committee's primary function would be to advise the University Council on all excavation matters and all other functions deemed necessary from time to time as requested when and where by the Council.[541] At this time, the University of Pretoria functioned as a two-tiered system of governance with the Council who controlled the finances and serviced the needs of society, and on the other hand the Senate composed of academics concerned with the teaching and research programme. Historically, these two internal bodies were often in conflict and had a stormy relationship. There were many bitter battles but were viewed as "the prime initiators of change".[542] It would appear from the records that Council, and not the Senate, had a much larger control over the Archaeological Committee. Behind the scenes however, since the Rector sat as Chairperson of the Senate and joint meetings were held between the Council and Senate, it can be deduced that this was a grey area, but nonetheless remained a dominant top-down approach to all institutional decision-making.

The original Archaeological Committee consisted of the following representatives who each played a specific and significant role both internally and externally. Governing the University of Pretoria at the time was its Council, chaired by J.S. Smit, a veteran Nationalist politician and the former Administrator of the Transvaal who held the Chairmanship of the Archaeological Committee until the end of 1933.[543] Fouché and D.E. Malan represented the University of Pretoria; J. de Villiers Roos and C. Maggs represented the public; T. Truter represented the Pretoria City Council; C. van Riet Lowe and J.H. de Wet represented the government; as well as A.E. du Toit who served as Chairperson of the Senate and as Rector (ex-officio) but was not compelled to attend these meetings.[544]

Throughout 1933, J.S. Smit served as the Chairperson, although at times the Chairmanship rotated in the absence of a member, and from 1934 Roos replaced Smit as Chairperson. The Secretary of the Archaeological Committee was Roelof L. Barry, who served as Secretary of the Council as well as the temporary Registrar from 1929 until May 1933.[545] Fouché's representation on the Committee had naturally emanated from the Van Graan discoverers who made the first contact with him, since Fouché had lectured on prehistory and made the link and he was thus recognised as the one for "whom the opening up of Mapungubwe is due in the first place", despite having no archaeological experience.[546] Fouché was primarily charged with the responsibility for the general direction of all the scientific research and publication thereof.

Prof. David Edward Malan, a professor from the Department of Zoology at the University of Pretoria was appointed as honorary director of field operations. Malan was a member of the South African Biological Society, the Pretoria Entomological Club and served as Chairman of the National Zoological Gardens of South Africa in Pretoria in 1926 and later again as Chairman of the Zoological Board until 1954.[547] In 1933, Malan held a seat on the University Council and his primary role on the Archaeological Committee was his external influence as an Associate Member of the Transvaal Museum Board.[548]

During this period, the Transvaal Museum was inseparably linked to the National Zoological Gardens, as zoo animals were kept at the back of the museum. They both shared the Daspoort farm property, but were further governed by the same board and reported to the Minister of the Interior, under whose jurisdiction the Committee fell. This association with the University of Pretoria and the Transvaal Museum was integral, as not only did Roos serve on the Board of Curators, but it was the only repository available in Pretoria at that time to appropriately store the Mapungubwe collection.[549]

In addition, as indicated there were two representatives from the government on the Committee. The first was C. van Riet Lowe, who held the position as appointed honorary director of excavations and served as the government archaeologist. Clarence van Riet Lowe (1894–1956) worked as a civil engineer for the Department of Public Works and was an avid Smuts supporter. He devoted thirty years to archaeology and became the first

---

[540] Mapungubwe Archive, Constitution of the Archaeological Committee, 1933.

[541] Mapungubwe Archive, UP/AGL/D/248, Constitution of the Archaeological Committee, 17 November 1933.

[542] B.L. Strydom, Broad South Africanism and Higher Education: The Transvaal University College (1909–1919), PhD History, University of Pretoria, 2013, pp. 27, 41.

[543] Jacobus Stephanus Smit's tenure as the Administrator of the Transvaal was from 1 March 1929 until 28 February 1934. He was successor to J.H. Hofmeyr (1924–1929). Smit was the Chairperson of the Transvaal University College and the University of Pretoria Council from 12 December 1932 until 17 November 1933.

[544] Mapungubwe Archive, Roos Archaeological Committee unappraised documents.

[545] C.H. Rautenbach, (ed.) et al, *Ad Destinatum. Gedenkboek van die Universiteit van Pretoria*. Johannesburg: Voortrekkerpers Beperk, 1960, p. 300.

[546] Mapungubwe Archive, UP/AGL/D/824, Archaeological Committee of the University of Pretoria, Annual Report for the year 1936–1937, R.1558, 1 April 1937.

[547] R.C.H. Bigalke, *The National Zoological Gardens of South Africa*. Pretoria: Central News Agency Ltd, 1954, p. 6.

[548] A.N. Pelzer also served on the Board of Trustees of the Transvaal Museum and held the position of Head of the Department of History. He is chiefly credited with writing up the University of Pretoria history for the first Volume of the *Ad Destinatum* under the editorship of C.H. Rautenbach.

[549] S. Tiley-Nel, "Sermons in stone, poetry in potsherds: the history of the Mapungubwe collection". In S. Tiley-Nel (ed.) *Mapungubwe remembered: contributions to Mapungubwe by the University of Pretoria*. Johannesburg: Chris van Rensburg Publications (Pty) Ltd, 2011, p. 185.

Director of the Bureau of Archaeology in 1935, which later became the Archaeological Survey.[550] Initially he was appointed to the Committee on an ad hoc basis and in this capacity advised on road construction, drew up site plans and was responsible for all the mapping. His tacheometric or rapid survey methods formed the basis for all the work at Mapungubwe. Whilst Van Riet Low, as director of excavations, further laid the groundwork for archaeological policy, which the Committee followed, he never took up the position of archaeologist for Mapungubwe because of his extensive duties for government. During this period, Van Riet Lowe already held three full-time administrative posts in archaeology at the Department of Public Works, the Bureau of Archaeology, as well as Secretary of the South African Historical Monuments Commission.[551]

Nonetheless, Van Riet Lowe was responsible for the three Honourable Ministers who visited the site between 1933 and 1937. They were Hertzog, Prime Minister in 1933, the Deputy Prime Minister and Minister of Justice, Smuts in July 1934 and the Minister of Finance, N.C. Havenga in July 1936. These State visitors "took lively interest in all they saw and tendered some wise advice", but were critical allies to ensure the University's compliance and success in terms of the mandate of the Archaeological Committee.[552] Unfortunately the second representative from the government, J.H. de Wet, of whom nothing is known nor his role on the Committee. He may have served with Van Riet Lowe in the Department of Public Works.

Other than Roos, the Committee member that represented the public was Mr Charles (Chas) Maggs.[553] Maggs, the only Englishman on the Committee, was extraordinarily prominent and affluent in the Pretoria business and financial sectors, which had a good relationship with Louis Botha, as well as with members of the former TUC as he was a major donor to the University.[554] He was the largest individual private donor of the University due

to his substantial financial contributions which funded new buildings and accommodation for students, as the institution grew and expanded after the First World War.[555]

In 1930, Maggs served on the first Council of the University of Pretoria and was actively involved in the controversy of the 50-50 language policy which the institution viewed as a means for unifying South Africa.[556] Maggs called for a "no change in policy" in order to "safeguard the interests" and for "all sections of the community" to receive "equal rights at the hand of the University of Pretoria".[557] Maggs formed part of the English-speaking alliance against the proposed change to an only Afrikaans medium institution, and what the *Pretoria News* declared as, "nothing more than a disgrace to the city".[558]

Subsequently, in October 1932, Maggs was not re-elected to represent the University donors on the University of Pretoria Council. Following this, on 25 October 1932, he led a public initiative and rallied ratepayers, students, parents and influential Pretoria residents against language segregation. He was instrumental in creating a furore in the English media about the discord of a "separatist education" and an "all Afrikaans university" as a "hot-bed of nationalism".[559] This was a decision shared by Smuts, the TUC founder, who also publicly expressed the move as "a lamentable decision".[560]

The outcome of the meeting with Maggs about language aimed to muster support from prominent residents who would appeal to the Minister of Education and the Council of the University to oppose and reverse the new one-language policy. They called for the immediate withdrawal of funding and the generous grants provided by the Pretoria City Council to the University.[561] Since 1920 Maggs had been a financier and Chairperson of the University's Buxton Hostel.[562] In 1932 he voluntarily withdrew, "in view of the utter impossibility of carrying on the ideal of the hostel owing to the new 100 percent Afrikaans policy adopted by the University Council", but his rash reaction was angrily received and caused a

[550] National Archives of South Africa (NASA), ASW, Vol. No.23, B11 Archaeological Survey, 1946.
[551] S. Tiley-Nel, "Clarence van Riet Lowe 1894–1956". In S. Tiley-Nel (ed.) *Mapungubwe remembered: contributions to Mapungubwe by the University of Pretoria*. Johannesburg: Chris van Rensburg Publications (Pty) Ltd, 2011, pp. 26–28.
[552] Mapungubwe Archive, J. de V. Roos Collection, Roos report to University of Pretoria Council, 1 April 1937.
[553] Charles Maggs (1863–1937) was distinguished in many spheres within London and when he moved to South Africa in 1880 he accumulated a fortune as he discovered the Zaaiplaats tin mine. He became a director and served on the boards of many enterprises, the Potgietersrus Town Council, Pretoria Portland Cement Company, the Silverton Tannery, Barclays Bank, the South African Iron and Steel Industrial Corporation and the Pretoria Chamber of Industries including the National Bank. Maggs was a well-known local benefactor, a conspicuous and successful businessman with immense generosity. In his time within Pretoria he donated thousands upon thousands of pounds to humanitarian and educational causes. Maggs built and lived in the house, "Greystoke" in Arcadia, Pretoria. Maggs later offered the house to the British High Commission as offices and he presented his house to the Majesty's Government in the United Kingdom as a token of honour to his country of birth; see *Western Daily Press*, England, 29 October 1937.
[554] "Death of Mr Charles Maggs: distinguished in many spheres". *Rand Daily Mail* 18 October 1937.

[555] C.H. Rautenbach, (ed.) et al, *Ad Destinatum. Gedenkboek van die Universiteit van Pretoria*. Johannesburg: Voortrekkerpers Beperk, 1960, p. 261
[556] "To unify South Africa. Ideal of the University of Pretoria. Chancellor's statement of policy". *Pretoria News*, 13 October 1930.
[557] C.H. Rautenbach, (ed.) et al, *Ad Destinatum. Gedenkboek van die Universiteit van Pretoria*. Johannesburg: Voortrekkerpers Beperk, 1960, p. 58–59.
[558] C.H. Rautenbach, (ed.) et al, *Ad Destinatum. Gedenkboek van die Universiteit van Pretoria*. Johannesburg: Voortrekkerpers Beperk, 1960, p. 70.
[559] See C.H. Rautenbach, (ed.) et al, *Ad Destinatum. Gedenkboek van die Universiteit van Pretoria*. Johannesburg: Voortrekkerpers Beperk, 1960, p. 54; "Politics and the T.U.C. Charge refuted". *Pretoria News*, 25 August 1922.
[560] "The University decision: deplored by Gen. Smuts". *Rand Daily Mail*, 15 September 1932.
[561] C.H. Rautenbach, (ed.) et al, *Ad Destinatum. Gedenkboek van die Universiteit van Pretoria*. Johannesburg: Voortrekkerpers Beperk, 1960, pp. 68–70
[562] C.H. Rautenbach, (ed.) et al, *Ad Destinatum. Gedenkboek van die Universiteit van Pretoria*. Johannesburg: Voortrekkerpers Beperk, 1960, p. 291.

storm within the University for years thereafter.[563] Maggs nonetheless remained on the Committee and in 1934 personally donated £50 towards the Excavation Fund.[564]

Perhaps the most interesting appointment on the Archaeological Committee was that of Colonel Theodore Gustav Truter (1873–1949), a former Resident Magistrate in the Transvaal and later Chief Commissioner of the Transvaal Police. Truter held this position for eighteen years as the first Commissioner of the South African Police, from his appointment on 15 October 1910 as Commissioner of the Transvaal Police, and then from 1913 until 1928 as Chief Commissioner of the Police forces of the four provinces. He retired on 30 November 1928 having served the state for thirty-six years.[565]

Truter was also one of the few South Africans to receive a British Knighthood, but little else is known about him.[566] Called upon by the University, the role of the South African Police Service was evident from the onset when Mapungubwe was placed under "European guard" to ensure that no looting occurred and to ensure protection of the site.[567] The Committee, most probably advised by Truter, were also tasked to investigate discrepancies of Mapungubwe gold allegedly and illegally sold in 1933 in Messina by H. van der Walt and then later again in 1940 by Van Tonder and some labourers.[568] These matters were reported to the Police Commissioner.[569] Roos was charged to investigate the allegations and liaised with the Deputy Commissioner of Police, Colonel Lendrum.[570]

The Archaeological Committee was legally bound by contract to the five original discoverers and, until 1938, annually paid them out half the metallic value of any gold objects found on *Greefswald*. The Van Graans were paid out an estimated amount of £670 between April 1933 and April 1938.[571] This greatly concerned Roos as he stated that, "under the first five years we were threatened by a potential court case by the Van Graans" because the contract with the government did not allow for any

rights to "treasure trove".[572] For the second five years and thereafter the Committee could simply not afford any further "finders fees" and felt threatened by this financial pressure as previously indicated, since the Van Graans perpetually proposed litigation.

Financially, the Committee did not only have to pay the discoverers, but also had to track the value of the gold recovered from excavations, which came to an estimated £1000 per year, and in addition had to cover the insurance policy which amounted to about £700 per annum.[573] On 10 December 1937, according to Mr H. Engelmohr, the University Accountant, the annual certificate of the total gold finds kept in the Royal Mint in Pretoria, as well as in the Transvaal Museum and in safe-keeping at the University amounted to 165.666 ounces troy (±5,152.788g).[574]

4.6. Collection endeavours: curatorship and co-operation with the Transvaal Museum

The Archaeological Committee, under the guidance of Prof. D.E. Malan, were responsible for the public exhibition of new finds as well as their storage and preservation.[575] In 1933, with the potential importance of the discoveries on Mapungubwe, arrangements were made by the authorities to stage an exhibition and additional financial contributions were solicited. The first exhibition held at the New Museum in Market Street, later the Transvaal Museum was entitled, "antiquities of a forgotten race" and had about £250 worth of gold on display.[576]

Large crowds were expected and included the Minister of Native Affairs, P.G.W. Grobler and the Mayor of Pretoria, Mr I. Solomon. *The Rand Daily Mail*, "treasures for exhibition" generated the public attention the Committee had predicted.[577] The Minister of the Interior, J.H. Hofmeyr officially opened the exhibition at the Transvaal Museum on 28 June 1933.[578] In his opening address, Hofmeyr stated that they had already granted five years' research for "fairly lavish financial support", and "hoped that its discoveries at Mapungubwe would make it world-famous" and "government felt that opportunity should be given to some academic body, in this case naturally the University of Pretoria".[579]

---

[563] C.H. Rautenbach, (ed.) et al, *Ad Destinatum. Gedenkboek van die Universiteit van Pretoria*. Johannesburg: Voortrekkerpers Beperk, 1960, p. 291

[564] Mapungubwe Archive, J. de Villiers Roos Collection, list of donations to cover expenses related to the archaeological discovery, including £25 from *The Star*, £10.10 from F.R. Paver and £185 pending from the Pretoria Municipality.

[565] Refer to the South African Mirror and history of the South African Police for a brief outline of T.G. Truter's administration, <http://www.samirror.com/sapolice-history.html>, access: 2018.07.24.

[566] R. Dix-Peek, A list of South African and Rhodesian born Baronets, Knight Bachelors, Dames and Peers, Live Journal 2010, < https://peek-01.livejournal.com/74468.html> access: 2018.07.24.

[567] Mapungubwe Archive, Roos unaccessioned documents.

[568] Mapungubwe Archive, Roos unappraised documents, interview with Deputy Commission CID, 29 March 1935.

[569] See Mapungubwe Archive, UP/AGL/D/22 and UP/AGL/D/578.

[570] Mapungubwe Archive, Roos unappraised documents, Affidavit from Pieter Willem van Tonder who called upon Roos at his home to prepare his statement and provide information in response to the allegations, 1 April 1935.

[571] Mapungubwe Archive, Roos unappraised hand-written notes and receipts of payments.

[572] Mapungubwe Archive, Roos unappraised note among Archaeological Committee papers, undated.

[573] Mapungubwe Archive, J. de Villiers Roos collection of finances, notes and hand-written documentation.

[574] Mapungubwe Archive, UP/AGL/D/973, Archaeological Committee Annual Report for the Financial Year 1937–1938.

[575] Mapungubwe Archive, UP/AGL/D/248, Constitution of the Archaeological Committee, 17 November 1933.

[576] See article, "Treasures for exhibition, found in koppie near Limpopo, contributions wanted". *Rand Daily Mail*, 27 June 1933; Mapungubwe Archive, Roos Collection, Inventory of Mapungubwe material, Annexure C (R.1007).

[577] "Treasures for exhibition, found in koppie near Limpopo, contributions wanted". *Rand Daily Mail*, 27 June 1933.

[578] Transvaal Museum Archive, Transvaal Museum Annual Report, 1933–1934; Mapungubwe Archive, UP/AGL/D/246.

[579] "Valuable finds at 'Mapumgubwe': Hofmeyr opens exhibition". *Rand Daily Mail*, 29 June 1933.

In August 1933, the Archaeological Committee further resolved that an attempt should be made to obtain co-operation in order to secure more effective protection for the archaeological site.[580] Subsequently, the ongoing and protracted legal negotiations regarding the gold compensation claims to the five discoverers were compounded by preservation endeavours which were of importance to the University of Pretoria.[581] On behalf of the Committee, Prof. D.E. Malan was asked to approach the Director of the Transvaal Museum, Dr C.J. Swierstra, the Principal of the University of the Witwatersrand, Dr H.R. Raikes and the Council of the South African Association for the Advancement of Science to state their views and called on the Minister of the Interior for the protection and preservation of antiquities.[582]

As a result, in October 1933, a co-operation body comprised of the Universities of Pretoria and the Witwatersrand, the Transvaal Museum and the Council of the South African Association for the Advancement of Science proposed that the Office of the Minister of the Interior would be requested to receive a deputation to consider legislation for more adequate protection of archaeological sites.[583]

The Council of the South African Association for the Advancement of Science delegated Fouché, as a member, to appoint two delegates of his choice. Fouché selected Prof. Raymond Dart (Head of the Department of Anatomy) and Prof. Louis Maingard (Professor of Anthropology), both from the University of the Witwatersrand, and leading academics to represent the Science Association and to join forces with both the University's and the Transvaal Museum.[584] The preservation of archaeological sites and historical monuments was sympathetically received by the Minister of the Interior.[585]

This initiative by the Archaeological Committee led to co-operation between the University of Pretoria and the Transvaal Museum who were approached for their services to provide secure storage, preservation of selected gold items, which were to be stored separately in a safe, and exhibition space for the expanding Mapungubwe Collection.[586] In October 1933 an agreement was entered into between the University of Pretoria and the Transvaal

Museum to collaborate, loan and accommodate the Mapungubwe Collection.[587] The Transvaal Museum, when relocated from the Old Museum in Boom Street to the New Museum in Market Street, displayed the Mapungubwe collection in the main entrance hall.[588]

A year later, towards the end of 1934, the Committee raised concerns to Council that, "the finds are getting to be too numerous to exhibit in the Pretoria [Transvaal] Museum and must be suitably arranged for archaeological study".[589] They further urged the Council to provide housing in a building in the university grounds. All arrangements with the Transvaal Museum had to be personally discussed with Roos, as Chairperson of the Archaeological Committee. In addition, all approvals for exhibition and storage space also filtered through Roos as well as instructions and authorizations by the Registrar under the approval of the Council. It was further agreed between the parties that the name of the University of Pretoria be mentioned in writing as the "owner of the collection" on all exhibition and publicity material.[590]

For decades, the expanding masses of accumulated archaeological material plagued and concerned the Archaeological Committee as the University maintained that the best position for the collection would be to remain in safekeeping and under preservation at the Transvaal Museum, with a small portion of gold deposited at the South African Mint in Pretoria. During this time, the Mapungubwe Collection comprised two sections, i.e. a smaller collection that was on permanent public exhibition, and a larger collection in safe storage. The material selected for exhibition not only consisted of photographs, maps, excavations plans and gold, but a very extensive range of examples of pottery, other ceramics such as clay figurines, iron and copper implements and bead assemblages, along with shell and organic remains.[591] The Transvaal Museum Archive does indicate at all, that fragments of human skeletal remains were also exhibited.[592]

[580] Mapungubwe Archive, UP/AGL/D/211, Co-operation in archaeology, August 1933.

[581] Transvaal Museum Archive, T.M. 12/37 (File 119) UP/MA/TVL/031, Agreement between the Transvaal Museum and the University of Pretoria; see also Mapungubwe Archive, Roos unappraised documents notes, 1933.

[582] Mapungubwe Archive, UP/AGL/D/211, Co-operation in archaeology, August 1933.

[583] Mapungubwe Archive, UP/AGL/D/235, Letter from L. Fouché to Private Secretary for the Minister of the Interior, 19 October 1933; UP/AGL/D/236, reply to Fouché from Office of the Minister of the Interior, 21 October 1933.

[584] Mapungubwe Archive, UP/AGL/D/237, Letter from L. Maingard to L. Fouché, 24 October 1933.

[585] "Historic spots in Union: deputation asks for preservation". *The Star*, 26 October 1933.

[586] Transvaal Museum Archive, T.M. 10/39 (File 100) UP/MA/TVL/002, Letter from Rector to Director, 28 August 1933.

[587] Transvaal Museum Archive, T.M. 12/37 (File 119) UP/MA/TVL/031, Agreement between the Transvaal Museum and the University of Pretoria in connection with the storage of the Mapungubwe Collection, signed C.J. Swierstra and C.F. Smit.

[588] The Transvaal Museum, formerly part of the *Staatsmuseum* of the ZAR was established in 1892, but was the only repository of archaeological, anthropological and historical material available in Pretoria. The University of Pretoria never had space or proper storage or exhibition areas for the Mapungubwe material until after 1994.

[589] Transvaal Museum Archive, T.M. 12/37 (File 119) UP/MA/TVL/033, Letter from Registrar to Museum Director, 18 March 1936.

[590] Transvaal Museum Archive, T.M. 12/37 (File 119) UP/MA/TVL/033, Letter from Registrar to Museum Director, 18 March 1936.

[591] Transvaal Museum Archive, T.M. 12/37 (File 119) UP/MA/TVL/037, for a full list of Mapungubwe material exhibited see extensive lists and inventories outlining contents of display cases.

[592] See T.M. 12/37 (File 119) List of material from Mapungubwe collection on exhibition in the New Museum. There are further records that mention that the human skeletal remains were also stored in the Transvaal Museum storage on shelves. Their fragility and preservation were of concern and the remainder of remains were sent to Prof. R.A. Dart, Head of the Department of Anatomy at the University of the Witwatersrand for analysis and further investigation. See also, T.M. 12/37 (File 119) UP/MA/TVL/040 and UP/MA/TVL/TVL/045.

On 24 April 1938, the University of Pretoria Archaeological Committee ended its five-year contract at Mapungubwe which was funded by the government through the Ministry of the Interior, with the option of a further five-year period ending April 1943. Roos re-negotiated on behalf of the University of Pretoria with the Secretary of the Interior, N.J. de Wet, for a new lease from government for the continuation of the Committee, their financial support of £1000 per annum, and to further scientific research.[593] This included Roos's renegotiations with the Mayor of the City of Pretoria who requested the annual Grant-in-aid funds from the Municipality of £300 for the continuation of exploration and excavations to ensure that "Pretoria's name will always be associated" with Mapungubwe.[594] This funding request was successful and was supplemented with further financial backing from the Minister of the Interior's office which continued until about 1940.[595]

In 1939, following the resignation of Roos as the government representative on the Archaeological Committee, speculatively as a result of his ailing health, the Director of the Transvaal Museum, Mr C.J. Swierstra, was seconded as the new government representative by the Minister of the Interior.[596] As the Mapungubwe material was the property of the Mapungubwe Archaeological Committee, together with the Archaeological Bureau under the Directorship of Van Riet Low, a second Mapungubwe exhibition was agreed to and arranged with Dr L. Wells and Dr Galloway from the Medical School at the University of Witwatersrand. This was considered to be a special display of skeletal material, a "loan of a few skulls" to be put on display at the Museums Association Conference, as well as that of the South African Association for the Advancement of Science in July 1946.[597]

In 1947, as further excavations were anticipated, and in response to handling the masses of the stored archaeological material, the exhibition space at the Transvaal Museum was improved and also expanded.[598] The Archaeological Committee was further obliged to ensure that all possible precautions were taken against potential theft and that contingency plans were in place since the Transvaal Museum waivered full responsibility for the safety of the archaeological material. Furthermore, the insurance of the Mapungubwe gold articles was further taken on by the University of Pretoria to an amount of £1000 against all risks whilst contained at the University, or stored in the Transvaal Museum or on exhibition anywhere in South Africa.[599]

The University of Pretoria merely expected the Transvaal Museum to provide as much space as possible in order to house the collection for several years, as sufficient space at the University was simply not adequate and impossible. The Transvaal Museum Board of Trustees expressed concerns that whilst "the collection occupied useful space", it ought to be put to more active use and enquired from the University as to the future of the collection for research purposes. The Museum Board felt that "the time had arrived for the University authorities to find suitable accommodation elsewhere".[600] The University also requested the Museum to bear full responsibility for exhibition, storage and its protection, but the Museum Board was explicit that they would not be responsible or held liable for "any damage or theft" and the Committee could go ahead on their own in terms of exhibition of the Mapungubwe collection.[601]

The University maintained its close connection with the South African Police, following Truter's position on the Archaeological Committee. The University held several discussions with the Deputy Commissioner of the Commanding Transvaal Division who advised on the safety of certain gold objects in the Transvaal Museum. Although the police could not place a permanent guard over the exhibits, they provided police guards for short periods. Two members of the Criminal Investigation Department advised on improvements to the glass display cases and all other security matters of the Mapungubwe gold held in the Transvaal Museum.[602] Security was of great concern to the University Council, as well as the Archaeological Committee, as during the late 1930s there were a spate of museum raids, vandalism, even cases of graffiti and theft of objects ranging from stones, whale bones to diamonds.[603]

Finally in May 1961, after nearly thirty years of strained co-operation and temporary curatorship under the new Directorship of Dr V. Fitz-Simons, the Transvaal Museum Board of Curators decided that the Mapungubwe Collection ought to be returned to the University of Pretoria.[604] The Transvaal Museum stored, exhibited and curated the Mapungubwe collection on behalf of the University of Pretoria from 1933 until 1961 with the option of reproductions or replica's being made available. The

[593] Mapungubwe Archive, J. de Villiers Roos Collection, Letter from J.H. de Wet Secretary of Interior to Roos, 25 May 1938.
[594] Mapungubwe Archive, J. de Villiers Roos Collection, Letter from Roos to His Worship the Mayor and Councillors of the Corporation of the City of Pretoria, 5 April 1938; see also National Archives of South Africa (NASA), MPA, 3/4/1518, file 108, Grant-in-aid University of Pretoria 1933–1938.
[595] Mapungubwe Archive, UP/AGL/D/1281, letter from Secretary for the Interior to the Registrar, 14 October 1940.
[596] Transvaal Museum Archive, T.M. 10/39 (File 100), UP/MA/TVL/010/012, Letter from Secretary for the Interior to C.J. Swierstra, 25 January 1939.
[597] Transvaal Museum Archive, T.M. 12/37 (File 119) UP/MA/TVL/068, Mapungubwe exhibit for the S.A. [sic] Meeting, 1 June 1946.
[598] E. Grobler, Collections management practices at the Transvaal Museum, 1913–1964: anthropological, archaeological and historical, PhD dissertation, University of Pretoria, 2005, p. 143.

[599] Transvaal Museum Archive, T.M. 12/37 (File 119) UP/MA/TVL/050, Letter from Accountant to Museum Director, 30 April 1948.
[600] Transvaal Museum Archive T.M. 12/37 (File 119) UP/MA/TVL/058, Letter from UP Registrar to Museum Director, 28 January 1948.
[601] Transvaal Museum Archive, T.M. 12/37 (File 119) UP/MA/TVL/023, Letter from Museum Director to UP Rector, 15 September, 1933.
[602] Transvaal Museum Archive, T.M. 12/37 (File 119) UP/MA/TVL/094, Letter from Deputy Commissioner to the Director, 29 October 1937.
[603] "Amazing story of museum raid". *The Star*, 18 October 1937; "Vandalism in Museums". *The Star*, 1 July 1937.
[604] Transvaal Museum Archive, T.M. 10/39 (File 119), UP/MA/TVL/016, Letter from Registrar to Dr. Fitz-Simons, 16 August 1961.

collection was officially returned in November 1961 under the archaeological care and arrangement of Prof. J.F. Eloff and Prof. P.J. Coertze from the Department of *Volkekunde*, who also served as the University representative on the Council of Curators.[605] The Transvaal Museum regarded the temporary loan of the Mapungubwe Collection as one of the most important loans and for three decades stored, preserved and exhibited the collection on behalf of the University of Pretoria.[606]

From the above discussions it is therefore evident that while the early Mapungubwe history had multiple trajectories, the influence of J. de Villiers Roos, and above that of L. Fouché, is evident. Furthermore, through the lens of the University of Pretoria Archaeological Committee, their actions and activities, it is also evident that they had a much wider and far-reaching role than just excavation at Mapungubwe. On behalf of the University Council Roos, upon advice from University legal counsel, further requested the government to exclude discoverers' rights to any undiscovered treasure, including any further rights to the University on any treasure trove since the State would assume ownership over it. Roos duly notified the five discoverers that their agreement with the University expired on 25 April 1938, and that no further compensation would be provided, as per the condition set by the Minister of the Interior.[607]

Following the economic recovery of the 1930s the financial navigation of the Archaeological Committee during its maiden years was not easy. Funding excavations were expensive and placed a major financial burden on the University, which had never attempted such an institutional endeavour as no precedent of its kind had ever existed before in South Africa. The exemplary way Roos as Chairperson assiduously maintained expenditures and scrutinised book-keeping records ensured the annual appropriation to the Archaeology Committee was warranted. Over the early years, the costs increased substantially, including all transport, travel costs, camping equipment, tools, stationary, salaries, equipment, vehicle maintenance, labour, subsidies to the newspapers, photographic material, including all legal and exhibition expenses, and other diverse outlays.[608]

In hindsight, the exorbitant running costs of the operation of excavations were underestimated and since there was no certainty of how much more gold would be recovered, the University of Pretoria erred on the side of caution to protect their institutional interests against uncertain circumstances. The Archaeological Committee continued to function from 1939 onwards, chaired by G. Moerdyk (1939–1942) who also held the position of Chairperson of the University of Pretoria Council from 1935 until 1942.[609] Over the next decade several factors slowed down the work of the Archaeological Committee, particularly since legislation affected archaeological excavations on *Greefswald* during 1938 and 1945 to control archaeological research.[610]

Furthermore, Mapungubwe excavations were forced to a stop mainly since the assistance of the Government subsidy had also ceased.[611] This more or less coincided with the time when the funding for Dongola also ceased as the Dongola Wildlife Sanctuary was deproclaimed by the new National Party.[612] Gardner had also been instructed by the University of Pretoria, as per his agreement prepared by Roos, to "publish nothing except topical newspapers articles for ten years after the completion of excavations".[613] Finally, around the time just after the Second World War (1939–1945), the official dissolution of the Archaeological Committee occurred formally in 1947.[614]

The University of Pretoria Archaeological Committee, with its multiple dimensions, significantly added to the understanding of the environment in which they operated within the University of Pretoria. These maiden years of the Archaeological Committee represented two types of historic self-fashioning: First, the archaeological justification for the research by means of large-scale, laborious and expensive excavations; and second, the justifications and validated efforts to truly institutionalise the discovery of Mapungubwe in order to "recognise the ownership of the University to all the gold finds" by consent of the State.[615]

The following chapter will highlight how the University of Pretoria's past legal chartering of Mapungubwe's scientific discovery not only led to national patrimony and patriation, but how the two approaches of stewardship versus ownership are consequently contested. It will consider how they were shaped by legal possession in conferring power, negotiating control and exclusive access to Mapungubwe.

---

[605] Transvaal Museum Archive, T.M. 10/39 (File 119), UP/MA/TVL/010/015. Letter of receipt of the Mapungubwe Collection by Prof. P.J. Coertze, 17 November 1961.

[606] E. Grobler, Collections management practices at the Transvaal Museum, 1913–1964: anthropological, archaeological and historical, PhD dissertation, University of Pretoria, 2005, pp. 270, 377.

[607] Mapungubwe Archive, J. de Villiers Roos Collection, Minutes of extraordinary Meeting of the Archaeological Committee, 2 April 1938.

[608] Mapungubwe Archive, J. de Villiers Roos Collection, Archaeological Committee financial statements, income and expenditure reports 1933–1938.

[609] Gerard Moerdyk (1890–1958), the South African architect served on the first Council of the University of Pretoria in 1930, he also held the position of Chairperson of University Council from 18 October 1935 until 25 June 1942. The Moerdyk family owned the farm, *Samaria* 28 MS which is situated adjacent to the west of *Greefswald* 37 MS.

[610] Mapungubwe Archive, UP/AGL/D/1482, Letter from Van Riet Lowe to Rector, 23 June 1952, see National Archives of South Africa (NASA), UOD, Vol. No. 417, X6/46/2/2, Archaeology *Greefswald* investigations file 1938–1950.

[611] "Mapungubwe excavations stopped". *Rand Daily Mail*, 26 May 1941.

[612] J. Carruthers, *National Park Science: a century of research in South Africa*. Cambridge: Cambridge University Press, 2017, p. 115.

[613] Mapungubwe Archive, UP/AGL/D/1483, Letter from G.A. Gardner to van Riet Lowe, 29 June 1952.

[614] Mapungubwe Archive, UP/AGL/ D/1201, Minutes of the Meeting of the Archaeological Committee, 4 March 1939.

[615] Mapungubwe Archive, UP/AGL/D/512, Archaeological Committee of the University of Pretoria Annual Report for the year 1934–1935, by J. de V. Roos to Chairman of the University Council, 2 April 1935.

5

Historical Ownership vs Heritage Stewardship

> We might inculcate a wiser regard for the future through active concern with the present. We don't simply save, we also fashion heritage... We make heritage our own by adding our stamp on it, that stamp is sometimes corrosive, sometimes creative. Heritage is not something just preserved or protected or conserved. It is modified all the time. It is enhanced, and it is also degraded by every new generation. David Lowenthal, 1998.

5.1. Legal chartering

Research emphasises that the early history of Mapungubwe seldom turns in an orderly fashion, not on a single development and neither does a single individual leave the only mark on the past. This truism is certainly the case when the complex early history of Mapungubwe is unpacked through the neglected lens of the Mapungubwe Archive. As has already been verified, the site of Mapungubwe and its "treasure trove" has been the centre of controversy since the discovery of gold there in 1933 under the helm and control of the Archaeological Committee.

Subsequently, the archaeology of Mapungubwe's past was of great scientific consequence to South African prehistory and contributed to the debates between the physical and cultural anthropologists as alluded to in the literature review. Moreover, many scholars' side-lined local knowledge and oral histories, Indigenous identities were marginalised and living heritage and traditional communities neglected, thereby adding to the later controversy over Mapungubwe as already mentioned. Nonetheless, the public hype over the gold discovery and the archaeological investigations overshadowed and skewed crucial legal issues, as South African historical and heritage legislation primarily played a didactic political role in the support of colonial white supremacy and Afrikaner Nationalism prior to democracy.[616]

Perhaps of greater ethical and moral consequence were the questions of legal title, rights to treasure trove, claims of discovery and other legitimate and legislative matters on heritage. From the outset, these legal issues required delicate manoeuvring by the University of Pretoria from Mapungubwe's discovery and scientific research which consequently came at a high cost, both financially and to the reputation of the institution. As discussed in the previous chapter, the formulation of the Archaeological

Committee as the guide of the University Council, served as an institutional instrument to exercise authority and power over Mapungubwe. Moreover, it also set in motion State concerns about other discoveries of gold on South African territory within wider historical contexts. In the 1930s, the former Director of the Archaeological Survey and Acting Secretary for the Commission for the Preservation of Natural and Historical Monuments, B.D. Malan, called for a commission into the enquiry about the discovery of gold on or near the Witwatersrand before 1886. He requested evidence and information about "by whom, when and where" the discovery of gold and its exploitation was made.[617]

By 1932 South Africa left the Gold Standard, the price of gold rose and was followed by a windfall in the mining of new gold deposits that resulted in an economic boost, followed by the so-called "seven golden years".[618] Furthermore, the protracted negotiations between the University lawyers and the discoverers were already strained, but lessened somewhat with the drafting of the Natural and Historical Monuments, Relics and Antiques Act, No. 4, which was passed by the Union parliament in 1934. Its precursor was the Historical Monuments Commission (HMC) that dated back to 1923. Yet, it was only later that a relatively modest effort began with monument declaration.[619]

These decades were a crucial period that brought about what Smuts referred to as a general "South Africanisation of science".[620] Politicians promoted the pursuit of science

---

[616] See for example discussions by K. Tomaselli and A. Mpofu, "The re-articulation of meaning of national monuments: beyond apartheid 'culture and policy'". *Journal of the Australian Key Centre for Cultural and Media Policy* 8(3), 1997, pp. 57–75; see also, D. Sibayi, Addressing the impact of the structural fragmentation on aspects of management and conservation of Cultural Heritage. MA thesis, University of Stellenbosch, 2009, p. 4.

[617] "Commission for the preservation of natural and historical monuments, relics and antiques". *Rand Daily Mail*, 21 December 1938; "Commission for the preservation of natural and historical monuments, relics and antiques". *Rand Daily Mail*, 18 January 1939.

[618] J. Lang, *Bullion Johannesburg: men, mines and the challenge of conflicts*. Johannesburg: Jonathan Ball, 1986, p. 509.

[619] Natural and Historical Monuments Act, No. 6 of 1923, this Act made provision for the preservation of natural and historical monuments of the Union and of objects of aesthetic, historical or scientific value or interest.

[620] In 1929, J.H. Hofmeyr as President of the South African Association delivered an address to the British Association in Cape Town titled, "Africa and Science", this theme was referred to as the "Africanisation of science" which Smuts re-iterated at the same meeting of the British Association in Johannesburg. See S. Dubow (ed.), *Science and society in southern Africa*. Manchester: Manchester University Press, 2000, pp. 84–85.

and funding was redirected to such efforts, by what Dubow called "knowledge-based institutions" that reaped benefits as the State increasingly drew on the sensibility of academic experts.[621] This period saw a rise in Smuts patronage to South African prehistory, the "reorientation of archaeology" and as one of the results, the first mobilisations of historical and heritage legislation.[622]

Furthermore, the breaking of "South Africanism" by the rise of Afrikaner nationalism served as a stimulus for the implementation of legislated segregation in the 1930s.[623] This overlapped with the discovery by physical anthropologists of early human fossils in South Africa. Morris points to this period as the "flowering of typology in South African physical anthropology" which unfortunately provided the scientific underpinning for the government's racial systems that followed.[624]

In the 1960s the Historical Monuments Commission was replaced by the National Monuments Council (NMC) and, under the narrow interests of archaeology, they brought about imbalances such as the over-representation of archaeological sites and other historical sites in monumentalisation.[625] This "selective monumentalisation" policy aimed to be a conservation strategy, yet mainly served white political strategies. In the early 1980s, at the height of apartheid, it is assumed (but as yet unsubstantiated) that the University of Pretoria was instrumental or involved in nominating Mapungubwe as a national monument.[626] According to F. Frescura, between 1983 and 1987, the years of some of the greatest government oppression also marked the highest point in the declarations of the National Monuments Council. During these years the number of proclamations trebled and over 826 nationalised monuments were created.[627] Frescura claims that during this time, the National Monuments Council members were

mainly white and so the bulk of declared monuments and memorials mostly reflected white culture, history and heritage.

Post 1994, when the State gave prominence to black liberation and legacy projects and struggle histories proliferated, representation and transformation of museums and heritage institutions came to the fore. The re-contestation of the past arose as more inclusive heritage received wider acknowledgment by means of legislative interventions for restorative justice.[628] When heritage was prioritised by the new democratic State, discord re-surfaced around Mapungubwe because of its connection to the University of Pretoria as a former defender of Afrikaner nationalism. Inevitably this gave rise to questions of access, repatriation and restitution as calls for redress were heightened. Following the new democracy, institutions of higher education such as universities fell outside the ambit of State heritage structures since they did not form part of declared cultural institutions.[629] Although the University of Pretoria is governed as an organ of the State by virtue of its exercises of public power and public function,[630] it was morally obliged to re-acknowledge its ownership of a declared national treasure including the Mapungubwe Archive. The result was an ultimate tipping point, as the University of Pretoria had to institutionally charter a new course forward, towards its present inclusive stewardship allowing for access and transformation, as opposed to its former exclusive ownership approach.

It is against this backdrop that the trajectory and shortfalls of South African historical and heritage legislation are outlined here, and how the fluctuations and variations in legislation affected Mapungubwe's historical past in the same way as it does its heritage present. Whilst the discovery of gold at Mapungubwe in the 1930s set in motion a legal approach that framed the protection of archaeological heritage, the legislative framework of heritage in South Africa is in itself a historically contested process and its efficacy is questioned.[631]

This chapter suggests that by means of the legal instrument process, historically Mapungubwe's gold "treasure trove" has evolved from a "treasure" value to that of "archaeological, cultural and historical value". More recently, also to a broader national patrimonial value of heritage that is passed on and inherited from one generation to the next. It further highlights two approaches, one the ownership and two the stewardship as the institutional concerns of the University in post apartheid South Africa elevated the 'discovery and

---

[621] See for example, S. Dubow, *A commonwealth of knowledge: science, sensibility and white South Africa 1820–2000*. Oxford: Oxford University Press, 2006, p. 8.

[622] See, N. Shepherd, "State of the discipline: science, culture and identity in South African archaeology, 1870–2003, *Journal of Southern African Studies* 29(4), 2003, pp. 831–832.

[623] For example, the Transvaal Asiatic Land Tenure Act of 1930; the Riotous Assemblies (Amendment) Act of 1930; the Native Services Contracts Act of 1932; the Slums (demolition of Slums) Act of 1934; the Representation of the Blacks Act of 1936 and the Representation of Natives Act of 1936.

[624] A.G. Morris, "Biological anthropology at the southern tip of Africa: carrying European baggage in an African context". *Current Anthropology* 53(5), 2011, pp. 152–160.

[625] See for example, J. Deacon, "Archaeological sites as national monuments in South Africa: a review of sites declared since 1936". *South African Historical Journal* 29(1), 1993, p. 119.

[626] If the University of Pretoria was instrumental in this nomination, there would be records of this nature. Nonetheless, it is possible that the records of the declaration are held in the archives of the former National Monuments Council which may or may not form part of SAHRA's registry. In 1983 and 1984, declaration was awarded by the National Monuments Council (NHC) to the sites of K2 and Mapungubwe and a small bronze plaque that cost R27.00 was placed on a stone at the proclaimed site, where it remains today. Mapungubwe Archive, UP/AG-/D/1846, "Legendariese kop bly behoue". *Beeld*, 20 August 1984.

[627] See for example, F. Frescura, "Monuments and the monumentalisation of myths" Paper presented at Myths, monuments, museums: new premises? University of the Witwatersrand, History Workshop, Johannesburg, 16–18 July 1992.

[628] See, T. Manetsi, State-prioritised heritage: governmentality, heritage management and the prioritisation of liberation heritage in post-colonial South Africa, PhD thesis, University of Cape Town, 2017.

[629] Cultural Institutions Act, No. 119 of 1998.

[630] The University of Pretoria is governed in terms of the Higher Education Act, No. 101 of 1997.

[631] See N. Ndlovu, "Legislation as an instrument in South African heritage management: Is it effective?" *Conservation and Management of Archaeological Sites* 13(1), February 2011, pp. 31–57.

scientific excavation' into a 'social and political' transformation domain.

Furthermore, it elucidates how Mapungubwe's early history had the potential to "both stimulate and act as a symbol of political struggle", including over time "how ownership of heritage objects, places and practices might be considered to give their possessors political power".[632] In closing, this chapter suggests that the institutional "possession" by the University of Pretoria upon the discovery of Mapungubwe as a "treasure trove" as well as the State's claim to "ownership of heritage", automatically placed and displaced "authorship" over Mapungubwe. This legal trend and its surrounding contestation have been carried over from one generation to the next since 1933, which mirrors the continued and evolving contestation of the past and present.

5.2. Controlling history: framing the legal approach

In South Africa, the first post Union attempt to protect heritage was the Bushmen Relics Protection Act, No. 22 of 1911.[633] At the time it was a very necessary protection against Western museums from filling their African treasuries from as early as the nineteenth century, if not earlier. Particularly with the imperial and European preoccupation of the looting and uncontrolled export of Bushman rock paintings and engravings.[634] Subsequently, as the result of a public outcry, this Act covered the prohibition and provided permits of rock painting and engravings exports.[635] As a consequence, this first piece of legislation was very narrow in scope, yet was in line with the early precolonial and colonial views of South African prehistory. Even though this only extended limited protection over a very small segment of South Africa, it did not include legislation for the removal or damage of objects nor over the collections in the possession of institutions.[636] Unfortunately, this era was also marred at the turn of the twentieth century by inhumane depictions of "Bushmen heritage" and the illegal free-trade in human skeletal remains to European museums.[637]

Twenty-three years later, the Bushmen Relics Protection Act, No. 22 of 1911 was followed by the slightly more inclusive Natural and Historical Monuments, Relics and Antiques Act, No. 4 of 1934.[638] This Act provided for the appointment of a Commission comprising of no less than seven members, who received no remuneration, and on recommendations of the Commission empowered the State as follows:

> The Minister of the Interior may from time to time proclaim any monuments, relics, or antiques, after which no person shall, without written consent of the commission, destroy or damage or remove or export any monument or relic. Any person who knowingly fails to comply with these provisions shall be guilty of an offence and liable on conviction to a fine of £100, with the alternative of six months imprisonment.[639]

This legislation protected, and was aimed once again at the preservation of mainly settler and colonial heritage, whilst a majority of prehistoric sites and many others remained historically marginalised and ignored by legislation. This Act merely emphasised the political nature of monument proclamation almost exclusively to bolster white heritage and later Afrikaner Nationalist interests. It was argued that as far as archaeological sites were concerned, there was a perception that declaration enhanced mainly the buildings of the colonial period up to ninety percent. Whilst there was some truth to the ignored "cultures of indigenous people" the choice of declaration was influenced by the interests and ideologies of the councillors, as well as public interest.[640]

As previously mentioned, C. van Riet Lowe was the Secretary of the Historical Monuments Commission until his retirement in 1955 and his dual position in the Department of Public Works and within the Bureau of Archaeology (established in 1934) influenced the selective declaration of archaeological sites during the 1930s to the 1950s. This coincided with Smuts, as Prime Minister and a friend of his, and in 1935 as they established the Archaeological Survey which was combined with the National Monuments Council.[641] However, Mapungubwe was never put forward or recommended for promulgation

[632] See for example the series of discussions of case studies in the politics of heritage and world heritage sites, as heritage is moved into the political arena as symbols of nationalism and class, for further discussion see, R. Harrison (ed.), *Understanding the politics of heritage*. Manchester: Manchester University Press, 2010, p. 154.

[633] The Bushmen Relics Protection Act, No. 22 of 1911 by modern standards of legislation was a simple statute, but importantly considered the first heritage legislation which comprised of a single page with five short articles, see further, A. Hall and A. Lillie, "The national Monuments Council and a policy of providing the protection for the cultural and environmental heritage". Paper presented at Myths, monuments, museums: new premises? University of the Witwatersrand, History Workshop, Johannesburg, 16–18 July 1992, p. 3. J. de Villiers Roos was also instrumental in the drafting of this Act.

[634] L. Henry, "A history of removing rock art in South Africa". *South African Archaeological Bulletin* 62(185), 2007, pp. 44–48.

[635] "Destruction of ancient relics: law to protect them". *Rand Daily Mail*, 5 August 1929; "Preserving old sites and relics". *Rand Daily Mail*, 31 July 1929.

[636] L. Kotze, and L.J. van Rensburg, "Legislative protection of cultural heritage resources: a South African perspective". *Queensland University of Technology Law and Justice Journal* 3(1), 2003, pp. 121–140.

[637] See for example, M. Legassick and C. Rassool. *Skeletons in the cupboard: South African museums and the trade in human remains 1907–1917.* Cape Town: South African Museum, 2000.

[638] The Natural and Historical Monuments, Relics and Antiques Act, No. 4 of 1934 was amended by Acts No. 9 of 1937 and later, No. 13 of 1967 and was eventually repealed in 1969.

[639] "S.A. Monuments and relics: preservation powers of the Minister". *Rand Daily Mail*, 6 February 1934.

[640] J. Deacon, "Archaeological sites as national monuments in South Africa: a review of sites declared since 1936". *South African Historical Journal* 29(1), 1993, p. 120.

[641] J. Deacon, "The professionalization of archaeology in the 1960". In P. Robertshaw (ed.), *A history of African archaeology*. London: James Currey Ltd. 1990, p. 73.

Past Imperfect

as a national monument until much later, even though Van Riet Lowe served on the Archaeological Committee.

Ironically, in the 1930s two other Iron Age archaeological sites were declared national monuments, championed mainly by Van Warmelo, the government ethnologist and probably supported by Van Riet Lowe as Secretary of the Commission. These two stone-walled settlements named Dzata and Verdun[642] were seen as "having historical and scientific interest" and were considered as exceptional objects both of "national interest".[643] Why Mapungubwe was not earmarked at the same time remains unknown, despite the fact that these two latter sites of Dzata and Verdun were far less significant and they certainly did not yield any remarkable "national treasures".

A majority of State institutions such as museums and archives, as well as institutions of higher education, supported the policy efforts of the Historical Monuments Commission and championed only "white", "settler" and "colonial heritage". This imbalance eventually called for revised legislation and catered for the growing demands to proclaim more memorials and monuments as a mechanism for forging Afrikaner national identity.[644] The rise of Afrikaner nationalism in the 1930s was further viewed as an expression of class interests to secure legal, political and economic interests which became embedded and entrenched in the segregatory legislation that was characteristic of the 1930s.[645]

The National Monuments Act, No. 28 then came into effect in 1969 and served to consolidate all previous South African historical legislation.[646] This Act broadened the range of sites to include historical sites, yet still concentrated predominantly on "select" archaeological sites and colonial monuments, a previous allusion to the legislative inheritance of the 1934 Relics and Antiques Act. Governed by the new National Monuments Council, the 1969 policy introduced the concept of provisions for site declaration, but was a State body that fell under

the Minister of National Education and was accused of discriminatory "monumentalisation".[647] For three decades, the National Monuments Act of 1969 guided the management of South Africa's historical, archaeological and cultural heritage through the "select and neglect" activities of the National Monuments Council.[648]

For the first time, the Council instituted a formal permit system for excavation, as well as generally protected heritage in terms of antiques, cultural treasures and shipwrecks. In essence it covered all archaeological, palaeontological and historical sites and claimed to be "not exclusive to European heritage".[649] However, by the 1980s, in "opposition to the grand narrative of official heritage" there were already alternative contestations and a small, but growing "vigorous archive of resistance, a counter archive, in various forms and at different sites, both private and public".[650] Up until then, the National Monuments Council was exclusively represented by whites, but soon after P.W. After Botha's introduction of the Tricameral Parliament (1984–1994), the Council later included one Indian and one Coloured representative.[651]

In reviewing the historical composition of the National Monuments Council between 1936 and 1989, Frescura criticised the political ideology of the exclusively white members of Council and their role in "giving legitimacy to past totalitarian and racist regimes".[652] Likewise, T. Manesti claimed that with the "professional archaeologists at the helm of the NMC", and what he termed the "privileging of archaeology", the selective nature of pre-colonial archaeological sites illustrated the extent to which "selective amnesia" occurred and one which was "steeped in personal biases".[653] He further referred to the operating policy of the National Monuments Council as a process of reflection of "authorised heritage discourse" at work with certain personalities in "positions of authority

---

[642] The Verdun ruins are associated with an early Venda chief settlement dating back to the 18th century and is today ranked as a Grade 2 Provincial Heritage Site. The Dzata ruins are also associated to an early Venda settlement that today forms part of the Dzanani Community and is recognised as an architectural link with Mapungubwe, and also dates to around the 18th century. Both are well-known, stone-walled early capital Venda sites associated with the Zimbabwe-style ruins and oral traditions can be linked to both sites.
[643] J. Deacon, "Archaeological sites as national monuments in South Africa: a review of sites declared since 1936". *South African Historical Journal* 29(1), 1993, pp. 125–126.
[644] See for example, S. Marschall, "Forging national identity: institutionalizing foundation myths through monument". *South African Journal of Cultural History* 19(1), 2005, pp. 18–35.
[645] H. Giliomee, *The Afrikaners: biography of a people*. London: Hurst & Company, 2012; see also H. Giliomee, "The growth of Afrikaner identity". In W. Beinart and S. Dubow (eds.), *Segregation and apartheid in twentieth century South Africa: rewriting histories*. London: Routledge, 1995, p. 189.
[646] The National Monuments Act, No. 28 of 1969 was amended several times in 1979, 1981 and in 1986 respectively. The National Monuments Council fell under the National Department of Education and after 1994, fell under the auspices of the Minister of Arts, Culture, Science and Technology.

[647] See F. Frescura, "Monuments and the monumentalisation of myths': new premises?" University of the Witwatersrand, History Workshop, Johannesburg, 1992.
[648] G. Whitelaw, "New legislation for cultural heritage". *Natalia* 30, Natal Society Foundation, 2010, pp. 58–63.
[649] J. Deacon, "Archaeological sites as national monuments in South Africa: a review of sites declared since 1936". *South African Historical Journal* 29(1), 1993, p. 120.
[650] See for example, H. Deacon, S. Mngqolo and S. Prosalendis, *Protecting our cultural capital: a research plan for the heritage sector*. Cape Town: Human Sciences Research Council (HSRC) Publishers, 2003, pp. 8–9.
[651] South African Government Gazette Notice No. 14048, 19 June 1992.
[652] B.D. Malan succeeded C. van Riet Lowe as the Director of the Bureau of Archaeology and Secretary of the Historical Monuments Commission in 1977, the archaeologist A.J. Humphries was then appointed in 1977 and thereafter J. Rudmar, an architect, sat on the National Monuments Council. Between 1969 about 71 people were nominated onto Council, of which 12 were known members of the *Broederbond*, 54 were Afrikaans speaking and only three women, see, F. Frescura, "National or Nationalist: the work of the Monuments Council, 1936–1989. Paper published as part of the proceedings of the National Urban Conservation Symposium, University of Witwatersrand, Johannesburg, 12–14 July 1990, available at, <https://www.sahistory.org.za/franco/historical-conservation-nationalist.html> *s.a.* access: 2018.08.15.
[653] See T. Manetsi, State-prioritised heritage: governmentality, heritage management and the prioritisation of liberation heritage in post-colonial South Africa, PhD thesis, University of Cape Town, 2017, p. 79.

78

Figure 5.1. Large bronze plaque commemorating excavations by the University of Pretoria 1933–1990 and the 1984 South African National Monument plaque.

and influence able to sway decisions in line with their interests and backgrounds".[654] This approach cemented the politicisation of both legislation and heritage.

Dr Janette Deacon, an acclaimed archaeologist and member of the National Monuments Council from 1989 to 1999, in her review of declared archaeological sites since 1936, stated that, "of the declared archaeological sites, only the Makapan Caves and Sterkfontein have been legally acquired (by purchase or lease) by an academic institution".[655] She cited at length several case studies of Stone Age and Iron Age sites from the Universities of the Witwatersrand and Cape Town respectively. Yet, she failed to mention Mapungubwe as a case study despite its major national interest and impact to archaeology, perhaps for other reasons? In addition, no mention was made that the University of Pretoria acquired research rights legally in 1933 from the State and, thereafter by the same powers of the National Monuments Council that extended permissions and legally granted permits to the University of Pretoria for their exclusive excavation rights at Mapungubwe from the 1960s until the end of the 1990s. Paradoxically, she concluded that "historians need to be persuaded that there is something to be learned from the archaeological record".[656]

As a consequence, it was during Deacon's tenure that the National Monuments Council made exceptional changes and advances in line with international practices that eventually shaped the current legislation for the protection of archaeology and wider national heritage. Dubbed "the mother of archival research" in the pursuit of heritage conservation of archaeological and rock art sites, she was also instrumental in later preparing Mapungubwe's nomination to the United Nations Education, Scientific and Cultural Organisation (UNESCO) for its world heritage status.[657]

For more than forty years, with biased council members, the National Monuments Act undoubtedly sheltered mainly white historical legacies and favoured built colonial heritage. During this "select and neglect" period, more than ninety-eight percent out of the 4000 national monuments gazetted nationally represented mostly white history. A small minority were natural heritage geological, palaeontological, and archaeological and rock art sites.[658] This legislation naturally showed clear signs

---

[654] T. Manetsi, State-prioritised heritage: governmentality, heritage management and the prioritisation of liberation heritage in post-colonial South Africa, PhD thesis, University of Cape Town, 2017, p. 79.

[655] J. Deacon, "Archaeological sites as national monuments in South Africa: a review of sites declared since 1936". *South African Historical Journal* 29(1), 1993, p. 129.

[656] J. Deacon, "Archaeological sites as national monuments in South Africa: a review of sites declared since 1936". *South African Historical Journal* 29(1), 1993, pp. 125–131.

[657] Dr Janette Deacon is an acclaimed Stone Age archaeologist, a distinguished scholar and widely published academic, particularly her award-winning contributions to the Bleek and Lloyd Archive at UCT. She was the editor of the *South African Archaeological Bulletin* from 1976 to 1993 and was instrumental in transforming the NMC into SAHRA in 1999. Through her work with the Getty Conservation Institute the SA Rock Art Initiative began at Mapungubwe. See further detail, <https://www.news.uct.ac.za/article/-2016-06-15-janette-deacon-ndash-the-xainki-or-mother-of-archival-< research> *s.a.* access: 2018.08.22; see also for example, Mapungubwe nomination dossier, <https://whc.unesco.org/uploads/nominations/1099.pdf> *s.a.* access: 2018.06.22.

[658] See, J. Deacon, South African heritage legislation in global perspective. Unpublished paper presented at the Management of Heritage Sites

of deficiencies, such as a lack of integration of heritage management, lack of understanding the importance of heritage conservation and narrowly defined heritage.[659] Essentially, the aim of legislation was ultimately for protection and preservation purposes.

In the 1960s, A.R. Willcox, a quantity surveyor by profession and an experienced rock art enthusiast or hobbyist conducted a sketchy study of recording and mapping rock art in the Limpopo Valley.[660] In 1966, Willcox representing the South African Association for the Advancement of Science, with the aim of preserving the rock art of this region, proposed twelve farms, including *Greefswald*, to be declared a private nature and archaeological reserve in the Limpopo Valley.[661] By May 1966, Willcox had approached the Director of Nature Conservation and requested whether their Department would administer a nature reserve in the Limpopo Valley.[662]

No objections were received from the Secretary for Agricultural Credit and Land Tenure and the initiative was backed and endorsed by the Registrar of the University of Pretoria.[663] In 1967, the Administrator of the Transvaal had added *Greefswald* 37 MS and its two neighbouring farms, *Den Staat* 27 MS and *Samaria* 28 MS to become part of the newly proclaimed Private Vhembe Nature Reserve under the Department of Nature Conservation.[664] This Reserve was the first military site in South Africa to be declared a nature reserve. *Greefswald* now part of the nature reserve, remained under direct military management of the apartheid era since it was considered a "threatened border area".[665]

In 1981, the Eloff five-volume reports on *Die Kulture van Greefswald* (The Cultures of Greefswald) had just been accepted and peer reviewed by the Human Sciences Research Council and were lauded as "one of the finest analyses of an African archaeological site in the history of African archaeology".[666] Following the conclusion of his research, in 1983, the University of Pretoria's Department of Archaeology requested formal permission from the SA Defence Force to hold their fifty-year celebrations at *Greefswald*.[667] This included a major student reunion to mark half a century of archaeological research, as well as Eloff's retirement as the first Head of the Department of Archaeology at the end of 1983.[668] This was followed by a public exhibition of Mapungubwe gold objects at the Gold Mining Museum in Johannesburg and the Intergold Organisation had just generously funded Dr W.A. Oddy from the British Museum to come to South Africa.[669]

During this flurry of activity and hype in the early 1980s, it was only fifty-years later following the gold discovery that Mapungubwe was eventually declared a national monument of South Africa in 1984 awarded by the National Monuments Council.[670] The site K2 was declared on 9 September 1983, promulgated in the South African Government Gazette Notice No. 1936. A year later, on 17 August 1984, Mapungubwe Hill and the adjacent southern Terrace were declared a national monument in the South African Government Gazette Notice No. 1756.[671] It remains unclear whether the nomination was actually submitted by the University of Pretoria, as the period of the 1980s is one of the greatest gaps in the Mapungubwe Archive. There is much silence and very little evidence in the declaration of Mapungubwe as a national landmark.

In 1986, the Minister's Office in the Department of Environment and Water Affairs proposed to convert the Vhembe Nature Reserve into a national park, but this move was opposed by the Department of Nature Conservation as well as the South African Defence Force.[672] In July 1992 Danie Hough, the Administrator of the Transvaal and W. Breytenbach, the Deputy Minister of Defence and of Environmental Affairs, symbolically handed over the Vhembe Training Area of the South African Defence Force to the Transvaal Provincial

---

seminar organised by the Heritage Assets Management Sub-Directorate of the Department of Public Works, Pretoria 21 September 1999.

[659] N. Ndlovu, "Legislation as an instrument in South African Heritage management: is it effective?" *Conservation and Management of Archaeological Sites* 13(1), February 2011, p. 32.

[660] See also, A.R. Willcox, "Painted petroglyphs at Balerno in the Limpopo Valley, Transvaal." *South African Journal of Science* 56, 1963, pp. 108–110. Van Riet Lowe after setting up the Archaeological Survey was also interested in recording and mapping rock art in South Africa, see C. van Riet Lowe, *The distribution of prehistoric rock engravings and paintings in South Africa*. Pretoria: Archaeological Survey, Archaeological Series 7, 1952.

[661] Mapungubwe Archive, UP/AGL/D/3706, Memo from Willcox to Registrar proposing Nature Reserve, January 1966. The National Parks Board had expressed its sympathy with the scheme but were not interested in the undertaking citing a lack of funds. See also Mapungubwe Archive, UP/AGL/D/3707, Second memorandum suggesting nature reserve and archaeological reserve in the Limpopo Valley, March 1966.

[662] Mapungubwe Archive, UP/AGL/D/3716, Letter from Wilcox to Department of Nature Conservation, 24 May 1966.

[663] Mapungubwe Archive, UP/AGL/D/3709, Letter from R. de Villiers, Secretary of for Agricultural Credit and Land Tenure to P.J. Coertze Department of Volkekunde, University of Pretoria, 25 March 1966; Mapungubwe Archive, UP/AGL/D/3713, Letter from Registrar to A.R. Willcox, 27 April 1966.

[664] Mapungubwe Archive, UP/AGL/D/3731/3, Transvaal Provincial Official Gazette Extraordinary, No. 281, declaration of private nature reserve in Limpopo Valley, 13 September 1967, p. 17.

[665] "Greefswald: UP vereer SAW en TPS met 'n goue simbool van vennootskap". *Tukkiewerf* 18 (3), 1992, pp. 6–7.

[666] Mapungubwe Archive, UP/AGL/D/1809, Letter from H.C. Marais, Director of the South African Institute for Research Development to Prof. J.F. Eloff, Department of Archaeology, 6 October 1981.

[667] Mapungubwe Archive, UP/AGL/D/1818, Letter from J.F. Eloff to Gen. Major F.E.C. van den Berg, Commander North Transvaal, Voortrekkerhoogte, 26 January 1983.

[668] Mapungubwe Archive, UP/AGL/D/ 1823, "Mapungupwe [sic] leef en lewer vondse". *Beeld*, 20 April 1983.

[669] Mapungubwe Archive, UP/AGL/D/ 1831, "Skatte uit ystertyd te sien". *Beeld*, 30 September 1983; see also Mapungubwe Archive, UP.AGL/D/1830 J.F. Eloff speech at the exhibition opening, 28 September 1983.

[670] A. Meyer, "K2 and Mapungubwe". *South African Archaeological Society Goodwin Series* 8, 2000, p. 4.

[671] Other than the two gazettes mentioned, the Mapungubwe Archive does not have any records pertaining to these declarations. The 1970s and 1980s periods present the largest gaps in the archives, unless these records are lodged in the National Monument Council Archives.

[672] L. Meskell, "A thoroughly modern park: Mapungubwe, UNESCO and indigenous heritage". In González-Ruibal A. (ed.) *Reclaiming archaeology: beyond the tropes of modernity*. London: Routledge, 2013, p. 249.

GREEFSWALD No, 37-MS.
L.G. Kaart No, A 3456/06

VEMBE—PRIVAATNATUURRESERVAAT. (Grootte:10,207 m.)
PRIVATE NATURE RESERVE. (Extent:10,207 m.)

SAMARIA No. 28-M.S.
L.G. Kaart No.A 3484/06

Limpoporivier

DEN STAAT No.27–M.S.
L.G. Kaart No. A 3448/06

Die bogenoemde reservaat beslaan die volgende gebiede soos op die bostaande kaart aangedui:—

1. Die plaas Den Staat 27 MS (distrik Soutpansberg).
2. Die plaas Samaria 28 MS (distrik Soutpansberg).
3. Die plaas Greefswald 37 MS (distrik Soutpansberg).

The above reserve comprises the following areas as indicated on the above diagram:—

1. The farm Den Staat 27 MS (District of Soutpansberg).
2. The farm Samaria 28 MS (District of Soutpansberg).
3. The farm Greefswald 37 MS (District of Soutpansberg).

3

Figure 5.2. Vhembe Private Nature Reserve, Provincial Gazette Extraordinary 13 September 1967.

Figure 5.3. SADF Vhembe Nature Reserve 1967–1992 with signatures of those attending.

Administration.[673] Military presence officially ceased at *Greefswald*[674] and excavation seasons by the University of Pretoria remained sporadic.

In 1997, under the same National Monuments Act, and sixty-three years after the discovery of Mapungubwe, a selection of artefacts associated with Mapungubwe and its related sites were declared a "cultural treasure".[675] The term "cultural treasure" was defined by the National Monuments Council as "any moveable property declared under the Act". The criteria to declare cultural treasures were based on items of "aesthetic, historical or scientific interest" that the Council considered to be of "national interest that relate specifically to the history and cultural or prehistory of the Republic".[676] This declaration implied that only a minor selection of cultural material from Mapungubwe now formed part of the national estate as a specifically declared heritage collection.[677] In terms of

the provisions of the National Monuments Act, No. 28 of 1969, while declared national heritage, the agreement with the National Monuments Council cited the University of Pretoria as "owners" of the "cultural treasures of Mapungubwe".[678]

Just before the turn of the twenty-first century, post apartheid legislation saw the statutory establishment of the South African Heritage Resources Agency (SAHRA) which replaced the former National Monuments Council as the new national administrative body for cultural heritage under the National Heritage Resources Act No. 25, of 1999.[679] This current legislation empowered them as an organ of State, to counter-challenge the Afrikaner Nationalist heritage legacies and aimed to transform the existing "mainstream heritage" to give "more voice to indigenous forms of heritage".[680] The essence of this Act not only regulates the management of heritage resources, but engages heritage at a three-tier governmental level for national, provincial and local authorities.[681] This so-called inclusive legislation hoped to encourage all

---

[673] Mapungubwe Archive, Handing-over of Vhembe invitation, Pretoria, Transvaal Provincial Administration, 24–25 July 1992.

[674] Post-1994 the military was still present at *Greefswald*.

[675] South African Government Gazette Notice No, 1306, 10 October 1997, a selection of cultural artefacts associated with the Iron Age settlements of Mapungubwe Hill and K2 were declared as heritage objects.

[676] According to the National Monuments Council, the definition of "cultural treasure" fell under a conservation category, despite no actual "conservation work" being done at Mapungubwe. This era was instead marked by destructive excavations and only later in 1996 did rehabilitation of the archaeological sites commence, see the National Monuments Council, "Cultural Treasures" definition, http://home.intekom.com/nmc/f9.htm *s.a.* access: 2018.08.21.

[677] The criteria for selection were not well-defined and were merely representative of cultural material from the main archaeological sites. Who decided what formed part of the declaration and what did not form part, remains unknown, but was most probably a decision taken by archaeologists at the time. This process appeared subjective and flawed, as only select or "best pieces" were earmarked resulting in some of the Mapungubwe Collection declared and a majority not. This is an ongoing

debate and has created discord among institutions and State parties, since no comprehensive definition is available for the entire Mapungubwe Collection; SAHRA appears only concerned with the nationally declared collection, which forms part of their mandate.

[678] Mapungubwe Archive, Copy of Memorandum of Agreement between the National Monuments Council and the University of Pretoria, 3 April 1996.

[679] Department of Arts and Culture, SAHRA, available, <www.dac.gov.za/sahra> *s.a.* access: 2018.08.22.

[680] E. Delmont, "South African Heritage development in the first decade of democracy". *African Arts* 37(4), 2004, p. 30.

[681] The term "heritage resources" is broadly defined by the National Heritage Resources Act (1999) as "any place or object of cultural significance", ideally it should refer to both tangible and intangible heritage forms and is a common term used within the heritage management sector in all three tiers of government.

communities to "nurture and conserve" their heritage and legacy, while it also contributed to the "redress of past inequities" and "imbalances of the past" through national reconciliation.[682]

To some extent, the Act also addresses socio-political debates and the issue of heritage ownership, which previous statutes failed to address and makes provision for repatriation and restitution.[683] In addition, other post 1994 legislative changes were further brought about when the National Archives and Record Service for the management and care of State records and governmental bodies in the form of the National Archives of South Africa Act, No. 43 of 1996 was promulgated and as amended by the Cultural Laws Amendment Act, No. 36 of 2001.[684] Unfortunately, not even eight years later this Act too has also been viewed as inadequate, as the state of the country's archival system is in jeopardy and not delivering its mandate.[685] Nonetheless, the year 1996 was considered a revolutionary year as the Constitution of the Republic of South Africa was promulgated in December of that year.[686] According to Manesti, the transformation of this heritage landscape after 1994 led to the emergence of a "common heritage" which became prioritised as a nationally rallying force for "national identity and national healing" in line with the principles of democracy as underpinned in the South African Constitution.[687]

In addition, the National Heritage Resources Act, No. 25 of 1999 makes provision for the "formal protection" of heritage objects, where the main mission of SAHRA as a parastatal of the Department of Arts and Culture (DAC) is mandated to coordinate the management and identification of the national estate.[688] The nation state is therefore deemed the legal custodian of the nation's diverse heritage resources that form part of the national estate.[689] These heritage resources are however not viewed nor defined as "national treasure". Instead, archaeological artefacts, objects or collections are rather declared as "types of heritage objects" and may be

"specifically declared" as heritage objects.[690] According to the National Heritage Resources Act (1999), whilst some heritage objects are located in public institutions, others are privately owned and declaration of a specifically declared heritage object does not change its ownership status since all heritage objects are deemed as "belonging" to the State.[691]

In a recent review of South African heritage legislation, it is clear that heritage management is heavily contested and gaps were identified in policy among critical aspects of redress, regarding not only monuments, but other contested issues such as repatriation, restitution, heritage conservation, communities and the role of living and intangible heritage.[692] This is further echoed in 2017 by Manetsi, as a disjuncture between international and national heritage instruments has been an inevitable source of tension. According to Manetsi, world heritage status declarations by UNESCO serves as a legal global instrument for "selective" world heritage sites, but has displaced local, nation-state policies and the African continent in particular has been neglected.[693]

Compounding the inadequacies of current heritage legislation is that both the South African Heritage Resources Agency (SAHRA) as well as the National Heritage Council (NHC), another agency of the Department of Arts and Culture, is dually mandated to "transform, protect and promote South African heritage".[694] The National Heritage Council is currently more focused inter alia on the decolonisation of heritage, resistance and liberation heritage. For example, the National Heritage Council is tasked with liaising with the World Heritage Committee (WHC), regarding UNESCO World Heritage Sites, a function of the Department of Environmental Affairs (formerly referred to as the Department of Environmental Affairs and Tourism or DEAT). Today there is a separate National Department of Tourism (NDT). Whereas, SAHRA is tasked with liaising with the Department of Arts and Culture (DAC) on National Heritage Sites and is not involved with World Heritage Sites.[695] Similarly, in 2017 Manesti points out that the, "policy-review process

---

[682] South African Government Gazette Notice No. 19974, 28 April 1999. See also, National Heritage Resources Act, No. 25 of 1999, preamble, p. 1.
[683] National Heritage Resources Act 25 of 1999, (section 41) restitution of heritage objects, p. 68; see also, J. Deacon, "South Africa's new heritage legislation". *World Archaeological Congress Newsletter* 5(1), 1997, p. 3.
[684] National Archives and Records Service of South Africa, No. 43 of 1996 as amended by Cultural Laws Amendment Act, No. 36 of 2001.
[685] See report titled, State of the Archives: an analysis of South Africa's national archival system, prepared by the Archival Platform, 2014, <http://www.archivalplatform.org/news/entry/state_of_the_archives/> *s.a.* access: 2018. 08.28
[686] The Constitution of the Republic of South Africa, No. 108 of 1996, here is often mention of the South African constitution as one of the best in the world, yet like all democratic institutional frameworks worldwide it has its flaws. See article by N. Runji, "Flaws of the world's best constitution laid bare". *Rand Daily Mail*, 7 April 2016.
[687] T. Manetsi, State-prioritised heritage: governmentality, heritage management and the prioritisation of liberation heritage in post-colonial South Africa, PhD thesis, University of Cape Town, 2017, p. 26.
[688] South African Heritage Resources Agency (SAHRA), available at <www.sahra.org.za>, access: 2018.08.23.
[689] National Heritage Resources Act No. 25 of 1999 (section 32), Heritage Objects, pp. 52–56

[690] Declared heritage objects are listed in the South African Government Gazette Notice No. 1512, 6 December 2002.
[691] National Heritage Resources Act No. 25, of 1999,(section 32), heritage objects, pp. 52–56
[692] Department of Arts and Culture, (n.d.), Review of Heritage Legislation Final report Vol. 1, prepared by the Heritage Agency cc and Cheadle Thompson and Hayson Inc. Attorneys, Cape Town.
[693] T. Manetsi, State-prioritised heritage: governmentality, heritage management and the prioritisation of liberation heritage in post-colonial South Africa, PhD thesis, University of Cape Town, 2017, pp. 56–57.
[694] In 1995, a heritage working group named the Arts and Culture Task Group (ACTAG) proposed the redrafting of the National Monuments Act and called for the formation of a National Heritage Council, as well as a National Heritage Trust to fund heritage projects as well as a National Commissions for Living Culture, Archives, Heritage Resources and Museums. The National Heritage Council Act No. 11 was approved in 1999; see <https://nationalgovernment.co.za/units/view/252/national-heritage-council-south-africa-nhc> access: 18.08.2018.
[695] Department of Arts and Culture, Review of Heritage Legislation Final report Vol. 1, prepared by the Heritage Agency cc and Cheadle Thompson and Hayson Inc. Attorneys, Cape Town, p. 25.

of the White Paper on Arts and Culture identified this problem of overlapping mandates".[696]

In 1996, this duplication of State resources and a "strong recommendation for the merger of state-funded organisations" were proposed under a single national body.[697] The Draft White Paper on Arts, Culture and Heritage of 2013 has yet to be ratified or passed into law by Parliament.[698] SAHRA's custodial responsibilities continue to look bleak and doubtful, as they demonstrate their own inability and incapacity to effectively manage South Africa's heritage resources.[699]

State claims to "national cultural patrimony" should be substituted with claims for better preservation, wider access and greater public interest in human heritage, cultural property and what is considered as national treasures.[700] This review of South African past heritage legislation has demonstrated what is seemingly a historical infliction determined by time, place and by people in power. Undoubtedly, not only legislation, but the discourse surrounding heritage has been globally influenced by Eurocentricity and heritage politics that is entrenched and "encoded in legal statutes".[701] For the sake of modernity and in keeping with the twenty-first century movements, concepts such as "heritage fluidity" and its multiple meanings should be considered.[702]

South Africa's national heritage remains particularly elusive to be defined and adequately legislated. Nonetheless, national cultural patrimony is not just legally necessary, but morally and ethically required. It should also be determined by society and community interest and not bound to academia or political posturing. As a result, heritage statutes and laws are revised, amended or remain unamended as and when the tide of national political imperatives wax and wane. As demonstrated in the trajectory of historical legislation, this attitude to heritage leaves South Africa seriously lagging behind on critical issues that are openly addressed in global discourse, such as heritage as a form of collective, social and community memory and identity.[703]

As previously discussed, the term "treasure" according to South African Law was once used in the legal definition of "ownership and property", where the finder could acquire ownership in accordance with Western legislative rules.[704] Yet, none of the above South African legislation or current Statutes mention the specific term "treasure" or define "national treasure", albeit the fact that globally cultural heritage is more directly linked to the term "cultural property".[705] Within a local context, although not legally defined as "national treasure" as such, the current heritage legislation was promulgated to protect and preserve "specifically declared treasures", even though *bone fide* ownership cannot be determined.[706]

Since the democratic dispensation in South Africa, heritage remains not only historically and legislatively unaddressed but also a politicised and contested issue. Therefore, until such time that the State develops a unified and centralised national heritage policy, there remains an intersection of responsibilities and mandates from conflicting views on the definitions of heritage, to the politicisation of what is deemed worthy as heritage and what is not. It further begs imperative questions to society about who owns heritage and who does not, and over two decades of democracy South Africa appears to not only be a "State in search of a nation" but also a State in search of its heritage identity.[707]

5.3. "A reversionary right"[708]: the ownership approach

Both historical and post democracy legislation have grappled with the contentious issue of ownership which has left a scar on how heritage is generally perceived and legally approached in South Africa. According to *Wille's Principles of South African law*, the basic definition, nature and limitations of ownership exclusively refer to the principle of property.[709] The comprehensive right of ownership embraces not only the powers to use, to enjoy and to consume, but also the power to possess and to dispose of property. This 'elasticity' of ownership is sometimes called a reversionary right, but despite its potentially comprehensive nature the definition, particularly of heritage ownership, has thus never been regarded as absolute. Manetsi explicitly states that, "in South Africa

[696] Department of Arts and Culture, White Paper on Arts and Culture, 1996.

[697] T. Manetsi, State-prioritised heritage: governmentality, heritage management and the prioritisation of liberation heritage in post-colonial South Africa, PhD thesis, University of Cape Town, 2017, p. 117.

[698] Department of Arts and Culture, Revised Draft White Paper on Arts, Culture and Heritage, 2013.

[699] The South African Heritage Resources Agency Annual Report, 2008, p. 46.

[700] See for example J. Merryman, "The public interest in cultural property". *California Law Review* 77(2), 1989, pp. 339–364.

[701] D.R. Peterson, K. Gavua and C. Rassool, (eds.). *The politics of heritage in Africa: economies, histories, and infrastructures.* Volume 48, Cambridge: Cambridge University Press, 2015, p. 10.

[702] C. Mathers, T.C. Darvill and B.J. Little, (eds.) *Heritage of value, archaeology of renown: reshaping archaeological assessment and significance.* Florida: University Press of Florida, 2005, pp. 89–113.

[703] For example, see B. Graham and P. Howard (eds.), *The Ashgate research companion to heritage and identity.* Aldershot: Ashgate Publishing Company, 2008.

[704] F. du Bois, (ed.), *Wille's Principles of South African Law.* Cape Town: Juta & Co, Ltd., 2007.

[705] J. Jokilehto, "*Definition of cultural heritage: references to documents in history*". 2005, ICCROM Working Group Heritage and Society'. Jokilehto traces the definition of cultural heritage back from the 6th century AD up until 2004. See for further information, <http://cif.icomos. org/pdf_docs/Documents%20on%20line/Heritage%20definitions.pdf> access: 2018.08.22.

[706] National Heritage Resources Act, No. 25 of 1999.

[707] L. Meskell and C. Scheermeyer, "Heritage as therapy: set pieces from the New South Africa". *Journal of Material Culture* 13(2), 2008, p. 153.

[708] The broad definition of "reversionary right" is the return of the rights of possession or considered as a vested interest, also a legal term, "Relating to the right, especially of the original owner or their heirs, to possess or succeed to property on the death of the present possessor", see definition of 'reversionary' in the Oxford English Dictionary, Oxford: Oxford University Press, 2018, see further <https://en.oxforddictionaries.com/ definition/reversionary> access: 2018.08.19.

[709] F. du Bois, (ed.), *Wille's Principles of South African Law.* Cape Town: Juta & Co, Ltd. 2007, pp. 470–471.

state institutionalisation of heritage legitimises state ownership of heritage resources and places heritage solely within the jurisdiction of the state".[710]

In South Africa, State claim to "ownership of heritage" is nothing new and has been an inherited infliction through the legislative changes. Yet heritage as pointed out by Lowenthal is, "not the sole link with the past".[711] Legislation cannot claim to neatly package heritage, as it includes history, memory, myth, living traditions, identity and intangibles that continually change and evolve through and over time. Worldwide, whilst countries employ national and international legislations to safeguard and to manage heritage, few are able to coherently grapple with the legitimate issue of heritage ownership.[712]

The South African issue of heritage ownership is viewed as something that has to be institutionalised, regulated, contained, transferred, or managed whereas in truth legal ownership confers rights to control and access as well as the use of heritage.[713] This inherently suggests that the practice of heritage as an economic, state or institutional resource goes against the notion that heritage "belongs" to a select group, community or culture, or even the noble idea that it belongs to the common heritage of humanity.[714] In the wake of post democracy thought and constitutional perceptions of broader ownership, the idea that, in truth, heritage is more "culturally" owned has also become increasingly important.[715] Whilst there can be arguments both for and against cultural ownership, there has evolved a fundamental shift towards a "common collective heritage" ownership by humanity.[716]

Current South African heritage legislation nonetheless serves a singular purpose in its approach towards the management and protection of Mapungubwe's heritage as a case study. Presently all heritage, both natural and cultural, are thus "owned" by State jurisdiction. To a certain extent this also exercises control and authority over the heritage resources placed under its national patrimony by constitutional right. While the National Heritage Resources Act of 1999 does not openly define the term "ownership", it loosely employs the term "belonging". This implies "a bestowing of value on something" that a group of people, culture or State consider their cultural

property or their cultural heritage.[717] In reality, the tension between legislation and ownership is not simple and a balance between the needs of heritage ownership and legal instruments needs to be a transparent and negotiated process.[718]

According to Hodder's views on *Rights of Descent,* in most international declarations ownership of heritage is generally vested in the sovereign nation state.[719] More recently in particular, Canadian and Australian declarations, rights of protection and use, if not ownership, are generally given to descendant communities and not to the nation State. Hodder argues that by placing ownership at the heart of cultural heritage rights, does not take into account the many different nuances of the notion of ownership. Thus heritage ownership is neither about the State nor an individual as it is often a collective, intangible and more about identity and less about control. Hodder emphasises that:

> This focus on the ownership of the past perhaps derives from the longer assumption that nation states have sovereign control of the heritage within their own borders. The discourse is so pervasive that we have perhaps turned a blind eye to the uncomfortable evidence from anthropology and history about the difficulties of making links between cultures and people. Culture is now seen as hybrid, flexible, in process, contextually changing, and transforming. Is this simply a post-modern, Western perspective that seeks to undermine the importance of tradition and descent to subject peoples?[720]

While approaches to heritage ownership are based on a variety of philosophies and vary from nation to nation, two common but divergent philosophies are cultural nationalism and cultural internationalism.[721] According to Roehrenbeck, adherents of cultural internationalism support the idea that cultural heritage belongs to the global community who have an interest in the preservation and enjoyment of all cultural heritage, wherever it is located. In contrast, cultural nationalists are of the view that a nation's cultural heritage belongs only within the borders of that nation where it was created, irrespective of provenance or title of ownership.[722]

[710] T. Manetsi, State-prioritised heritage: governmentality, heritage management and the prioritisation of liberation heritage in post-colonial South Africa, PhD thesis, University of Cape Town, 2017, p. 210.

[711] D. Lowenthal, *The heritage crusade and the spoils of history.* Cambridge: Cambridge University Press, 1998, p. 3.

[712] See for example, C. Renfrew, *Loot, legitimacy and ownership.* London: Duckworth, 2000.

[713] L. Smith, *The uses of heritage.* London: Routledge, 2006, p. 22.

[714] L. Stroud, *Common heritage of mankind: a bibliography of legal writing.* Malta: Foundation de Malte, 2013.

[715] R. Harrison, *"The politics of heritage".* In R. Harrison (ed.), *Understanding the politics of heritage.* Manchester: Manchester University, Press, 2010, p. 188.

[716] C. Renfrew, *Loot, legitimacy and ownership.* London: Duckworth, 2000, p. 19.

[717] See for example, L. Prott and P. O'Keefe, "Cultural heritage or Cultural property?" *International Journal of Cultural Property* 1(2), 1992, pp. 307–320; see also J. Carman, *Against cultural property: archaeology, heritage and ownership.* Bloomsbury: Bristol Classical Press, 2005.

[718] See for example, L. La Follette, *Negotiating culture: heritage, ownership and intellectual property.* Massachusetts: University of Massachusetts Press, 2013.

[719] See for example, I. Hodder, "Cultural heritage rights: from ownership and descent to justice and well-being". *Anthropological Quarterly* 83(4), 2010, pp. 861–882.

[720] I. Hodder, "Cultural heritage rights: from ownership and descent to justice and well-being". *Anthropological Quarterly* 83(4), 2010, p. 869.

[721] J.H. Merryman, "Two ways of thinking about cultural property". *American Journal of International Law* 7, 1986, p. 831.

[722] C.A. Roehrenbeck, "Repatriation of cultural property–who owns the past? An introduction to approaches and to selected statutory instruments". *International Journal of Legal Information* 38(2) Article 11, 2010, p. 190.

Historically, and certainly presently, South Africa in general takes on the cultural nationalist approach to heritage ownership. This emphasises national interest above world interest, where patriotic pride and national values contend that heritage, even if the owner is unknown, are important to cultural definition and expressions of a shared identity about the past.[723] Despite the fact that South Africa is a signatory to the World Heritage Convention Act, 1999 and other conventions, national legislation takes precedence above all.[724]

A leading proponent of cultural internationalism is James Cuno, the Director of the Art Institute of Chicago. He argues that "nationalist retentionist cultural property laws conspire against our appreciation of the nature of culture".[725] Unlike the Canadian and Australian perspectives, Cuno's grand notion finds worldwide support and suggests that heritage should rather be owned and lodged in "encyclopaedic museums" where they can be cared for and be available for the world to see and not with descendant communities.[726] This outwardly Western-centric argument claims that such museums are like state instruments of power. Cuno argues that these museums are ' precisely not an instrument of the state, but stand as symbols against an essentialised, state-derived cultural identity" as they reflect liberal institutions that openly share all the heritage of humanity. In a globalised age of contention around cultural heritage ownership, Cuno proposes the value for the "encyclopaedic museum" as a truly cosmopolitan institution, promoting tolerance, understanding, and a shared sense of history for the whole of humankind.[727]

Whilst all nations take different approaches to ownership or cultural property, often for historical reasons or for cultural historiographical reasons, they also vary in how they view the past and which elements of the past are considered more significant to modern society and to which society. It also depends on whether a nation takes the view of cultural nationalism or cultural internationalism, and whether or not they opt to intersect with international treaty regimes

in lieu of their own legislations.[728] It is clear from the diversity of legal systems adopted within nations that the system adopted by a particular nation on heritage depends on the circumstances of that nation. In other words, one size does not fit all.[729] Yet, the debate on who should keep, own, protect and enjoy heritage in any country is ongoing, because "at its base is a conflict over identity, and over the right to reclaim objects that are tangible symbols of that shared identity".[730]

Even if there is a clear sense of whether or not South Africa has a shared identity, is not the issue here, but there can be no dispute that there is a shared history and Mapungubwe's past represents a collective heritage that has symbolic value to South Africa's sense of cultural heritage. This view might be debatable too. Yet, as a solution L. Smith offers and promotes a consensus approach to history as a means of addressing contested pasts, conflicts and social differences. Referred to as "authorised heritage discourse" this has become ubiquitous to the understanding of heritage as its resonance is found in state heritage agencies, government policy, national legislation, international charters, statutes and policies.[731]

Despite ongoing heritage discourses, the University of Pretoria remains a legal guardian over contested cultural heritage. The defining historical moment that Mapungubwe was translated into national heritage and world heritage status, the State adopted "authorised discourse of the past" and in turn exercised control and jurisdiction over that heritage. The argument is that, within legal parameters, State "ownership of heritage", besides providing promotion and protection, has also provided power and authority.[732] Contending claims over not only ownership, but stewardship of heritage is characteristic of the twenty-first century discourse.[733]

5.4. A responsible right: the stewardship approach

In simple terms, stewardship is the careful, sound and responsible management of heritage which is entrusted into the care of a museum or institution, which incurs legal, social and ethical obligations for the possession or ownership of collections or cultural heritage.[734] Historical

---

[723] R. Anglin, "The world heritage list: bridging the cultural property nationalism- internationalism divide". *Yale Journal of Law* 2, 2008, pp. 241–242.

[724] UNESCO Convention on World Heritage Property 1972, South Africa became a signatory to this convention in 1997 mainly as a means of un ocking the economic and tourism potential of heritage, a strategy by the National Department of Tourism. See also, South African World Heritage Convention Act, No. 49 of 1999.

[725] J. Cuno, *Who owns antiquity? Museums and the battle over our ancient heritage.* Princeton: Princeton University Press, 2008, p. 5.

[726] Encyclopaedic museums are defined as cosmopolitan museums dedicated to the proposition that by gathering and presenting some examples of the world's diverse artistic cultures all placed under one roof in a single museum. In fact, these museums are also seen as imperial institutions, built for and by the wealthiest nations. Examples of such encyclopaedic museums are the world's most renowned and visited museums such as the British Museum, The Louvre, National Museum of China, the Smithsonian Institution, the Metropolitan Museum of Arts, the Vatican Museum, and the Art Institute of Chicago. In India and Africa encyclopaedic museums are absent.

[727] J. Cuno, *Museums matter: in praise of the Encyclopaedic Museum.* Chicago: University of Chicago Press, 2011.

[728] For example, as of 2009, 122 nations have signed the main 1954 Hague Convention, 121 nations have signed the 1970 UNESCO Convention and 22 nations have signed the 1995 UNIDROIT Convention.

[729] P. Gerstenblith, "Identity and cultural property: the protection of cultural property in the United States". *Boston University Law (B.U.L) Review* 75, 1995, pp. 596–597.

[730] S. Waxman, *Loot: The battle over the stolen treasures of the ancient world.* New York: Times Books, 2008.

[731] See for example, L. Smith, *Archaeological theory and the politics of cultural heritage.* London: Routledge, 2004; L. Smith, *The uses of heritage.* London: Routledge, 2006, p. 22.

[732] See, for example, F.X. Blouin, and W.G. Rosenberg, *Processing the past: contesting authorities in history and the archive.* Oxford: Oxford Scholarship, 2011.

[733] See for example L. La Follette, *Negotiating culture: heritage, ownership and intellectual property.* Massachusetts: University of Massachusetts Press, 2013.

[734] There is no definitive definition for stewardship, yet the general meaning is broad and taken from the American Alliance of Museums

discourse contends that, together with the issue of heritage ownership, is the reconsideration of what is implied and meant by stewardship, a form of cultural heritage ethics. The issue of whose heritage is it, and can history be owned, possessed or assigned, therefore adds a complex dimension to what is already considered a controversial debate about heritage ethics and its diverse contexts.[735]

In *Negotiating culture: heritage, ownership and intellectual property*, La Follette in 2013 chronicles controversies over who should have legal rights of ownership and control over heritage ownership, and argues for the idea of stewardship versus ownership. Since museums and other institutions are increasingly at the epicentre of cultural ownership issues, La Follette considers whether, as in line with legal ownership, culture should be treated as cultural property which can be purchased and sold.[736] Adding to the controversial debate over ownership versus stewardship is the argument that the past essentially belongs to the world and is not that of a particular modern state or nation. According to Cuno, "the past comprises antiquity, and antiquity knows no borders" he further maintains that nationalistic retention of heritage impedes "access to common heritage" and encourages a "dubious and dangerous politicization" of heritage and of ultimately the end of culture itself.[737] Therefore, the contention of cultural heritage should not only be limited to protection and politics, but engage more meaningfully on other ethical issues such as stewardship, custodianship, trusteeship and guardianship of the past.

As stated previously, the ramifications of Mapungubwe's declaration as a national "treasure trove" in 1933, and later as a "national cultural treasure" were at the time made in the nation's best interests to protect archaeological heritage. Yet, when declared as "national treasures", this resulted in prickly debate and a critical re-evaluation of not only the role of heritage in the country as a whole, but also directed attention to responsibilities of institutions that have heritage under their care. Whilst the State "owns heritage", the University of Pretoria remains responsible for the stewardship over that heritage. Although this does not imply sole stewardship, it suggests the need for an integrative perspective that is not entirely legal on one side nor political on the other. The University of Pretoria has embraced its stewardship and signed a tri-partied agreement with South African national parks who are responsible for the cultural landscape of Mapungubwe and the South African Heritage Resources Agency for heritage authority oversight- this then provides collective responsibility for Mapungubwe.

This approach over ownership towards stewardship would encourage deliberation on heritage issues which are not owned or ownable. Today such battles over heritage are not simply about practical politics, but also theoretically embedded in complex moral and ethical debates and difficult questions.[738] In considering the thorny questions of stewardship opens many new debates about not only who owns the past, but in whose hands cultural heritage should be, or rather "who controls the past" and whether or not the past should be owned or can be re-authored?[739]

So where does this leave the debate on ownership and stewardship? It is not dependent on 'where' the issue of ownership lies, but rather opens another argument that heritage cannot be owned. Is this not then a rhetorical debate when owning the "unownable"? There is no immediate answer to this question. Current South African legislation was enacted to redress the wrongs of the past and to counter-balance the dominance of power struggles, although the powers are now in a different and political guise. This inviolability of Mapungubwe as national patrimony has to be addressed alongside issues of ownership and stewardship and legislation, as guiding instruments, have to be amended and promulgated. Whether or not the scholarly divide between a heritage ownership and stewardship approach can be bridged remains unanswered.

If one favours the notion of stewardship, re-owning or re-authoring the past, cultural heritage cases such as Mapungubwe will require both political and social negotiation as well as compromise, because neither legal recourse nor political arbitration will advance any argument for or against. Instead, the principle of stewardship could speak out in favour of unified perspectives for the protection of the past and recognition of the collective past, as a common human legacy of South Africa. If not, a kind of promotion of internal cultural warfare will further fuel bitter debates and will divide us further as a shared nation, and this would certainly not be a democratic ideal.[740]

Looking ahead to the future in the twenty-first century, heritage will increasingly be about intellectual property rights, copyright, institutional rights, ethical and moral "rights" that one will have to be cognisant of. As alluded to in previous chapters, there were exclusive rights to treasures, rights to land, rights to borders, rights to research, rights to minerals, rights to heritage, and, in general, rights to authorised heritage discourse by either the State or that which forms part of its constitutional memory. Thus, the politics of Mapungubwe's heritage is not about ownership or stewardship. It involves the legitimisation of where heritage is assigned, and includes the power, authority and

(AAM), definition, and <www.aam-us.org/resources/ethics-standards> access: 2018.08.20.

[735] See for example, S. Constantine, (ed.) *Cultural heritage ethics: between theory and practice.* Cambridge: Open Book Publishers, 2014.

[736] L. La Follette, *Negotiating culture: heritage, ownership and intellectual property.* Massachusetts: University of Massachusetts Press, 2013.

[737] J. Cuno, *Who owns antiquity? Museums and the battle over our ancient heritage.* Princeton: Princeton University Press, 2008, pp. 1–8.

[738] S. Constantine, (ed.) *Cultural heritage ethics: between theory and practice.* Cambridge: Open Book Publishers, 2014, pp. 131–134.

[739] I. McBryde, *Who owns the past?* Papers from the Annual Symposium of the Australian Academy of the Humanities, Melbourne. Oxford: Oxford University Press, 1985, p. 2.

[740] K. Baslar, *The concept of the common heritage of mankind in international law.* The Hague: Kluwer Law International, 1997.

dist nction as well as the exclusion of those who do not have access to its heritage.

The next chapter considers how the "Mapungubwe Archive" as an extension of contested heritage has become a metaphor for the institutional memory and reputation of Mapungubwe within the University of Pretoria. It elucidates how the Mapungubwe Archive, as a modern construct of the twenty-first century was first developed, created, examined and constructed and has the potential to be reconsidered not just as an institutional depository, but also as a "space of memory". The University of Pretoria's past exclusive "ownership" has over time morphed into a responsibility of inclusive "stewardship". This serves as a reminder that the Mapungubwe Archive has enhanced our understanding of the early history of Mapungubwe's contested past and how the Archive can be utilised to inform present debates on both heritage and history as approaches to that past.

6

Epilogue

There is no remembering without forgetting. They open each other, light becoming darkness, darkness becoming light. Verne Harris, 2007.

6.1. An imperfect Mapungubwe Archive past

This book sets out to examine the contested early history of the Mapungubwe Archive from the period prior to 1933 and the subsequent years following the discovery of the gold "treasure trove" through the instrumental work of the University of Pretoria Archaeological Committee. Furthermore, before setting out a brief recapitulation of this research, its implications and recommendations, it is important to elucidate slightly more about the Mapungubwe Archive itself. This epilogue provides a brief overview of the origins, development and the creation of the only Mapungubwe Archive in South Africa which is held at the University of Pretoria.

The overview of the Mapungubwe Archive is left for the final chapter because the Archive as such is mainly viewed as a modern construct that was only established as recently as 2005. Before then, as mentioned in the beginning, it is not possible to absolutely determine when an archive becomes an archive as such. The Mapungubwe Archive at the University of Pretoria has thus predominantly been a metaphorical archive in the sense that it formed an unidentified and uncohesive part of the institution's memory bank. After a brief history of the archive was outlined, this chapter offers some reflective insight into what the Mapungubwe Archive is and what it is not, as well as its value and what it is considered to represent. Finally, the emphasis is on the key elements that are distinctive to this book and how these can contribute to some directions for future research on the Mapungubwe Archive.

One of the key themes to emerge from the archival research is the complex multiplicity of narratives surrounding the "discoveries" of Mapungubwe and its exceptional gold "treasure trove" that occurred during a critical period in South Africa's past. This mirrors Nesmith's identification of the "cracks" that let light in and in "seeing" archives from an unconventional perspective.[741] Following the decades after the formation of the Union, post First World War recovery and the economic depression of the 1930s, Mapungubwe was hailed as one of most significant prehistoric discoveries of the twentieth century in South Africa. This significance has been perpetuated

and escalated into the twenty-first century currently symbolising national identity.

It is argued that after the euphoria following the 1933 gold discovery, the subsequent ramifications and repercussions unfolded many contested issues such as ownership, legal rights, racial discrimination and marginalisation, because some national identities were deeply forged and others forgotten in both a public and scholarly landscape. The conclusions of this research further suggest that the Archive speaks only partially to the establishment, control and the authority of the Archaeological Committee that acted on behalf of the University of Pretoria Council and the State. These powers decided who, how, when, where and why early Mapungubwe history should unfold and how it should be told. Some of these key notions and narratives are expressed in the preceding chapters and reflect more on the context rather than the content of the Mapungubwe Archive.

Another key finding in the research is that the Mapungubwe Archive also found itself to be a manifestation of colonial and Afrikaner Nationalist politics and social ideology. This has become evident and supports other historical legacies about the history of the University of Pretoria. Its early foundations are set within the apex of transformation from the 1910 English Transvaal University College (TUC) ideals that strived for broader South Africanism, and finally evolved into the 1932 "Afrikanerised" University of Pretoria. As stated above, this institution epitomised the "forgetting and remembering" of its own history, as Afrikaans and English were pitted against one another in the 50-50 language policy struggles. Included in these struggles were the battles between anti-colonials and anti-nationalists, and those who did not realise it at the time seemingly forged, controlled and created Mapungubwe's contested past and could ultimately be held responsible for its contested present.[742]

This publication has shown the direct nationalising role played by the University of Pretoria among the flurry of nationalisms, and the professionalization of some disciplines such as history, archaeology, anthropology and ethnology in which the research fashioned discourse and compounded

---

[741] See T. Nesmith, "Seeing archives: postmodernism and changing intellectual place of archives". *The American Archivist* 65, (Spring/Summer 2002), pp. 24–41.

[742] See, B.L. Strydom, Broad South Africanism and Higher Education: The Transvaal University College (1909–1919), PhD History, University of Pretoria, 2013; M. Schoeman, "Co-operation, conflict and the University of Pretoria Archaeological committee". In S. Tiley-Nel (ed.) *Mapungubwe remembered*. Johannesburg: Chris van Rensburg Publications (Pty) Ltd, 2011, pp. 89–101.

contestation. In contrast to previous Mapungubwe research, which has been largely dominated by the discipline of Archaeology as mentioned in the literature review, and supports the notion that the re-examination of Mapungubwe's early history need not be solely in the domain of a single discipline. The endless potential of archival science and historical scholarship in the reassessment of the past is not specific to any discipline mentioned, since nuanced studies of the contested past are increasingly found in many archival studies in South Africa. Likewise, research on the Mapungubwe Archive has reconsidered the place of historical knowledge and emphasised the very flawed nature of history and its many imperfections.

As stated in the first chapter, the Mapungubwe Archive serves as both repository and depository to identify, collect and preserve records of archival value that relate to the history, past and present, of the University of Pretoria. It has been officially curated and managed by the University of Pretoria Museums since 2000, and the Mapungubwe Archive is earmarked, long-term, for final assimilation into the University of Pretoria Archives where it will be held in perpetuity as a reflection of the institution's stewardship over the Mapungubwe Collection since 1933. The Mapungubwe Archive is also recognised for its historical, cultural and archaeological value, but more importantly, it holds crucial institutional heritage as both a form of scholarly debate and public memory.

In closing, this chapter mentions the future value of the Mapungubwe Archive, its preservation and the importance of its research potential, looking forward into the next

Figure 6.1. Formal opening of the Mapungubwe Archive on 24 February 2022 by (from left to right) Prof. Tawana Kupe, Vice Chancellor and Principal of the University of Pretoria and Mr Todd Haskell, Charge d'Affaires US Embassy, Pretoria.

century. For over eight decades, the Mapungubwe Archive has contained historical records of a documentary and photographic nature about the University of Pretoria and the subject of Mapungubwe. Yet, despite its extraordinary and unique records, until now it has had little impact upon academic thought as few scholars are aware of its existence or the role which the University of Pretoria has played in its untapped complex history.

The genesis of the Mapungubwe Archive initially began through the activities generated by the University of Pretoria Archaeological Committee in February 1933, and the first correspondence between the five discoverers, the resultant negotiations and legal engagements. The most common types of documents are the primary records between the Committee and the University of Pretoria Council, and the State. Included are a multitude of newspaper clippings from the *Rand Daily Mail*, *The Star* and the *Pretoria News* as public interest spread about the scientific discoveries made at Mapungubwe.[743] Within its first decade and a half between 1933 to about 1947 the Archive expanded significantly to include all written, drawn and photographic documentation that comprised over 10 000 historical records.[744] Broadly speaking, the Mapungubwe Archive cannot solely be defined as all or just parts of the archaeological record of Mapungubwe. The Archive is today much more than just a collection of historical records or old papers, deteriorating documents and ageing photographs. It can be viewed as the archival canon or body of research knowledge and memory generated by the University of Pretoria in its research and civic stewardship of both the Mapungubwe Collection and Mapungubwe Archive[745], marking nearing 90 years in 2023.

Nonetheless, the Archive has been shaped by the institution, and not created by single individuals because it reflects a long succession of efforts by a collective to retain their historicity. Outwardly, the Mapungubwe Archive comprises historical records, photographs, maps, field reports, written and typed letters of correspondence, newspaper clippings, memoranda, annual reports, legal papers, financial papers, and minutes of meetings, agendas and departmental records among others. Over time, the Archive has expanded considerably in depth and range, to include electronic and digital records, ephemera, oral history, biographical sections, tape recordings and other sub-sections and what is regarded to be the only comprehensive Mapungubwe reference section in the country.

The Archive continues to develop, grow and expand as the years add more and more layers to the body of knowledge on Mapungubwe. In addition, the Archive is far from

perfectly structured as there is a backlog of masses of historical records that still require appraisal, sorting and cataloguing. Imperfect in its state, like any archive, it contains gaps, has missing records and has undergone damage owing to the ongoing years of neglect as there has been very low levels of engagement with the Mapungubwe Archive until more recently.

After World War II, the Mapungubwe Archive became symptomatic of archaeological tendencies to keep some, but not all, field records, lists of inventories and generic research data used specifically for archaeological field projects. Gradually it became the building block for research data for archaeologists to eventually publish the results of their excavation and fieldwork. For example Eloff's 1979 five-volume study on *Die Kulture van Greefswald* (The Cultures of Greefswald) and Meyer's 1998, *The Archaeological sites of Greefswald*. Thus the historical papers, not the Archive, became a research tool for descriptive and interpretative approaches to the drawing up of chronologies, typologies and stratigraphies of the archaeological sites and presenting them as research reports.[746]

As far as can be ascertained, the historical records in the Mapungubwe Archive were only referenced for the first time by Meyer in 1998, where the archive became a systematic category as an extension of the archaeological collection under study as an administrative instrument and research tool. As Senior Lecturer in the Department of Anthropology and Archaeology at the University of Pretoria who dedicated over thirty years of his career to Mapungubwe, Meyer was the first to take decisive steps in the late 1980s to collate and file the administrative records which fitted into three filing cabinets. His pioneering attempts, albeit without realising it, were the beginnings of constructing an archive and signalled a significant move in the theory of accession and record selection which shaped the evolution of the Mapungubwe Archive onwards.[747]

Throughout the 1980s and 1990s, the Mapungubwe Archive was considered to be the paper trail that was generated by the University of Pretoria's excavations at the sites of K2, Mapungubwe and its southern Terrace. During this time Meyer organised, somewhat chronologically, and allocated a "numbering system" using an abbreviated method referred to as, UP/AGL/D/. This abbreviation stood for the University of Pretoria (UP), Archaeology (AGL), Document (D) and was then allocated a number, yet only the first 3 812 were numbered. This system only divulges a marginalised component of the totality of

[743] Mapungubwe Archive, unappraised newspaper clippings (1933–1999).
[744] Mapungubwe Archive, unappraised document collection.
[745] Tiley-Nel, S., Imperfect Past: The contested early history of the Mapungubwe Archive, PhD History, University of Pretoria, 2019.

[746] A. Meyer, *The Iron Age sites of Greefswald: stratigraphy and chronology of the sites and a history of investigations*. Pretoria: University of Pretoria, 1998.
[747] For an overview of biography of A. Meyer, see A. van Vollenhoven, "Andrie Meyer". In S. Tiley-Nel (ed.), *Mapungubwe remembered: contributions to Mapungubwe by the University of Pretoria*. Johannesburg: Chris van Rensburg Publications (Pty) Ltd, 2011, pp. 35–39.

Mapungubwe's historical records and largely excluded photographic records.

Meyer created his own type of Dewey classification system, but there is no "key" to unlocking the myriad of abbreviations, no glossary or legends of descriptions and in a sense no practical order upon which it was created. This approach mainly reflected the administration system of the Department of Archaeology as the abbreviation, "AGL" for the Afrikaans "*argeologie*" (archaeology), also referred to all teaching modules for that subject. During this period the Mapungubwe Archive was thus departmentalised and not institutionalised. The historical manuscripts for at least the first fifty years were completely dismembered. The original order of the papers was lost through time, as the principle of provenance or *respect des fonds* was unknown to archaeologists who were certainly not attentive in respect of the theoretic dimensions of the Mapungubwe Archive. It was merely a means to an end.[748]

Towards the nearing of the turn of the twenty-first century, the Mapungubwe Archive was stored in the Humanities Building on level eight within the Department of Anthropology and Archaeology at the University of Pretoria. Some internal departmental changes were rejected outright by some archaeologists as *volkekunde* was still given more prominence than archaeology. Severe discord arose with the Head of the Department of Anthropology, Prof. J.B. Hartman, who in desperation offered to transfer the Mapungubwe Collection to the National Cultural History Museum in Pretoria.[749] From 1996, the Department of Anthropology and Archaeology had changed their curriculum, in view of a downward trend in student numbers. The Department introduced new modules for Heritage and Cultural Tourism, Cultural Resource Management and there was a strong focus on Ethno-Archaeology. The updated University of Pretoria's *Ad Destinatum IV* of 1993–2000 once again barely mentioned Mapungubwe and there is no mention of its Archive.[750]

In these later years, the Department was thrown into further turmoil, staff changed, archaeologists retired or resigned, teaching modules both in archaeology and *volkekunde* were modified and as mentioned in chapter one internal academic politics had a stranglehold on the situation. Unfairly, many of the anthropologists were tarred as "apartheid anthropologists"[751] and by default this included the archaeologists working in the same department. The criticism against *volkekunde* at the University of Pretoria as previously conceived as "one volk one culture" was

disseminated in several literature studies, particularly from social anthropological angles that called for the "end of culture".[752]

Volkekunde as a subject was eventually discontinued at the University of Pretoria in reaction to the demise of the wider *volkekunde* paradigm which signalled the closure of a specific era of cultural anthropology. Towards the end of the twentieth and the start of the twenty-first century, liberal, anti-culture social anthropologists now headed the Department who did not take kindly to departmental funding being spent on masses of excavated cultural material and the dissonance with the institutions contested history and Mapungubwe.[753]

To compound these problems at the end of the 1990s were larger institutional concerns about the future care and protection of the Mapungubwe Collection and its associated Archive. This period was aggravated by public demand for a permanent Mapungubwe display in line with the State's new democratic priority of African heritage which was also affected by changes in heritage legislation. As highlighted in Chapter Five, these legislative changes increased demands for wider accessibility to that which was deemed Mapungubwe heritage, not only in general by society and the State, but also by some renewed academic interest in Mapungubwe which was no longer exclusive to the University of Pretoria. Fortunately, due to the efforts of the Vice Principal and Rector, Prof. J. van Zyl, the University of Pretoria secured corporate and external funding from Dr Anton Rupert, the well-known businessman and benefactor to the University, to establish the SASOL African Heritage Exhibition.[754]

As a result of a major financial injection directed towards the Mapungubwe Collection and at the cost of trying to minimise the University of Pretoria's "gatekeeping" reputation, in 1999 there was a physical movement of the Mapungubwe Collection and its "associated records". This included moving the Archive away from the Department of Anthropology and Archaeology to a better suited location with the aim of creating more public access. This was done under a museum setting to the dedicated management by the University of Pretoria's Bureau of Cultural Affairs, directed by Dr André Breedt. His department was charged to establish a permanent public

[748] Personal appraisal of the Mapungubwe Archive by S. Tiley-Nel, 20 June 2017.
[749] Mapungubwe Archive, Letter from S. Bezuidenhout, National Monuments Council to Prof. Hartman, Head of the Department of Anthropology and Archaeology, 23 July 1998.
[750] F. van der Watt (ed.), *Ad Destinatum IV 1993–2000. Historical developments and events at the University of Pretoria*. Pretoria: University of Pretoria, 2002, pp. 78–79.
[751] R. Gordon, "Apartheid's anthropologists: the genealogy of Afrikaner anthropology". *American Ethnologist* 15(3), 1988, pp. 535–553.

[752] See for example arguments against *volkekunde* by a former Head of the Department of Anthropology and Archaeology, J. Sharp, "The end of culture? Some directions for anthropology at the University of Pretoria". *Anthropology Southern Africa* 29(1–2), 2006, pp. 17–23; J. Sharp, "Two separate developments: anthropology in South Africa". *Royal Anthropological Institute of Great Britain and Ireland (RAIN)* 36, 1980, pp. 4–6; J. Sharp, "Can we study ethnicity? A critique of fields of study in South African anthropology". *Social Dynamics* 6 (1), 1980, pp. 1–16; J. Sharp, "One nation, two anthropologies? A response to Coertze's' Kommentaar op geignoreerde kritiek". *South African Journal of Ethnology* 2(1), 2000, pp. 30–33.
[753] Personal recollections, 1999–2004.
[754] Mapungubwe Archive, unappraised, funds for Mapungubwe collection "cultural treasures" for permanent exhibition, 16 March 1999.

exhibition for the University of Pretoria.[755] Ironically, the institution's "gatekeeping" of Mapungubwe status was amplified further when they became the proprietor of the trade mark of the gold rhino in 2001.[756]

From June 2000, the archival records were formally curated within the beginnings of a small university museum, with better care and a monitored environment. The Archives began to lose their organic contact with active administration and broke cleanly away from the Department of Anthropology and Archaeology. Finally, it moved closer towards inclusion in the wider Mapungubwe Collection held by the University of Pretoria. There was a dire need to recognise the continuation of the Mapungubwe Archive as a living institutional heritage. This was a crucial period for the "life" of the Mapungubwe Archive and allowed for scrutinising of the appraisal process of institutional records, determining whether records and other materials have permanent archival value or not. This is when archival and museum practice shaped the records into the Mapungubwe Archive, fundamental to forming part of the institutional memory of the University of Pretoria.

A series of important steps were taken within the first few years following transfer and gained momentum between the years 2002 and 2004. A dedicated space in metal cabinets was made available for the historical records. The documents were broadly sorted into chronological order, divided and placed into more secure boxes and, where funding permitted, acid-free paper was interleaved between the most fragile and older manuscripts. Access to the original documents was still restricted in lieu of photocopies for those needing to access the Mapungubwe Archive for research purposes.[757] A minor pilot digitisation programme was initiated for an online institutional repository, a type-of research platform that was created by the Department of Library Services of the University of Pretoria.[758]

Minimum handling was crucial as media, public and general access in the past had resulted in the theft of historical documents, while photographs were even physically ripped out, and some even cut out of the photo albums.[759] Original documents also went missing in an uncontrolled and unmonitored environment. Gradually, proper management systems and governance structures were put in place that guided the initial stages of a research archive into the Mapungubwe Archive. Researchers had

access and could submit motivations for postgraduate and undergraduate use. External researchers were also invited to utilise the Archive in exchange for copies of their research which would be lodged into the reference section to grow and expand the Mapungubwe Archive as a repository.[760]

The Mapungubwe Archive gradually developed alongside formal curation plans for Mapungubwe within the institution, but became increasingly difficult to manage as much of the transferred archaeological collection were without associated documentation. Research was hampered as primary sources could not be traced or linked to the material. Publications and research results were disjointed as museum research on Mapungubwe was increasing beyond the confines of the discipline of archaeology moving more towards other disciplines such as historical, heritage and museum studies. In 2005, the Mapungubwe Archive was formally listed as "an archive" in the directory entries of Archival Repositories of South Africa.[761] Where appropriate and possible, compliance with the Promotion of Access to Information Act, No. 2 of 2000, the National Archives and Record Services of South Africa Act, No. 43 of 1996, coincided with the establishment of the University of Pretoria Archives.[762]

In the following years, there was a concerted drive to internally consolidate the University of Pretoria Mapungubwe records which had over decades been dispersed and dissociated among various departments. It was critical to collate, gather and acquire Mapungubwe historical records that had been spread across departments and libraries, including storerooms, random filing cabinets and even documentation in the personal possession of former students, employees and staff, and sometimes even with individuals outside of the University. This curatorial movement saw the rise of the first preservation efforts as the Archive was sorted and stored, and documents were separated from the photograph collection.

The storage environment was monitored and handling of original material was reduced as a result of a reprography or reproduction section. It is common for archival institutions to reproduce materials and make copies available for research use when archival materials are fragile or heavily used. Incremental changes could only be effected with a very small operational budget and virtually no staff. A portion of the Mapungubwe Archive was placed onto an electronic database for quick retrieval and accessibility, researchers were monitored and careful handling and proper archival procedures were introduced. Slowly and gradually the establishment of the Archive was begun

[755] Mapungubwe Archive, unappraised, letter from University of Pretoria requesting President Mbeki to be guest of honour at the opening of the "Africa Exhibition", 6 January 1999.
[756] Mapungubwe Archive, unappraised current records, Licence of Agreement Adams & Adams to the Registrar, 13 August 2001.
[757] There are a number of archival methods of reprography or reproduction, including microfilming, photocopying, photographic reproduction and digitization.
[758] See Department of Library Services, University of Pretoria, UPSpace, institutional repository, available at <https://repository.up.ac.za/handle/2263/21577> *s.a.* access: 2018.08.31.
[759] Mapungubwe Archive, see Neville Jones 1934 photographic albums.
[760] Mapungubwe Archive, Summary Guide to the Mapungubwe Archive, 2006.
[761] Directory Entries of Archival Repositories 2005, <http://www.nationalarchives.gov.za/dir_entries_pg7_2005.htm> *s.a.* access: 2016.05.26.
[762] Constitution of the Archives of the University of Pretoria, 2008, see further, <https://www.up.ac.za/media/shared/413/ZPImages/UP%20Archives/constitution-of-the-up-archives.zp50349.pdf> *s.a.* access: 2018.08.31.

Figure 6.2. Commemorative plaque of the U.S. Ambassadors Fund for Cultural Preservation for the grant to the University of Pretoria Museums preservation of the Mapungubwe Archive 2018–2021.

and in 2008 the first draft policy as a means of governance was developed for the Mapungubwe Archive.[763]

Establishing a Mapungubwe Archive comes with the task of creating wider research, access and preservation, which pertains to the storehouse of preserved body of knowledge. This notion has become a key curatorial focus, not merely in the inherited usage of "keeping of the archive", but in the "making" of a more dynamic Mapungubwe Archive. The Mapungubwe Archive as a formal repository is the result of a major grant allocated to the University of Pretoria Museums over 2018 and 2021, for the preservation of historical records, yet fortunately funding allowed for the creation of a permanent African archival repository. Debt is owed to the US Embassy and to the US Ambassadors Fund for Cultural Preservation (AFCP) in making this a reality and a centre of research excellence at the University of Pretoria. More philosophically the Mapungubwe is a remnant of the collective memory of the University of Pretoria and over time it has transcended its purpose and is aimed to be future-focused, yet predications are hard to be make. Once limited to historical texts, or mere research data, to becoming more institutionally valued owing to the swathes of its archival memory not just for the 'scholar's domain" but as a public heritage resource.[764]

The Mapungubwe Archive stands as an African archive repository for not only South Africa, but the wider continent and for global access.

Just as the Mapungubwe cultural landscape can be said to represent the past, so can the Archive too, but only if it is cared for, accessed, utilised and sustained. Currently, the Mapungubwe Archive is curated, yet the challenges that remain are perhaps similar to the state of South Africa's national archival system, seen elsewhere in also private and institutional historical archives. For example, transforming archives, accessibility, limited resources, finances, proper archival facilities and qualified archivists.[765]

This publication is the first of its kind solely on the Mapungubwe Archive. Research has demonstrated that the Archive was not bound to be an "archaeological archive" nor an administrative records facility. It is, instead, a reflection on the University of Pretoria's institutional memory that is embedded in the intersections of both the past and present. The emphasis here is rather on how the Mapungubwe Archive has not only been utilised as a research instrument, but also as a political wand to address its contested past. As a term or as a theory of the

[763] Mapungubwe Archive Policy 2006, University of Pretoria.
[764] V Harris, *Exploring archives: an introduction to archival ideas and practice in South Africa*. 2nd ed. Pretoria: National Archive of South Africa, 2000.

[765] See report, State of the archives: an analysis of South Africa's national archival system, prepared by the Archival Platform, 2014, <http://www.archivalplatform.org/news/entry/state_of_the_archives/> access: 2018.08.28.

twenty-first century, the "Mapungubwe Archive" has the ability to be re-figured. The Archive's fluidity has changed and continues to change in ever-evolving forms up to the present, therefore it is never fixed. The Mapungubwe Archive is also not guaranteed by time or place or space. Instead, it blurs the boundaries of time and the role of the past in the present that suggests that the past is constantly unfinished as the title suggests, a Past Imperfect? The contested early history of the Mapungubwe Archive – is also accentuated and a greater need for the Mapungubwe Archive to be researched from transdisciplinary perspectives, both from the continent and by the global community.

This book acknowledges but does not delve further into the remainder years of the role of the Archaeological Committee and the magnitude of the University of Pretoria's role after the 1940s. The apartheid period and institutionalised *Volkekunde* part in Mapungubwe's history has yet to be addressed in-depth by future research. This line of enquiry raises significant questions on how Mapungubwe's oral histories were neglected and how local knowledge was represented, captured, archived and interpreted by the anthropologists who were at the helm of Mapungubwe research.

In terms of what was covered in the literature review, shifting between the broad chronological themes provided not only a detailed overview of the chronological progression of previous Mapungubwe research and its intellectual trajectory, but augmented how the archive fits into other wider disciplinary conversations. This chapter added many more archival "layers" and can build on the particular work already echoed by the distinguished anthropologist, Lynn Meskell in her research on post colonial theory and global heritage as well as that of the environmental historian, Jane Carruthers.[766] Both of these scholars did not have access or the privilege thereof to the Mapungubwe Archive to inform their research which has only superficially scratched the apartheid era of Mapungubwe history at the University of Pretoria.

A major challenge therefore is the reluctance of some academics already involved with Mapungubwe research to engage directly with the Mapungubwe Archive. One of the problems already alluded to, is the many gaps and deliberate silences about the Archive, particularly for the period of the 1980s, and is the result of gatekeeping and the needless destruction of Department of Archaeology and Anthropology records leading up to, before and even after 1994. Although many of these records may not have been directly about Mapungubwe, the Department of *Volkekunde* records and the trajectory of their influence on Mapungubwe research from after the 1950s remains a significant challenge. In addition, the contestation

between the physical anthropologists and cultural anthropologists calls for an archival research topic on its own. The academic discord surrounding the Mapungubwe human skeletal remains,[767] the neglect of oral histories[768] and non-engagement with local communities in the past and the present, appeals for an entirely new direction of contested historical research which could inform the backbone of future research potentials.[769] For this purpose, the contestation for this publication did not include the above, but rather focused on the gold "treasure trove" and legal ramifications which could not be separated from the parallel discoveries as covered in Chapter Three and Chapter Four.

It is anticipated that in coming years, there will be a witness of significant change and turn towards the Mapungubwe Archive, as a physical repository and as a space of memory that can be adapted and re-created to ensure the future of this Archive at the University of Pretoria. Future research directions that might usefully focus on the Archive include the oral history; the early ethnographic history, in particular the Van Warmelo Archive;[770] the apartheid era and *Volkekunde* periods; the history of the Vhembe Nature Reserve; perhaps an analyses of the historical media discourse from the wealth of newspaper reports; the hidden history of Greefswald and the SANDF; the archive as a site of memory; archival gender studies; or even Mapungubwe's legal history in shaping a heritage discourse.

Another avenue for other research could be into specific biographical or micro-histories. It would be relevant to further delve into the J. de Villiers Roos historical manuscript collection; as well as the Transvaal Museum Archive in relation to Mapungubwe's early history; and perhaps even the many illustrations, colour slides and photographs to infiltrate scientific discourse on Mapungubwe's early photographs that carry fragmented histories of exchange, archive, memory and identity. These proposed future studies on the Mapungubwe Archive have endless possibilities.

In addition to the provision of some directions for future research, this book has made a contribution to the historical literature on Mapungubwe, since this research is new in terms of archival studies, related archival literature and historical enquiry on Mapungubwe's early history that is thus still limited. Firstly, the key theme of

---

[766] See for example, L. Meskell, (ed.), *Global heritage: a reader*. Oxford: Wiley-Blackwell, 2015; J. Carruthers, "Mapungubwe: an historical and contemporary analysis of a World Heritage cultural landscape". *Koedoe* 49(1), 2006.

[767] M.H. Schoeman and I. Pikirayi, "Repatriating more than Mapungubwe human remains: archaeological material culture, a shared future and an artificially divided past". *Journal of Contemporary African Studies* 29(4), 2011, pp. 389–403.

[768] See MISTRA, *Mapungubwe Reconsidered: a living legacy- exploring beyond the rise and decline of the Mapungubwe state*. Johannesburg: Mapungubwe Institute for Strategic Reflection (MISTRA), 2013, pp. 13–17.

[769] I. Pikirayi, "Sharing the past: archaeology and community engagement in southern Africa". In P. Stone and Z. Hui (eds.), *Academe, practice and the public*. London: Routledge, 2014, pp. 157–159.

[770] The Van Warmelo Archive, Special (Africana) Collections, Department of Library Services, University of Pretoria, see, <https://repository.up.ac.za/handle/2263/52076> access: 2018.08.31.

"treasure trove" which is woven throughout the research process, argues that the contestation of Mapungubwe is not a recent notion and stems from the State claims of ownership back in 1933. Secondly, in understanding the trajectory of historical legislation, its overview and deficiencies of the current heritage legislation supports the idea of contestation surrounding heritage ethics such as ownership, stewardship and engages other wider debates on intangible heritage, such as whose heritage is it and who does the past belong to? Through the early legal instruments, the Archaeological Committee navigated and chartered the University of Pretoria's initial claims to ownership and sole research rights.

The above approaches are discussed as the right of the State in "owning" heritage together with the University of Pretoria's responsibility of stewardship and serves as an embedded notion of re-authoring Mapungubwe's past. Moreover, the twenty-first century has called for open and balanced discussions that do not necessarily focus on legal or practical disputes, but rather ethical and more moral arguments in heritage debates on stewardship, power, status and control. The centrality of the Mapungubwe Archive, its gaps and omissions during the "monumentalisation" apartheid period is clear. With an absence of primary records and how legislative instruments enabled the manoeuvrings by the University of Pretoria in this current debate is an evidential factor that can no longer be ignored.

Thirdly, this book contributes to the argument against the traditional early history of Mapungubwe as outlined by Fouché's *Mapungubwe Volume I* of 1937, including, those research studies which followed this ""official history" for several decades in proposing that Mapungubwe was first ""discovered" in 1933. Furthermore, research confirms that Jacob de Villiers Roos was a key unknown historical figure in the early Mapungubwe narrative and the conclusions of research confirmed that much of the University of Pretoria's approach to Mapungubwe was through his influence and not that of Fouché as has been previously suggested by other research.[771] The present struggles and discord around Mapungubwe suggests that the past has to be negotiated as the institution's stewardship and reputation on Mapungubwe remains an issue of contestation which may never be concluded.

Some of the findings of research thus confront the classical narrative of Mapungubwe's early history, taking on an archival perspective to start thinking across disciplines towards multiplicity as South African society dramatically changes and transforms each decade. In the past decade, "life" has been awarded to the Mapungubwe Archive as

research has looked at the processes of change within the archive and how it has changed and shaped public and academic discourse. This approach mirrors modern archival theory, gleaned and supported from postmodern approaches commonly located in Archival Science, taking cues from Ann Stoler, Jacques Derrida, Carolyn Hamilton, Verne Harris, and Terry Cook.

This research caught the "Mapungubwe Archive fever" as it has challenged the insular perspectives of traditional archives looking away from the historical record towards its more functional context and not just its content. Finally, this first investigation and re-examination of the Mapungubwe Archive as not only an untapped historical source of academic enquiry but rather, as a critical discourse within local and global archival trends of "reading against the grain", is perhaps the most significant contribution this book has attempted to make within the historical discipline.

In undertaking this research on the Mapungubwe Archive there is now a better understanding of the deep nature of archival research and the disordered research process. Research validates the important contribution the Mapungubwe Archive can make to revisiting Mapungubwe research and to wider South African historical and archival studies. Whilst, the archival research has demonstrated that which has already been published on Mapungubwe, it also emphasises that research can be viewed as incomplete or even subjective. In many cases, this is a personal reflection about the value of Mapungubwe held by many scholars, and how they interpret and critique the research process has the potential to be clearly flawed and cannot be objectively presented as the "unvarnished truth". Yet, the process has questioned my own existing perceptions about my knowledge of Mapungubwe's early history and a greater respect and recognition of how much there is still to learn, to correct and to sensitise. So much in fact, that much of our existing knowledge of this early history has been falsified, incorrectly presented and inadequately addressed.

Many of the nuanced findings and implications of this book are by default unintended and unapologetic, yet will hopefully open up debate and question new avenues of research on Mapungubwe's subaltern histories and greater awareness of the Mapungubwe Archive. It is anticipated that there will be a growing awareness and greater attention in future studies to address the unsung heroes and marginalised voices contained within the archival narrative and within the University of Pretoria Archive. As an institutional example, the Mapungubwe Archive has stimulated not only new research interests, but a greater appreciation for exploring and preserving the archival "landscapes of the past", as well as its struggles within South African history.

South African archives are indeed in distress. Despondently, the "insidious process underway that is contributing to the stripping away the records of democratic South Africa's

---

[771] L. Fouché, (ed.), *Mapungubwe: ancient Bantu civilization on the Limpopo: Reports on excavations at Mapungubwe (Northern Transvaal) from February 1933 to June 1935*, Volume I. Cambridge: Cambridge University Press, 1937; M. Schoeman, "Co-operation, conflict and the University of Pretoria Archaeological Committee. In, S. Tiley-Nel (ed.) *Mapungubwe remembered: contributions to Mapungubwe by the University of Pretoria*. Johannesburg: Chris van Rensburg Publications (Pty) Ltd, 2011, pp. 88–101.

Figure 6.3. Interior of the contemporary Mapungubwe Archive at the University of Pretoria.

historical, political, administrative and cultural heritage" is evident.[772] Archival records are destroyed, or they are lost or simply not retained in safekeeping, actually destroying vital links between a people and their past. Despite the multiplicity of criticisms that have been levelled against the University of Pretoria, the strongest single element or saving grace is their institutional tenacity, intentionality and unintentionality to promote, protect and preserve a small part of South African archival history. In the process, this has demonstrated that the past is severely flawed and imperfect, it cannot be changed or amended, but recognition of the many wrongs, as well as the rights are continually formed and shaped by ongoing discourse.

The significance of the Mapungubwe Archive is in the changing context of growing heritage debates around issues such as access, inclusion, redress and decoloniality. The Mapungubwe Archive has the power to transform knowledge around Mapungubwe's historical past, as well as its heritage present as the legacy of eighty-five years by the University of Pretoria and Mapungubwe is marked 1933 to 2018.[773] The Mapungubwe Archive has become in recent years, a fruitful ground for historical research and it is encouraging that in the future, scholars will attempt

to conceptualise it, in that it will become a recurring reference in many studies across disciplines and will become a transdisciplinary resource.

In order to ensure the survival of the Mapungubwe Archive, it will need to be better resourced, better valued and more widely used by scholars as an archival frontier to expanding knowledge on South African history and in particular its prehistory. There is a changing need within Humanities scholarship towards archives, an archival turn towards the notion of "archives as artefacts of evidence" and the process of making an archive, not just keeping the archive in place. The life of the Mapungubwe Archive must still be re-articulated, re-considered, re-positioned, re-constructed and deconstructed if necessary. The Mapungubwe Archive provides the raw primary material for rewriting important chapters and some new chapters to broaden South African history and has the potential to be a valuable heritage resource as a contested site, since it has both the power to remember and "unremember" the past.

---

[772] R. Pather, "Activists fight to keep SA's historical documents safe". *Mail & Guardian*, 6 March 2016.

[773] Tiley-Nel, S. & H. Steenkamp. *Eighty-Five Years: The University of Pretoria through the lens of the Mapungubwe Archive*. 1933–2018. University of Pretoria: Pretoria, 2018.

Bibliography

1. ARCHIVAL SOURCES

Mapungubwe Archive (MA), University of Pretoria, Pretoria

Minutes of Meeting of the Archaeological Committee of the University of Pretoria, 1933–1947

X File Nos. 1–3, J de V Roos Collection (1933–1938), uncatalogued

UP/MAP/VGC, Van Graan Collection, uncatalogued

UP/AGL/D/1 – UP/AGL/D/3777, accessed records

National Archives of South Africa (NASA), Pretoria

A9, Adv. J. de V Roos

UOD, Vol. No. 417, X6/46/2/2, Archaeology Greefswald Investigations (1938–1950)

ASW, Vol. No. 23, B11, Archaeological survey Mapungubwe (1946)

MPA, 3/4/1518, 108, Grant-in-aid University of Pretoria (1933–1938)

Special Collections (Africana), Department of Library Services, University of Pretoria

A.M. van Ryneveld, "Die Adv. J de V. Roos Versameling in die Staatsargief 1884–1940", 1969.

E. Klopper and J. Coetzee, "Gids op aanwinste in die Merensky Biblioteek", Universiteit van Pretoria

Jacob de Villiers Boekery, 13 Junie 1979.

J. de V. Roos Manuscript Collection, JDV Boxes 1–22, uncatalogued.

Van Warmelo Collection

South African History Archive (SAHA), Historical Papers Department

University of the Witwatersrand (Wits), William Cullen Library, Johannesburg

Special Projects A1 Gays in the Apartheid Military

A1.1 SADF correspondence file: training management, regulations and instructions: Greefswald 1969–1973.

A1.2 SADF correspondence file: handling of drug addicts: Greefswald 1973–1976.

Transvaal Museum (TM) Archive, Pretoria

DITSONG Museums of South Africa (DMSA)

T.M. 10/39 (File 100), Archaeological Committee University of Pretoria

T.M. 12/37 (File 119), Mapungubwe Enquiries

University of Pretoria Archive (UPA), Pretoria

A-1, Overview histories

B-4-1-2 Minutes of Council, 1933–1940

University of Witwatersrand Library, Johannesburg

Historical Papers Research Archive (HPRA)

A842, Smuts, Jan Christiaan, 1854–1950.

A28f, A842, A1337, Van Riet Lowe, Clarence

Nos. 233, Frobenius, L, *Forschungsinstitut fur Kultur morphologie* (Frankfurt, Germany)

2. NEWSPAPER ARTICLES

Anon

"Men of the moment: Mr J. de V. Roos". Anon, 3 January 1925.

Beeld

"Mapungupwe leef en lewer vondse". *Beeld*, 20 April 1983.

"Skatte uit ystertyd te sien". *Beeld*, 30 September 1983.

"Legendariese kop bly behoue". *Beeld*, 20 August 1984.

"UP ontken artefakte is weggesteek". *Beeld*, 12 January 1999.

Business Day

"The horrors of the vault". *Business Day*, 9 December 2014.

Cape Argus

"Mystery of the hill of the ancient dead". *Cape Argus*, 18 March 1939.

City Press

"Ancient rulers remains to return to royal graves: famed gold pieces go 'home' too". *City Press*, 28 October 2007.

"A joyful welcome for ancient rulers returning home". *City Press*, 4 November 2007.

Daily Maverick

"Dr Shock is in the dock- and now his wife is under lock". *Daily Maverick*, 29 January 2013.

Die Brandwag

"Mapoengoebwe: 'n oorblyfsel van die ryk van Monomotapa". *Die Brandwag*, 17 September 1937.

Die Burger

"Apartheid thinking in academia". *Die Burger*, 8 June 2013.

Die Vaderland

"Hy's nog nie klaar met die heuwel en goue skatte". *Die Vaderland*, 3 November 1979.

"Afrika se skatte is dalk deur jagter weggedra". *Die Vaderland,* 21 April 1983.

"Na 52 jaar is die glans nog nie daar". *Die Vaderland*, 27 October 1984.

Die Volkstem

"'n Romantiese figuur verdwene". *Die Volkstem*, 13 March 1917.

'Lotrie: Baas olifantjagter". *Die Volkstem*, n.d. October 1948.

Farmer's Weekly

'Dispute between coal miner and conservation coalition". *Farmer's Weekly*, 11 December 2012

Flying Springbok

"The face of South Africa: Mapungubwe". *Flying Springbok*, June 1984.

Mail & Guardian

"Activists fight to keep SA's historical documents safe". *Mail & Guardian*, 6 March 2016.

Pretoria News

"Politics and the T.U.C. Charge refuted". *Pretoria News*, 25 August 1922

"To unify South Africa. Ideal of the University of Pretoria. Chancellor's statement of policy". *Pretoria News*, 13 October 1930.

"Exploration at the Limpopo", *Pretoria News*, 18 June 1934.

"Tuks denies 'hiding' artefacts". *Pretoria News*, 12 January 1999.

"Historical row". *Pretoria News*, 13 January 1999.

"Remains returned to Mapungubwe descendants: families celebrate symbolic gesture by Tuks and others". *Pretoria News*, 31 October 2007.

Primary Producer

"Dongola Reserve controversy: Zoutpansberg farmers state their case". *Primary Producer*, February 1946.

Rand Daily Mail

'Preserving old sites and relics". *Rand Daily Mail*, 31 July 1929.

'Destruction of ancient relics: law to protect them". *Rand Daily Mail*, 5 August 1929.

'The University decision: deplored by Gen. Smuts". *Rand Daily Mail*, 15 September 1932.

'Discovery of gold ornaments: claimed by Pretoria University". *Rand Daily Mail*, 11 March 1933.

'Treasures for exhibition, found in koppie near Limpopo, contributions wanted". *Rand Daily Mail*, 27 June 1933.

"Valuable finds at 'Mapumgubwe': Hofmeyr opens exhibition". *Rand Daily Mail*, 29 June 1933.

"Death of Mrs J. E. Roos". *Rand Daily Mail*, 4 August 1933.

"Discoveries of ancient civilisation: Professor Leo Fouché speaks on Mapungubwe". *Rand Daily Mail*, 11 September 1933.

"S.A. Monuments and relics: preservation powers of the Minister". *Rand Daily Mail*, 6 February 1934.

"Death of Mr Charles Maggs: distinguished in many spheres". *Rand Daily Mail*, 18 October 1937.

"Commission for the preservation of natural and historical monuments, relics and antiques". *Rand Daily Mail*, 21 December 1938.

"Commission for the preservation of natural and historical monuments, relics and antiques". *Rand Daily Mail*, 18 January 1939.

"Funeral of Mr J De Villiers Roos". *Rand Daily Mail*, 5 August 1940.

"Mapungubwe excavations stopped". *Rand Daily Mail*, 26 May 1941.

"Funeral of Prof. Fouché: tribute by Smuts". *Rand Daily Mail*, 21 March 1949.

"Flaws of the 'world's best constitution' laid bare". *Rand Daily Mail*, 7 April 2016.

Sunday Argus

"Fight to save 'SA's lost city of gold". *Sunday Argus*, 1 June 2015.

Sunday Times

"The case against the Ancients". *Sunday Times*, 3 January 1926.

"The eremite on the Limpopo". *Sunday Times*, 10 March 1933.

"The hermit of the Limpopo". *Sunday Times*, 7 May 1933.

The Illustrated London News

"The mystery grave of Mapungubwe: a remarkable discovery in the Transvaal. A grave of unknown origin containing much gold-work, found on the summit of a natural stronghold in a wild region". *The Illustrated London News*, 8 April 1933.

The New Age

"How western economics took over". *The New Age*, 2 March 2018.

The Star

"Human origins". *The Star*, 6 February 1925.

"Mapungubwe natural fortress of the Limpopo: an impregnable hill Pretoria party's research experiences". *The Star*, 15 March 1933.

"Transvaal treasure ownership puzzle: whose are the gold ornaments found in the north?". *The Star,* 26 March 1933.

"Akin with Zimbabwe? Discoveries at Mapungubwe: aerial survey in progress". *The Star,* 29 August 1933.

"Treasures of Mapungubwe: finds of utmost importance". *The Star,* 11 September 1933.

"Historic spots in Union: deputation asks for preservation". *The Star,* 26 October 1933.

"First Transvaal Bantu? 'Bronze Age site' new development in the Limpopo Valley". *The Star,* 12 October 1935.

"Archaeology on the Limpopo: results of excavations at Mapungubwe". *The Star,* 17 October 1935.

"Vandalism in Museums". *The Star,* 1 July 1937.

"Amazing story of museum raid". *The Star,* 18 October 1937.

The Walrus

"Dr Shock: How an apartheid-era psychiatrist went from torturing gay soldiers in South Africa to sexually abusing patients in Alberta". *The Walrus,* 19 September 2015.

Tukkiewerf

"Greefswald: UP vereer SAW en TPS met 'n goue simbool van vennootskap". *Tukkiewerf* 18(3), 1992, pp. 6–7.

3. BOOKS

Agnew, N. & J. Bridgland (eds.), *Of the past, for the future: integrating archaeology and conservation.* Los Angeles: Getty Publications, 2006.

Allan, K., (ed.), *Paper Wars: access to information in South Africa.* Johannesburg: Witwatersrand University Press, 2009.

Anderson, K., *Heroes of South Africa.* Johannesburg: AD Donker, 1983.

Baslar, K., *The concept of the common heritage of mankind in international law.* The Hague: Kluwer Law International, 1997.

Beard, C.R., *The romance of treasure trove.* London: Sampson Low, Marston & Co Ltd, 1933.

Beinart, W. & S. Dubow (eds.), *Segregation and apartheid in twentieth century South Africa: rewriting histories.* London: Routledge, 1995.

Bergh, J.S., (ed.), *Geskiedenisatlas van Suid-Afrika: die vier Noordelike Provinsies.* Pretoria: van Schaik, 1999.

Berry, M. & M. Cadman. *Dongola to Mapungubwe: the 80-year battle to conserve the Limpopo valley.* Swartwater: Mmabolela Press, 2007.

Bigalke, R.C.H. *The National Zoological Gardens of South Africa.* Pretoria: Central News Agency, 1954.

Blazevic, M. & L.C. Feldman (eds.), *Misperformance: essays in shifting perspectives.* Ljubljana: MASKA Institute of Publishing, Production and Education, 2014.

Blouin, F.X. & W.G. Rosenberg. *Processing the past: contesting authorities in history and the archive.* Oxford: Oxford Scholarship, 2011.

Braun, L.F., *Colonial survey and native landscapes in rural South Africa 1850–1913: the politics of divided space in the Cape and Transvaal.* Leiden: Brill, 2015.

Brumann, C. & D. Berliner (eds.), *World heritage on the ground: ethnographic perspectives.* New York: Berghahn Books, 2016.

Bryan. C.F. Jr., *Imperfect past: history in a new light.* Virginia: Dementi Milestone Publishing, 2015.

Calabrese, J.A., *The emergence of social and political complexity in the Shashi-Limpopo Valley of southern Africa, AD 900 to AD 1300: ethnicity, class and polity.* Oxford: BAR Publishing, International Series 1617, 2007.

Cameron, T., *Jan Smuts: an illustrated biography.* Pretoria: Human & Rousseau (Pty) Ltd, 2004.

Carman, J., *Valuing ancient things.* Leicester: Leicester University Press, 1996.

Carman, J., *Against cultural property: archaeology, heritage and ownership.* Bloomsbury: Bristol Classical Press, 2005.

Carnes, M.C. (ed.), *Past imperfect: history according to the movies.* New York: Henry Holt, 1995.

Carr, E.H., *What is history?* London: Penguin, 1961.

Carruthers, J., *National Park science: a century of research in South Africa.* Cambridge: Cambridge University Press, 2017.

Caton-Thompson, G., *The Zimbabwe culture.* Oxford: Clarendon Press, 1931.

Constantine, S. (ed.), *Cultural heritage ethics: between theory and practice.* Cambridge: Open Book Publishers, 2014.

Craven, L., *What are archives? Cultural and theoretical perspectives: a reader.* Burlington: Ashgate, 2008.

Cuno, J., *Who owns antiquity? Museums and the battle over our ancient heritage.* Princeton: Princeton University Press, 2008.

Cuno, J., *Museums matter: in praise of the Encyclopaedic Museum.* Chicago: University of Chicago Press, 2011.

Deacon, H., S. Mngqolo & S. Prosalendis, *Protecting our cultural capital: a research plan for the heritage sector.* Cape Town: Human Sciences Research Council Publishers, 2003.

De l' Estoile., B., F. Neiburg & L. Sigaud (eds.), *Empires, nations and natives: anthropology and state-making.* Durham & London: Duke University Press, 2002.

De Kock, W.J., *Jacob de Villiers Roos, 1869–1940, Lewenskets van 'n veelsydige Afrikaner.* Cape Town: A.A. Balkema, 1958.

Derrida, J., *Archive fever: a Freudian impression.* Chicago: University of Chicago Press, 1998.

De Villiers, C.C., *Die Geslacht Registers de Oude Kaapsche Familien.* Kaapstad: Van de Sandt de Villiers & Co. Beperkt, Drukkers, 1894.

Du Bois, F. (ed.), *Wille's Principles of South African law.* Cape Town: Juta & Co. Ltd, 2007.

Dubow, S., *Scientific racism in modern South Africa.* Cambridge: Cambridge University Press, 1995.

Dubow, S., *A commonwealth of knowledge: science, sensibility and white South Africa 1820–2000,* Oxford and New York: Oxford University Press, 2006.

Dubow, S. (ed.), *Science and society in southern Africa.* Manchester: Manchester University Press, 2000.

Eastwood, T. & H. MacNeil, (eds.), *Currents of archival thinking.* Santa Barbara: Libraries Unlimited, 2010.

Fagan, B., *Writing archaeology: telling stories about the past.* Walnut Creek: Left Coast Press, 2006.

Fage, J.D. & R. Oliver, (eds.), *Papers in African Prehistory.* Cambridge: Cambridge University Press, 1970.

Fouché, L. (ed.). *Mapungubwe: ancient Bantu civilization on the Limpopo: reports on excavations at Mapungubwe (Northern Transvaal) from February 1933 to June 1935.* Volume I. Cambridge: Cambridge University Press, 1937.

Frobenius, L., *Madsimu Dsangara Südafrikanische Felsbilderchronik.* Berlin: Atlantis, 1931.

Frobenius, L., *Erythräa Länder und Zeiten des heiligen Königsmordes.* Berlin: Atlantis, 1931.

Galloway, A., *The skeletal remains of Bambandyanalo.* Johannesburg: Witwatersrand University Press, 1959.

Gardner, G.A., *Mapungubwe, Volume II, Report on excavations at Mapungubwe and Bambandyanalo in the Transvaal from 1935–1940.* P.J. Coertze (ed.), Pretoria: Van Schaik Publishers, 1963.

Gilliomee, H., *The Afrikaners: biography of a people.* London: Hurst & Company, 2012.

González-Ruibal, A. (ed.), *Reclaiming archaeology: beyond the tropes of modernity.* London: Routledge, 2013.

Graham, B. & P. Howard, (eds.), *The Ashgate research companion to heritage and identity.* Aldershot: Ashgate Publishing Company, 2008.

Guha, S., *Artefacts of history: archaeology, historiography and Indian Pasts.* London: Sage Publications Pty. Ltd, 2015.

Haberland, E. (ed.), *Leo Frobenius on African history, art, and culture: an anthology.* Princeton: Markus Wiener Publishers, 2007.

Hall, M., *The changing past: farmers, kings, and traders in southern Africa, 200–1869.* Cape Town: David Philip, 1987.

Hamilton, C., V. Harris, J. Taylor, M. Pickover, G. Reid & R. Saler, (eds.), *Refiguring the archive.* Cape Town: David Phillip, 2002.

Hammond-Tooke, W.D., *Imperfect interpreters: South Africa's anthropologists 1920–1990.* Johannesburg: Witwatersrand University Press, 1997.

Harris, V., *Exploring archives: an introduction to archival ideas and practice in South Africa.* (2nd ed.). Pretoria: National Archives of South Africa, 2000.

Harris, V., *Archive and justice: a South African perspective.* Chicago: Society of American Archivists, 2007.

Harrison. R. (ed.), *Understanding the politics of heritage.* Manchester: Manchester University Press, 2010.

Hill, G.F., *Treasure trove in law and practice, from the earliest time to the present day.* Oxford: Clarendon Press, 1936.

Hodgkin, K. & S. Radstone, (eds.), *Contested pasts: the politics of memory.* London: Routledge, 2003.

Huffman, T.N., *Handbook to the Iron Age: the archaeology of pre-colonial farming societies in southern Africa.* Kwa-Zulu Natal: University of Kwa-Zulu Natal Press, 2007.

Inskeep, R.R., *The peopling of Southern Africa.* Cape Town: David Philip, 1978.

Jenkins, E., *Symbols of nationhood.* Braamfontein: South African Institute of Race Relations, 2003.

Kotzé, D.J., *Dapper kinders van Suid-Afrika.* Bloemfontein: Die Sondagskool-boekhandel, 1962.

Kruger, D.W. (ed.), *Dictionary of South African Biography.* Cape Town: Human Sciences Research Council, 1972.

Kruger, D.W. & C.J. Beyers, (eds.), *Dictionary of South African Biography.* (Part 3), Cape Town: Nasionale Boekhandel, 1977.

Lang, J., *Bullion Johannesburg: men, mines and the challenge of conflicts.* Johannesburg: Jonathan Ball, 1986.

La Follette, L., *Negotiating culture: heritage, ownership and intellectual property.* Massachusetts: University of Massachusetts Press, 2013.

Lee, R.W., *The elements of Roman law: with a translation of the Institute of Justinian.* (4th ed.), London: Sweet & Maxwell, 1956.

Legassick, M. & C. Rassool, *Skeletons in the cupboard: South African museums and the trade in human remains 1907–1917.* Cape Town: South African Museum, 2000.

Leslie, M. & T. Maggs, (eds.), *African Naissance: the Limpopo Valley 1000 Years Ago.* Johannesburg: South African Archaeological Society Goodwin Series 8, 2000.

Lowenthal, D., *The heritage crusade and the spoils of history.* Cambridge: Cambridge University Press, 1998.

Manyanga, M., *Resilient landscapes: socio-environmental dynamics in the Shashe-Limpopo basin, Southern Zimbabwe c. AD to the present.* Studies in Global Archaeology 11, Uppsala: Uppsala University, 2007.

Marks, S. & A. Atmore (eds.), *Economy and society in pre-industrial South Africa.* London: Longman, 1980.

Mathers, C., T.C. Darvill & B.J. Little. (eds.), *Heritage of value, archaeology of renown: reshaping archaeological assessment and significance.* Florida: University Press of Florida, 2005.

Meskell, L., *The nature of heritage: the new South Africa.* Oxford: Wiley-Blackwell, 2012.

Meskell, L. (ed.), *Global heritage: a reader.* Oxford: Wiley-Blackwell, 2015.

Meyer, A., *The Iron Age sites of Greefswald: stratigraphy and chronology of the sites and a history of investigations.* Pretoria: University of Pretoria, 1998.

Mitchell, P., *The archaeology of Southern Africa.* Cambridge: Cambridge University Press, 2002.

Moerschell, C.J., *Und de Grenze der Zivilisation: Sudafrikanische Skizzen.* Würzburg: Stürtz, 1910.

Moerschell, C.J., *Afrikanische Fahrten und Abenteuer und Beobachtungen des Buren Bernard Francois Lotrie.* Würzburg: Stürtz, 1912.

Moerschell, C.J., *Der Wilde Lotrie.* Begleiter Livingstones Voortrekker: Würzburg, 1912.

Mouton, F.A. (ed.), *History, historians and Afrikaner nationalism*: *essays on the History Department of the University of Pretoria, 1909–1985.* (1ˢᵗ ed.). Vanderbijlpark: Kleio, 2007.

Murray, B.K., *Wits: the early years: a history of the University of the Witwatersrand, Johannesburg, and its precursors 1896–1939.* Johannesburg: Wits University Press, 1982.

Ndoro, W., S. Chirikure & J. Deacon. (eds.), *Managing heritage in Africa: who cares?* New York: Routledge, 2017.

Peterson, D.R., K. Gavua & C. Rassool. (eds.), *The politics of heritage in Africa: economies, histories, and infrastructures.* Vol. 48. Cambridge: Cambridge University Press, 2015.

Pikirayi, I. *Tradition, archaeological heritage protection and communities in the Limpopo Province of South Africa.* Addis Ababa: Ethiopia: Organisation for Social Science Research in eastern and Southern Africa (OSSREA), 2011.

Randall-MacIver, D., *Medieval Rhodesia.* London: MacMillan, 1905.

Rautenbach, C.H. (ed.) et al. *Ad Destinatum. Gedenkboek van die Universiteit van Pretoria.* Johannesburg: Voortrekkerpers Beperk, 1960.

Renfrew, C., *Loot, legitimacy and ownership.* London: Duckworth, 2000.

Robertshaw, P. (ed.), *A history of African Archaeology.* Oxford: James Currey Ltd, 1990.

Rosenthal, E., *The hinges creaked; true stories of South African treasure, lost and found.* Cape Town: H. Timmins, 1951.

Roth, M.P., *Historical dictionary of war journalism.* London: Greenwood Press, 1953.

Runyan, W.M. (ed.), *Psychology and historical interpretation.* Oxford: Oxford University Press, 1988.

Saunders, C. & N. Southey. *A dictionary of South African history.* Cape Town: David Philip, 1998.

Schofield, J.F., *Primitive pottery: an introduction to the South African ceramics, prehistoric and protohistoric.* Cape Town: South African Archaeological Society, 1948.

Schmidt P.R. & I. Pikirayi (eds.), *Community archaeology and heritage in Africa: decolonizing practice.* London: Routledge, 2016.

Skeates, R., J. Carman, & C. McDavid (eds.), *The Oxford Handbook of Public Archaeology.* Oxford: Oxford University Press, 2012.

Smith, A., *An inquiry into the nature and causes of the wealth of nations (1776).* S.M. Soares (ed.) New York: MetaLibri Digital Library, 2007.

Smith, L., *Archaeological theory and the politics of cultural heritage.* Routledge: London, 2004.

Smith, L., *The uses of heritage.* Routledge: London, 2006.

Stoler, A.L., *Along the archival grain: epistemic anxieties and colonial common sense.* New Jersey: Princeton University Press, 2009.

Stone, P. & Z. Hui (eds.), *Academe, practice and the public.* London: Routledge, 2014.

Stroud, L., *Common heritage of mankind: a bibliography of legal writing.* Malta: Foundation de Malte, 2013.

Taylor, W.P., *African treasures: sixty years among diamonds and gold.* London: John Long Limited, 1912.

Tempelhoff, J.W.N., *Die okkupasiestelsel in die distrik Soutpansberg, 1886–1899.* Archives yearbook for South African History 60. Pretoria: Government Printers, 1997.

Tiley-Nel, S. (ed.), *Mapungubwe Remembered: contributions to Mapungubwe by the University of Pretoria.* Johannesburg: Chris van Rensburg Publications (Pty) Ltd, 2011.

Tiley-Nel, S. & H. Steenkamp. Eighty-Five Years: The University of Pretoria through the lens of the Mapungubwe Archive. 1933–2018. University of Pretoria: Pretoria, 2018.

Torr G., *Kill yourself and count to 10*. Cape Town: Penguin Random House, 2014.

Towner, L.W., *Past imperfect: essays on history, libraries and humanities*. Chicago: University of Chicago Press, 1993.

Van der Watt, F., (ed.) *Ad Destinatum IV 1993–2000. Historical developments and events at the University of Pretoria*. Pretoria: University of Pretoria, 2002.

Van Riet Lowe, C., *The distribution of prehistoric rock engravings and paintings in South Africa*. Pretoria: Archaeological Survey, Archaeological Series 7, 1952.

Van Riet Lowe, C., *The glass beads of Mapungubwe*. Union of South Africa, Department of Education, Arts and Science. Pretoria: Archaeological Survey, 1955.

Van Schalkwyk, J.A. (ed.), *Studies in honour of Professor J.F. Eloff*. Pretoria: National Cultural History Museum, 1997.

Van Warmelo, N.J., (ed.) *Copper miners of Messina and the early history of the Zoutpansberg*. Vernacular accounts by S.M.D. Dzivhani, M.F. Mamadi, M.M. Motenda and E. Modau. Pretoria: Department of Native Affairs, Union of South Africa, 1940.

Voigt, E.A., *Guide to archaeological sites in the northern and eastern Transvaal*. Pretoria: Transvaal Museum, 1981.

Voigt, E.A., *Mapungubwe: an archaeo-zoological interpretation of an Iron Age community*. Pretoria: Transvaal Museum, 1983.

Von Leibbrandt, H.C., *Rambles through the archives of the Colony of the Cape of Good Hope 1688–1700*. Cape Town: J.C. Juta & Co, 1887.

Waxman, S., *Loot: the battle over the stolen treasures of the ancient world*. New York: Times Books, 2008.

4. ARTICLES AND JOURNALS

Anglin, R., "The world heritage list: bridging the cultural property nationalism- internationalism divide". *Yale Journal of Law*, 20(2), 2008, pp. 241–242.

Anon, Obituary, "Gérard Paul Lestrade: 1897–1962". *African Studies* 22(2), 2007, pp. 91–95.

Antonites, A.R., J. Bradfield & T. Forssman., "Technological, functional and contextual aspects of K2 and Mapungubwe worked bone industries". *African Archaeological Review* 33(4), 2016, pp. 437–463.

Bard, J.A. & L. McFadyen., "Towards an archaeology of archaeological archive". *Archaeological Review* 29(2), 2014, pp. 14–32.

Banks, A., "Fathering *Volkekunde*: race and culture in the ethnological writings of Werner Eiselen, Stellenbosch University, 1926–1936." *Anthropology Southern Africa* 38(3), 2015, pp. 163–179.

Bland, R., "Rescuing our neglected heritage: the evolution of the government's policy on portable antiquities in England and Wales". *Cultural Trends* 14(4), 2005, pp. 257–296.

Bland, R., "Treasure Trove and the case for reform". *Art, Antiquity and Law* 1 (February 2006), pp. 11–26.

Bland, R., "Response: the Treasure Act and Portable Antiquities Scheme". *Internet Archaeology* 33, 2013.

Boot F.H., "Obituary: H.F. Sentker". *South African Archaeological Bulletin* 39(140), Dec.1984, p. 143.

Brothman, B., "The past that archives keep: memory, history, and the preservation of archival records". *Archivaria* 51, 2001, pp. 48–80.

Carleton, J., "Protecting the national heritage: the implications of the British Treasure Act 1996". *International Journal of Cultural Property* 6(2) 1997, pp. 343–352.

Carruthers, J., "The Dongola Wild Life Sanctuary: 'psychological blunder, economic folly and political monstrosity' or more valuable than rubies and gold?" *Kleio* XXIV, 1992, pp. 82–100.

Carruthers, J., "Mapungubwe: an historical and contemporary analysis of a World Heritage cultural landscape". *Koedoe* 49(1), 2006, pp. 1–13.

Carruthers, J., "Trouble in the garden: South African botanical politics ca. 1870–1950". *South African Journal of Botany* 77(2), 2011, pp. 258–267.

Chirikure, S., "Metals in society: iron production and its position in Iron Age communities of southern Africa". *Journal of Social Archaeology* 7, 2007, pp. 72–100.

Chirikure, S., "'Where angels fear to tread': ethics, commercial archaeology, and extractive industries in southern Africa". *Azania: Archaeological Research in Africa* 49(2), 2014, pp. 218–231.

Chirikure, S., M. Manyanga., A.M. Pollard., F. Bandama., G. Mahachi & I. Pikirayi., "Zimbabwe culture before Mapungubwe: new evidence from Mapela Hill, south-western Zimbabwe". *PloS One* 9(10), 2014, e111224 [sic].

Chirikure, S., M. Manyanga., W. Ndoro & G. Pwiti, "Unfulfilled promises? Heritage management and community participation at some of Africa's cultural heritage sites". *International Journal of Heritage Studies* 16(1–2), 2010, pp. 30–44.

Chisholm, L.C., "Crime, class and nationalism: The criminology of Jacob de Villiers Roos, 1869–1918". *Social Dynamics: a Journal of African Studies* 13(2), 1987 pp. 46–59.

Cleere, H., "The CBA: the first fifty years". *Council for British Archaeology Annual Report* 44, 1994, pp. 108–109.

Cocks, M., S. Vetter & K.F. Wiersum., "From universal to local: perspectives on cultural landscape heritage in South Africa". *International Journal of Heritage Studies* 24(1), 2017, pp. 35–52.

Coertze, P.J., "Ras en Kultuur", *Hertzog-Annale van die Suid-Afrikaanse Akademie vir Wetenskap en Kuns: Jaarboek* V, Pretoria: Suid-Afrikaanse Akademie vir Wetenskap en Kuns, 1958, pp. 53–56.

Coertze, P.J., "'n Prinsipiële en feitelike inleiding tot studie van die bevolkingsverhoudings-vraagstuk in Suid-Afrika". *Tydskrif vir Rasse-Aangeleenthede* 22(3) 1971, pp. 106–108.

Coertze, R.D., "Obituary N.J. van Warmelo 1904–1989". *South African Journal of Ethnology* 12(3), 1989, pp. 85–90.

Cook, T., "From information to knowledge: an intellectual paradigm for archives". *Archivaria* 19, Winter 1984–1985, pp. 28–49.

Cook, T., "What is past is prologue: a history of archival ideas since 1898 and the future paradigm shift". *Archivaria* 43, 1997, pp. 17–63.

Cook, T., "Archival science and postmodernism: new formulations for old concepts". *Archival Science* 1, 2001, pp. 3–24.

Cook, T., "Electronic records, paper minds: the revolution in information management and archive in the post-custodial and post-modern era". *Archive and Social Studies: A Journal of Interdisciplinary Research* 1(0), 2007, pp. 399–443.

Cook, T., "Archival principles and cultural diversity: contradiction, convergence or paradigm shift? A Canadian perspective". *International Journal of Archive* 3/4, 2007, pp. 37–38.

Cook, T., "We are what we keep; we keep what we are: archival appraisal past, present and future". *Journal of the Society of Archivists* 32(2), 2011, pp. 173–189.

Cook, T., "Evidence, memory, identity, and community: four shifting archival paradigms". *Archival Science* 13(2–3), 2013, pp. 95–120.

Cookson, N., "Treasure trove: dumb enchantment or new law?" *Antiquity 66,* 1992, pp. 399–405.

Davison, C.C., "Chemical resemblance of garden roller and M1 glass beads". *Journal of African Studies* 32(4), 1973, pp. 247–257.

Deacon, J., "Archaeological sites as national monuments in South Africa: a review of sites declared since 1936". *South African Historical Journal* 29(1), 1993, pp. 118–131.

Deacon, J., "South Africa's new heritage legislation". *World Archaeological Congress Newsletter* 5(1), 1997, pp. 3–4.

Delmont, E., "South African Heritage development in the first decade of democracy". *African Arts* 37(4), 2004, p. 30.

Dubow, S., "Racial irredentism, ethnogenesis, and white supremacy in high-apartheid South Africa". *Kronos* 41(1), 2015, pp. 236–264.

Eastwood, E.B. & G. Blundell., "Re-discovering the rock art of the Limpopo-Shashe confluence area, southern Africa". *Southern African Field Archaeology* 8, 1999, pp. 17–27.

Fagan, B.M., "Review of Mapungubwe, Volume II by G.A. Gardner". *Journal of African History* 5(2), 1964, pp. 314–316.

Fagan, B.M., "The Greefswald sequence: Bambandyanalo and Mapungubwe". *Journal of African History* 5(3), 1964, pp. 337–361.

Forsmann, T., "Missing pieces: Later Stone Age surface assemblages on the greater Mapungubwe landscape, South Africa". *Southern African Humanities* 25(1), 2013, pp. 65–85.

Gardner, G.A., "Hottentot culture on the Limpopo". *South African Archaeological Bulletin* 4(16), 1949, pp. 116–121.

Gardner, G.A., "Mapungubwe 1935–1940". *South African Archaeological Bulletin* 10(39), 1955, pp. 73–77.

Gardner, G.A., "Mapungubwe and Bambandyanalo". *South African Archaeological Bulletin* 11(42), 1956, pp. 55–56.

Gardner, G.A., "The shallow bowls of Mapungubwe". *South African Archaeological Bulletin* 14(53), 1959, pp. 35–37.

Genovese, T.R., "Decolonizing archival methodology: combating hegemony and moving towards a collaborative archival environment". *AlterNative: An International Journal of Indigenous People* 12(1), 2016, pp. 32–42.

Gerstenblith, P., "Identity and cultural property: the protection of cultural property in the United States". *Boston University Law Review* (B.U.L), 75, 1995, pp. 596–597.

Gilliland-Swetland, A.J. & S. McKemmish., "Building an infrastructure for archival research". *Archival Science* 4(3/4), 2004, pp. 149–197.

Gordon, R., "Apartheid's anthropologists: the genealogy of Afrikaner anthropology". *American Ethnologist* 15(3), 1988, pp. 535–553.

Hall, M., "The burden of tribalism: the social context of southern African Iron Age studies". *American Antiquity* 49(3), 1984, pp. 455–467.

Hamilton, C., "Backstory, biography, and the life of James Stuart". *History in Africa* 38, 2011, pp. 319–341.

Hamilton, C., "Forged and continually refashioned in the crucible of ongoing social and political life: archives and custodial practices as subjects of enquiry". *South African Historical Journal* 65(1), 2013, pp. 1–22.

Harris, V., "The archival sliver: power, memory, and archives in South Africa". *Archival Science* 2, 2002, pp. 63–86.

Harris, V., "Redefining archives in South Africa: public archive and society in transition, 1990–1996". *Archivaria* 42 (Fall 1996), pp. 6–27.

Harris, V., "Claiming less, delivering more: a critique of positivist formulations on archives in South Africa". *Archivaria* 44, 1997, pp. 132–141.

Hedstrom, M., "Archives, memory, and interfaces with the past". *Archival Science* 2, 2002, pp. 21–43.

Henry, L., "A history of removing rock art in South Africa". *South African Archaeological Bulletin* 62(185), 2007, pp. 44–48.

Hodder, I., "Cultural heritage rights: from ownership and descent to justice and well-being". *Anthropological Quarterly* 83(4), 2010, pp. 861–882.

Hubbard, P., "The Ancient Ruins Company". *Prehistory Society of Zimbabwe Newsletter*, Issue 144, May 2010, pp. 2–4.

Huffman, T.N., "Climate change during the Iron Age in the Shashe Limpopo Basin, southern Africa". *Journal of Archaeological Science* 35(7), 2008, pp. 2032–2047.

Huffman, T.N., "Mapungubwe and Great Zimbabwe: the origin and spread of social complexity in southern Africa". *Journal of Anthropological Archaeology* 23(1), 2009, pp. 37–54.

Huffman, T.N., "Historical archaeology of the Mapungubwe area: Boer, Birwa and Machete". *Southern Africa Humanities* 24(1), 2012, pp. 33–59.

Huffman, T.N., "Mapela, Mapungubwe and the origins of states in southern Africa". *South African Archaeological Bulletin* 2015, pp.15–27.

Huffman, T.N. & S. Woodborne., "Archaeology, baobabs and drought: cultural proxies and environmental data from the Mapungubwe landscape, southern Africa". *The Holocene* 26(3), 2016, pp. 464–470.

Ita, J., "Frobenius in West African history". *Journal of Africa History* 13(4), 1972, pp. 673–688.

Kaplan, R.M., "The Aversion Project - psychiatric abuses in the South African Defence Force during the apartheid era". *South African Medical Journal* 91(3), 2001, pp. 216–217.

Kaplan, R.M., "The bizarre career of Aubrey Levin: from abuser of homosexual conscripts to molester of male prisoners". *Forensic Research and Criminological International Journal* 2(5), 2016, pp. 69–71.

Ketelaar, E., "Archives as spaces of memory". *Journal of the Society of Archivists* 29(1), April 2008, pp. 9–27.

King, R., "Archaeological naissance at Mapungubwe". *Journal of Social Archaeology* 11(3), 2011, pp. 311–333.

King, R., "Teaching archaeological pasts in South Africa: historical and contemporary considerations of archaeological education". *Archaeologies* 8(2), 2012, pp. 85–115.

Koleini, F., F. De Beer., M.H. Schoeman., I. Pikirayi., S. Chirikure., G. Nothnagel., & J.M. Radebe., "Efficiency of neutron tomography in visualizing the internal structure of metal artefacts from Mapungubwe museum collection with the aim of conservation". *Journal of Cultural Heritage* 13, 2012, pp. 246–253.

Kolen, J., "The 'anthropologization' of archaeological heritage". *Archaeological Dialogues* 16 (2), 2009, pp. 209–225.

Kotze, L. and L.J. Van Rensburg., "Legislative protection of cultural heritage resources: a South African perspective". *Queensland University of Technology Law and Justice Journal* (QUTLawJJl) 3(1), 2003.

Kriel, L., "The scramble for the Soutpansberg? The Boers and partition of Africa in the 1890s". *Scientia Militaria South African Journal of Military Studies* 31(2), 2003, pp. 74–91.

Kriel, M., "Culture and power: the rise of Afrikaner nationalism revisited". *Journal of the Association for the Study of Ethnicity and Nationalism* (ASEN) 16(3), 2010, pp. 402–422.

Kuman, K., J.C. Baron & R.J. Gibbon., "Earlier Stone Age archaeology of the Vhembe-Dongola National Park (South Africa) and vicinity". *Quaternary International* 129, 2005, pp. 23–32.

Lestrade, G.P., "Some notes on the ethnic history of the VhaVenda and their Rhodesian affinities". *South African Journal of Science* 24, 1927, pp. 486–495.

Lewsen, P., "What history means to me". *South African Historical Journal* 28, 1993, pp. 3–14.

Lucas, G., "Time and the archaeological archive". *Journal of Theory and Practice* 14(3), 2010, pp. 343–359.

Malan, B.D., "Remarks and reminiscences on the history of archaeology in South Africa". *South African Archaeological Bulletin* 25 (99/100), 1970, pp. 88–92.

Manoff, M., "Theories of the archive from across the disciplines". *Libraries and the Academy* 4(1), 2004, pp. 9–25.

Marks, S., "South Africa: The myth of the empty land". *History Today* 30(1), 1980, pp. 7–12.

Marschall, S., "Forging national identity: institutionalizing foundation myths though monument". *South African Journal of Cultural History* 19(1), 2005, pp. 18–35.

Martin W. & G. Lushington, "The law of treasure trove". *Journal of the Royal Society of Arts* 56 (2883), 1908, pp. 348–359.

Merriman, N. & H. Swaine., "Archaeological archives: serving the public interest?" *European Journal of Archaeology* 2(2), 1999, pp. 249–267.

Merryman, J.H., "Two ways of thinking about cultural property". *American Journal of International Law* 7, 1986, pp. 831–853.

Merryman, J. H., "The public interest in cultural property". *California Law Review* 77(2), 1989, pp. 339–364.

Meskell, L., "Negative heritage and past mastering in archaeology". *Anthropological Quarterly* 75, 2002, pp. 557–574.

Meskell, L., "Recognition, restitution and the potentials of post colonial liberalism for South African heritage". *South African Archaeological Bulletin* 60, 2005, pp. 72–78.

Meskell, L., "Falling walls and mending fences: archaeological ethnography in the Limpopo". *Journal of Southern African Studies* 33, 2007, pp. 383–400.

Meskell, L. & C. Scheermeyer, "Heritage as therapy: set pieces from the new South Africa". *Journal of Material Culture* 13(2), 2008, pp. 153–173.

Meyer, A., "Mapungubwe: the Smuts connection". *South African Archaeological Society Newsletter* 3(2), 1980, pp. 8–10.

Meyer, A., "Stand van argeologiese insig in die volkerebewegings in Suid Afrika". *Suid-Afrikaanse Tydskrif vir Etnologie* 12(2), 1989, pp. 69–75.

Meyer, A., "Stratigrafie van die ystertydperkterreine op Greefswald". *Suid-Afrikaanse Tydskrif vir Etnologie* 17(4) 1994, pp. 137–160.

Meyer, A., "K2 and Mapungubwe". *South African Archaeological Society Goodwin Series* 8, 2000, pp. 4–13.

Miller, D., "Metal assemblages from Greefswald areas, K2, Mapungubwe Hill and Mapungubwe southern Terrace". *South African Archaeological Bulletin* 56, 2001, pp. 83–103.

Miller, D., "Pioneering metallographic analyses of indigenous metal artefacts from southern Africa: collected by the Frobenius expedition 1929–1930". *South African Archaeological Bulletin* 4(156), 1992, pp. 108–115.

Morris, A.G., "Biological anthropology at the southern tip of Africa: carrying European baggage in an African context". *Current Anthropology* 53(5), 2011, pp. 152–160.

Mortensen, P., "The place of theory in archival practice". *Archivaria* 47, 1999, pp. 1–26.

Mouton, F.A., "Professor Leo Fouché, the History Department and the Afrikanerization of the University of Pretoria". *Historia* 38(1), 1993, pp. 92–101.

Mouton, F.A., "A.N. Pelzer: a custodian of Afrikanerdom". *South African Historical Journal* 37(1), 1997, pp. 133–155.

Mouton, F.A., "A free, united South Africa under the Union Jack": F.S. Malan, South Africanism and the British Empire, 1895–1924". *Historia* 51(1) 2006, pp. 2–48.

Murray, B., "Leo Fouché and history at Wits University 1934–1942". *African Historical Review* 48(1), 2016, pp. 83–99.

Ndlovu, N., "Legislation as an instrument in South African heritage management: Is it effective?" *Conservation and Management of Archaeological Sites* 13(1), February 2011, pp. 31–57.

Nesmith, T., "Seeing archives: postmodernism and changing intellectual place of archives". *The American Archivist* 65, (Spring/Summer 2002), pp. 24–41.

Nesmith, T., "What's history got to do with it? Reconsidering the place of historical knowledge in archival work". *Archivaria* 57, (Spring 2004), pp. 1–26.

Nesmith, T., "Archives from the bottom up: social history and archival scholarship". *Archives and Social Studies: Journal of Interdisciplinary Research* 2(1) March 2008, pp. 41–82.

Nienaber, W.C., N. Keough., M. Steyn & J.H. Meiring, "Reburial of the Mapungubwe human remains: an overview of process and procedure". *South African Archaeological Bulletin* 63(188), 2008, pp. 164–169.

Oddy, A., "On the trail of Iron Age gold". *Transvaal Museum Bulletin* 19 (November 1983), pp. 24–26.

Oddy, A., "Gold in the southern African Iron Age". *Gold Bulletin* 17(2), 1984, pp. 70–78.

Palmer, N.E., "Treasure trove and title to discovered antiquities". *International Journal of Cultural Property* 2(2), 1993, pp. 275–318.

Pikirayi, I., "Ceramics and group identities; towards a social archaeology in southern African Iron Age studies". *Journal of Social Archaeology* 7, 2007, pp. 286–301.

Prinsloo, L.C., N. Wood., M. Loubser., S.M.C. Verryn & S. Tiley., "The re-examination of Chinese celadon sherds from Mapungubwe a thirteenth century Iron Age site in South Africa using Raman spectroscopy, XRD and XRF". *Journal of Raman Spectroscopy* 36(8), 2005, pp. 806–816.

Prinsloo, L.C. and P. Colomban., "A Raman spectroscopic study of the Mapungubwe oblates: glass trade beads excavated at an Iron Age archaeological site in South Africa". *Journal of Raman Spectroscopy* 39(1), 2008, pp. 79–90.

Prott, L. & P. O' Keefe., "Cultural heritage or Cultural Property?" *International Journal of Cultural Property*, 1(2), 1992, pp. 307–320.

Renfrew, C., "Art fraud: raiders of the lost past". *Journal of Financial Crime* 3(1), 2007, pp. 7–9.

Rightmire, G.P. "Iron Age skulls from southern Africa reassessed by multiple discriminant analysis". *African Journal of Physical Anthropology* 33(2), 1970, pp. 147–168.

Roehrenbeck, C.A., "Repatriation of cultural property–who owns the past? An introduction to approaches and to selected statutory instruments". *International Journal of Legal Information* 38(2) Article 11, 2010, pp. 185–200.

Roff, S., "Archives, documents, and hidden history: a course to teach undergraduates the thrill of historical discovery real and virtual". *The History Teacher* 40(4), 2007, pp. 551–558.

Schoeman, M.H., "Imagining rain-places: rain control and changing ritual landscapes in the Shashe-Limpopo confluence area, South Africa". *South African Archaeological Bulletin* 61(184), 2006, pp. 152–165.

Schoeman, M.H. & I. Pikirayi., "Repatriating more than Mapungubwe human remains: archaeological material culture, a shared future and an artificially divided past". *Journal of Contemporary African Studies* 29(4), 2011, pp. 389–403.

Schoonraad, M., "Preliminary survey of the rock-art of the Limpopo Valley". *South African Archaeological Bulletin* 15(57), 1960, pp. 10–13.

Schwartz, J.M. & T. Cook., "Archive, records, and power: from (postmodern) theory to (archival) performance". *Archival Science* 2(3), 2002, pp. 171–185.

Schultz, E.H., "Zuzammensetzung und Aufbau einiger Metallfunde der Afrika-Expedition von Leo Frobenius 1928/30". *Paideuma* 5, 1950, pp. 131–134.

Sharp, J., "Two separate developments: anthropology in South Africa". *Royal Anthropological Institute of Great Britain and Ireland (RAIN)* 36, 1980, pp. 4–6.

Sharp, J., "Can we study ethnicity? A critique of fields of study in South African anthropology". *Social Dynamics* 6(1), 1980, pp. 1–16.

Sharp, J., "The roots and development of *Volkekunde* in South Africa". *Journal of Southern African Studies* 18 (1), 1981, pp. 16–36.

Sharp, J., "One nation, two anthropologies? A response to Coertze's' Kommentaar op geignoreerde kritiek". *South African Journal of Ethnology* 2(1), 2000, pp. 30–33.

Sharp, J., "The end of culture? Some directions for anthropology at the University of Pretoria". *Anthropology Southern Africa* 29(1–2), 2006, pp. 17–23.

Shepherd, N., "The politics of archaeology in Africa". *Annual review of Anthropology* 31, 2002, pp. 189–209.

Shepherd, N., "Disciplining archaeology; the invention of South African prehistory, 1923–1953". *Kronos* 28, November 2002, pp. 127–145.

Shepherd, N., "Heading south, looking north: why we need a post-colonial archaeology". *Archaeological Dialogues* 9, 2002, pp. 74–82.

Shepherd, N., "State of the discipline: science, culture and identity in South African archaeology, 1870–2003". *Journal of Southern African Studies* 29(4), 2003, pp. 823–844.

Shepherd, N., "Who is doing courses in archaeology at South African universities? And what are they studying?" *South African Archaeological Bulletin* 60, 2005, pp. 123–126.

Sleen, W.G.N. "Trade-wind beads". *Man* 65, February 1956, pp. 27–29.

Smith, J., J. Lee-Thorp & S. Hall., "Climate change and agropastoralist settlements in the Shashe-Limpopo river basin, southern Africa AD 880 to 1700". *South African Archaeological Bulletin* 62(186), 2007, pp. 115–125.

Sparrow, C., "Treasure trove: a lawyer's view". *Antiquity* 56, 1982, pp. 199–201.

Steyn, M., "A reassessment of the human skeletal remains from K2 and Mapungubwe (South Africa). *South African Archaeological Bulletin* 52(165), 1997, pp. 14–20.

Steyn, M., "The Mapungubwe gold graves revisited". *South African Archaeological Bulletin* 62(186), 2007, pp. 140–146.

Steyn, M. & M. Henneberg. "Preliminary report on the paleodemography of the K2 and Mapungubwe populations (South Africa). *Human Biology* 66(1), 1994, pp. 105–120.

Steyn, M. & M. Henneberg, "Odontometric characteristics of the people from the Iron Age sites at Mapungubwe and K2 (South Africa). *Homo, Journal of Comparative Human Biology* 48(3), 1997, pp. 215–226.

Steyn, M. & M. Henneberg. "Cranial growth in the prehistoric sample from K2 at Mapungubwe (South Africa) is population specific". *Homo, Journal of Comparative Human Biology* 48(1), 1997, pp. 62–71.

Stiebel, L., "A treasure story: Thomas Baines's map to the gold fields of south eastern Africa 1877'". *English Studies in Africa* 45(1), 2002, pp. 1–17.

Stoler, A.L., "Colonial archives and the arts of governance". *Archival Science* (2), 2002, pp. 87–109.

Summers, R., "Armchair archaeology". *South African Archaeological Bulletin* 5(19), 1950, pp. 101–104.

Thornton, R., "Evolution, salvation and history in the rise of the ethnographic monograph in Southern Africa 1860–1920". *Social Dynamics* 6(2), 1981, pp. 14–23.

Tiley-Nel, S. & H. Botha., "The conservation of the Mapungubwe gold collection, South Africa". *Journal of the Institute of Conservation* 36(1), 2013, pp. 65–80.

Tomaselli, K. & A. Mpofu., "The re-articulation of meaning of national monuments: beyond apartheid 'culture and policy'". *Journal of the Australian Key Centre for Cultural and Media Policy* 8(3), 1997, pp. 57–75.

Tournié, A., L.C. Prinsloo, & P. Colomban., "Raman classification of glass beads excavated on Mapungubwe Hill and K2, two archaeological sites in South Africa". *Journal of Raman Spectroscopy* 43(4), 2012, pp. 532–542.

Van der Waal, C.S., "Long walk from volkekunde to anthropology: reflections on representing the human in South Africa". *Anthropology Southern Africa* 38(3–4), 2015, pp. 216–234.

Van Eeden, E.S., "Pioneering regional history studies in South Africa: reflections within the former section for regional history at the Human Sciences Research Council (HSRC)". *Historia* 59(1), 2014, pp. 118–140.

Van Onselen, C., "Crime and total institutions in the making of modern South Africa: the life of 'Nongoloza' Mathebula, 1867–1948". *History Workshop* (Spring 1985), pp. 62–81.

Van Riet Lowe, C., "Mapungubwe: first report on excavations in the Northern Transvaal". *Antiquity* 10(39), 1936, pp. 282–291.

Van Riet Lowe, C., "Beads of the water". *Journal of Bantu Studies* 11(1), 1937, pp. 367–372.

Van Zyl Smit, D., "A legitimate prison system in a future South Africa?" *Legal Studies* 16(2), 1992, pp. 178–192.

Whitelaw, G., "New legislation for cultural heritage". *Natalia* 30, Natal Society Foundation, 2010, pp. 58–63.

Willcox, A.R., "Painted petroglyphs at Balerno in the Limpopo Valley, Transvaal." *South African Journal of Science* 56, 1963, pp. 108–110.

Willcox, A.R. & H. Pager., "More petroglyphs from the Limpopo valley, Transvaal." *South African Archaeological Bulletin* 23, 1968, pp. 50–51.

Wintjes, J., "The Frobenius expedition to Natal and the Cinyati archive". *Southern African Humanities* 25, 2013, pp. 167–205.

Wintjes, J., "Frobenius discovered before crossing Limpopo ruins: ancient fortificated settlements, beautiful pottery mountains stop". *De Arte* 52(1), 2017, pp. 31–67.

Wintjes, J. & S. Tiley-Nel, "The Lottering connection", *South African Archaeological Bulletin*, No. (210), 2019, pp. 101–110.

Woodborne, S., M. Pienaar, & S. Tiley-Nel., "Dating the Mapungubwe Hill Gold". *Journal of African Archaeology* 7(1), 1999, pp. 99–103.

Zwernemann, J., "Leo Frobenius and cultural research in Africa". *Institute of African Studies, Research Review* 3(2), 1967, pp. 2–20.

5. UNPUBLISHED REPORTS, PAPERS AND OTHER WORKS

Bonner, P. & J. Carruthers., The recent history of the Mapungubwe area, Mapungubwe Cultural Heritage Resources Survey. Report commissioned by the Department of Environmental Affairs and Tourism, 2003.

Cape of Good Hope, Report of the Council of the University of the Cape of Good Hope for the 1896. Colonial Secretary's Ministerial Division, 1897.

Carruthers. J., Jan Smuts and the Dongola Wild Life Sanctuary. Talk to the Friends of Smuts Foundation, Irene, 21 May 2003.

Centre for Applied Legal Studies (CALS). Changing corporate behaviour: the Mapungubwe case study, a research report. University of the Witwatersrand, Johannesburg: Raith Foundation, 2014.

British Association for the Advancement of Science, Report of the Office of the British Association. London: Burlington House, 1930.

Cook, T., "Landscapes of the past: archivists, historians and the fight for memory". Public lecture for the Ministry of Culture for Spain and the National Historical Archives Madrid, Spain, 23 June, 2010.

Deacon, J., South African heritage legislation in global perspective, unpublished paper presented at the Management of Heritage Sites Seminar organised by the Heritage Assets Management Sub-Directorate of the Department of Public Works, Pretoria, 21 September 1999.

Department of Arts and Culture (DAC), (n.d.). Review of heritage legislation final report Vol. 1. Cape Town: Heritage Agency cc, Cheadle Thompson and Hayson Inc. Attorneys.

Evans, D. N., An eco-tourism perspective of the Limpopo River Basin with particular reference to the Greater Mapungubwe Transfrontier Conservation Area given the impact thereon by the proposed Vele colliery. Tourism Working Group of the GMTFCA 18, 2010.

Eloff, J.F., *Die Kulture van Greefswald*, Vols. I-V. Ongepubliseerde verslag aan die Raad vir Geesteswetenskaplike Navorsing. Pretoria: Universiteit van Pretoria, 1979.

Eloff, J.F., Greefswald-opgrawing 1980, Ongepubliseerde verslag, Pretoria: Universiteit van Pretoria, 1980.

Eloff, J.F., Verslag oor opgrawingswerk op die plaas Greefswald gedurende April 1981, ongepubliseerde verslag, Pretoria: Universiteit van Pretoria, 1981.

Eloff, J.F., Verslag oor argeologiese navorsing op Greefswald gedurende April 1982, Ongepubliseerde verslag, Pretoria: Universiteit van Pretoria, 1982.

Eloff, J.F., Verslag oor argeologiese navorsing op Greefswald gedurende April 1983, Ongepubliseerde verslag, Pretoria: Universiteit van Pretoria, 1983.

Frescura, F., National or nationalist: the work of the Monuments Council, 1936–1989. Paper published as part of the proceedings of the national Urban Conservation Symposium, University of Witwatersrand, 12–14 July, Johannesburg, 1990.

Frescura, F., Monuments and the Monumentalisation of Myths' New Premises? University of the Witwatersrand History Workshop, 16–18 July, Johannesburg, 1992.

Hall, A. and A. Lillie., "The national Monuments Council and a policy of providing the protection for the cultural and environmental heritage". Paper presented at "Myths, monuments, museums: new premises?" University of the Witwatersrand, History Workshop, Johannesburg, 16–18 July 1992.

Hamilton, C., The public life of an archive: archival biography as methodology, unpublished paper, presented at the Archive and Public Culture Workshop, University of Cape Town, Cape Town, 2 September 2009.

Kemmish, S., M. Piggot., B. Reed, & F. Upward, (eds.), Archives: Recordkeeping in Society, Charles Stuart University, Centre for Information Studies, Series: Topics in Australasian Library and Information Studies, No. 24 Elsevier, 2005.

Mapungubwe Institute for Strategic Reflection., Mapungubwe Reconsidered: Exploring beyond the rise and decline of the Mapungubwe state, Mapungubwe research report, Executive Summary, Johannesburg: MISTRA, 2012.

McEryde, I., "Who owns the past?" Papers from the Annual Symposium of the Australian Academy of the Humanities, Melbourne, Oxford University Press, 1985.

Meyer, A., *Inligtingformate vir argeologie veldwerk*. Pretoria: Universiteit van Pretoria, 2003.

Raltshai, N.M.N., Preliminary report on the oral history of the Mapungubwe area, unpublished report for the Department of Environmental Affairs and Tourism, Pretoria, 2002.

Raltshai, N.M.N., Additional information on the oral history of Mapungubwe, unpublished addendum to the World Heritage Nomination Dossier for Mapungubwe, Department of Environmental Affairs and Tourism, Pretoria, 2003.

Sentker, H.F., Mapungubwe 1953–1954, Ongepubliseerde verslag. Pretoria: Universiteit van Pretoria, 1969.

Summers, R., Mapungubwe Reconsidered, unpublished report, Mapungubwe Archive, Pretoria: University of Pretoria, 1966.

Tiley-Nel, S., The reconnection: on Smuts and Mapungubwe's early history. Paper presented to the Friends of the Smuts Foundation, Irene, 24 April 2014.

Union of South Africa., Report of the Select Committee on the Dongola Wild Life Sanctuary Bill (Hybrid Bill), Vol. 1, section 12, Cape Town, 1945.

Union of South Africa, Report of the Select Committee on the Dongola Wild Life Sanctuary Bill (Hybrid Bill), Vol. 2, section 6–46, Cape Town, 1946.

Van Zyl, M., J. De Gruchy., S. Lapinsky., S. Lewin, & G. Reid., The aVersion project: Human rights abuses of gays and lesbians in the SADF by health workers during the apartheid era. Cape Town: Simply Said and Done, 1999.

6. THESES AND DISSERTATIONS

Antonites, A., Political and economic interactions in the hinterland of the Mapungubwe polity, c. AD 1220–1300 South Africa. PhD dissertation, Yale University, 2012.

Chisholm, L., Reformatories and industrial schools in South Africa: a study of class, colour and gender, 1882–1939. Ph.D. thesis, University of the Witwatersrand, 1989.

De Bruyn, P.P., Die Geskiedenis van Potchefstroom Gimnasium 1907–1982. Master's Degree, North West University, 1988.

Forssman, T.R., The Later Stone Age occupation and sequence of the Mapungubwe landscape. MSc. dissertation, University of Witwatersrand, 2010.

Gibson, J.L., A critical study of the report of the de Villiers Commission on technical and vocational education. Unpublished MA of Education degree, University of Natal, 1968.

Grobler, E., Collections management practices at the Transvaal Museum, 1913–1964: anthropological, archaeological and historical. PhD thesis, University of Pretoria, 2005.

Hanisch, E.M.O., An archaeological interpretation of certain Iron Age sites in the Limpopo-Shashi valley. Unpublished MA dissertation, University of Pretoria, 1980.

Hutten, L., K2 Revisited: An archaeozoological study of an Iron Age Site in the Northern Province, South Africa. Unpublished Msc Anatomy dissertation, University of Pretoria, 2005.

Kashe-Katiya, X., Carefully Hidden Away: Excavating the archive of the Mapungubwe dead and their possessions". MA minor dissertation, University of Cape Town, 2013.

Koleini, F., Mapungubwe metals revisited: a technical and historical study of Mapungubwe material culture with an emphasis on conservation. PhD thesis, University of Pretoria, 2014.

Manetsi, T., State-prioritised heritage: governmentality, heritage management and the prioritisation of liberation heritage in post-colonial South Africa. PhD thesis, University of Cape Town, 2017.

Murimbika, M., Sacred powers and rituals of transformation: an ethnoarchaeological study of rainmaking rituals and agricultural productivity during the evolution of the Mapungubwe state, AD 1000 to AD 1300. Unpublished PhD thesis, University of Witwatersrand, 2006.

Phillips, H., 'Black October': the impact of the Spanish Influenza Epidemic of 1918 in South Africa. PhD thesis, University of Cape Town, 1984.

Reddy, V., Moffies, stabanis, and lesbos: the political construction of queer identities in Southern Africa. PhD dissertation, University of Kwa-Zulu Natal, 2005.

Scott, S.S., A 'Ware Afrikaner' – an examination of the role of Eugene Marais (1871–1936) in the making of Afrikaner identity. PhD Modern History, University of Oxford, 2001.

Sibayi, D., Addressing the impact of the structural fragmentation on aspects of management and conservation of Cultural Heritage. MA thesis, University of Stellenbosch, 2009.

Sinclair, R., The office treatment of white, South African, homosexual men and the consequent reaction of Gay liberation from the 1930s to 2000. PhD thesis, Rand Afrikaans University, 2004.

Steyn, M., An assessment of the health status and physical characteristics of the prehistoric population from Mapungubwe. PhD dissertation, University of the Witwatersrand, 1994.

Strydom, B.L., Broad South Africanism and Higher Education: The Transvaal University College (1909–1919). PhD History, University of Pretoria, 2013.

Tiley-Nel, S., A technological study and manufacture of ceramic vessels from K2 and Mapungubwe Hill, South Africa. Unpublished MA thesis, University of Pretoria, 2013.

Tiley-Nel, S., Past Imperfect: The contested early history of the Mapungubwe Archive, PhD History, University of Pretoria, 2019.

Van Doornum, B., Changing places, spaces and identity in the Shashe-Limpopo region of Limpopo Province, South Africa. PhD thesis, University of Witwatersrand, 2005.

Voigt, E.A., The faunal remains from Greefswald as a reflection of Iron Age economic and cultural activities. MA dissertation, University of Pretoria, 1978.

Zipkin, A., Archaeology under apartheid: a preliminary investigation into the potential politicization of science in South Africa. Honors thesis, Cornell University, 2009.

7. ELECTRONIC AND ONLINE SOURCES

American Alliance of Museums (AAM), 2018, definition. <www.aam-us.org/resources/ethics-standards>, Access: 2018-08-20.

Archives at the crossroads, 2007. Open report to the Minister of Arts and Culture, Archival Conference "National System, Public Interest", co-convened by the National Archives, the Nelson Mandela Foundation and the Constitution of Public Intellectual Life Research Project, April 2007. <https://www.nelsonmandela.org/images/uploads/NMF_Dialogue_-Archives_at_the_Crossroads1.pdf>, *s.a.* Access: 2018-09-26.

Archival Platform, 2014, "State of the Archives: an analysis of South Africa's national archival system", prepared by the Archival Platform. <http://www.archivalplatform.org/news/entry/state_of_the_archives_/ >, *s.a.* Access: 2018-08-28.

Brown, D.H. 2007, "Archaeological archive: A guide to best practice in creation, compilation, transfer and curation". Archaeological Archive Forum (AAF), London: Institute of Field Archaeologists. <http://www.archaeologyuk.org/archives/aaf_archaeological_archives_2011.pdf>, Access: 2016-06-24.

Business Dictionary, "Thrift paradox", definition. <https://www.businessdictionary.com/definition/paradox-of-thrift.html> Access: 2018-07-31.

Cambridge Advanced Learner's Dictionary and Thesaurus, 2015, Cambridge University Press, Cambridge. <http://dictionary.cambridge.org/dictionary/english/imperfect>, Access: 2015-10-29.

Carruthers, J. 2015. "The 'Battle of Dongola' and the Mapungubwe National Park". Royal Society of South Africa. <http://www.royalsocietysa.org.za>, *s.a.* Access: 2015-01-28.

Cunningham, R.B. 2000, "The slow death of treasure trove", The Archaeological Institute of America, Archaeology Archive. <https://archive.archaeology.org/online/features/trove/>, Access: 2018-06-11.

Directory Entries of Archival Repositories, 2005. <http://www.national.archives.gov.za/dir_entries_pg7_2005.html>, Access: 2016-05-26.

Dix-peek, R. 2010, "A list of South African and Rhodesian born baronets, Knight Bachelors, Dames and Peers". Live Journal. <https://peek-01.livejournal.com/74468.html>, *s.a.* Access: 2018-07-24.

Frobenius Institute, <https://frobenius-institut.de/en/collections-and-archives/legacies>, Access: 2018.07.10.

Knight, B. 1999, "History of the Medieval English Coroner System, Crowner Part 6: Treasure trove and nautical activities". <www.britannia.com/history/articles/coroner6>, Access: 2018-03-27.

Leonard, L. & Lebogang. T., "Exploring the impacts of mining on tourism growth and local sustainability: the care of Mapungubwe Heritage site, Limpopo, South Africa", *Sustainable Development*, Wiley Online Library, 2017. <https://doi.org/10.1002.sd.1695>, *s.a.* Access: 2018-04-04.

Mapungubwe Institute for Strategic Reflection (MISTRA), 2011, "Mapungubwe Reconsidered: a living legacy exploring beyond the rise and decline of the Mapungubwe State". <http://www.mistra.org.za/Library/Publications/Pages/Mapungubwe-Reconsidered-Exploring-beyond-the-rise-and-decline-of-the-Mapungubwe-state.aspx>, *s.a.* Access: 2016-05-18.

National Heritage Council South Africa (NHC), 2012–2018, "Overview and core functions". <https://nationalgovernment.co.za/units/view/252/national-heritage-council-south-africa-nhc>, *s.a.* Access: 2018-08-20.

National Monuments Council (NHC), "Cultural Treasures definition", Conservation Category. <http://home.intekom.com/nmc/f9.htm>, *s.a.* Access: 2018-08-21.

Jokilehto, J. 2005, "Definition of cultural heritage: references to documents in history", ICCROM Working Group 'Heritage and Society'. <http://cif.icomos.org/pdf_docs/Documents%20on%20line/Heritage%20definitions.pdf>, Access: 2018-08-21.

Oxford English Dictionary, 2018, Oxford University Press, Oxford. <https://en.oxforddictionaries.com/definition/treasure_trove>, Access: 2018-06-06.

Queen's & Lord Treasurer's Remembrancer, 2016, ' Treasure Trove". <http://www.qltr.gov.uk/content/treasure-trove>, Access: 11-06-2018.

South African Broadcasting Corporation (SABC) Education, "Mapungubwe: Echoes in the Valley", July 2017, See, <https://www.mediaupdate.co.za/media/139923/sabc-3-announces-the-arrival-of-mapungubwe-echoes-in-the-valley>, *s.a.* Access: 2017-04-17.

South African National Narks (SANParks), 2017, "Mapungubwe National Park and World Heritage Site Management Plan". <https://www.sanparks.org/assets/docs/conservation/park_man/mapungubwe-draft-plan.pdf>, *s.a.* Access: 22-06-2017.

Sentinel Projects, "The abuse of psychiatry in the SADF: 'I am first a soldier and then a psychiatrist'". <http://sadf.sentinelprojects.com/1mil/thug1.html>, *s.a.* Access: 2016-05-26.

South African Heritage Resources Agency (SAHRA), 2018, <www.sahra.org.za>, *s.a.* Access: 2018-08-23.

South African History Archives (SAHA), <http://foip.saha.org.za/static/paper-wars-access-to-information-in-south-africa>, *s.a.* Access: 2018-06-06.

South African History Online (SAHO), "Defining the Bantu"', 2011. <http://www.sahistory.org.za/article/defining-term-bantu>, *s.a.* Access: 2018-05-30.

South African Mirror, "History of the South African Police 1913–1944".<http://www.samirror.com/sapolice-history.html>, *s.a.* Access: 2018-07-24.

The Economist, 2008 "Armchair archaeology", see <https://www.economist.com/node/11999379>, *s.a.* Access: 2018-06-06.

United Nations Education, Scientific and Cultural Organisation (UNESCO), Mapungubwe Nomination Dossier, Mapungubwe Cultural Landscape, 5 July 2003. <https://whc.unesco.org/uploads/nominations/1099.pdf>, Access: 2017-06-22.

University College of London, 2015, "Past Imperfect". <http://ucl.ac.uk/art-history/news-events/past-imperfect>, Access: 2015-09-03.

University of Oxford, 2017, "Hidden histories in the archives".<https://www.history.ox.ac.uk/article/hidden-histories-archives>, Access: 2018-04-03.

UPSpace, Department of Library Services, University of Pretoria. <https://repository.up.ac.za/handle/2263/21577>, Access: 2018-08-31.

Woods, G. 2014, "The legacy book: the Auditor General's 100 year publication". Auditor General of South Africa (AGSA), Johannesburg. <https://www.agsa.co.za/Portals/0/AG/AGSA%20Legacy%20Book.pdf> *s.a.* Access: 2018-07-25.

8. GOVERNMENT PUBLICATIONS, POLICIES AND LEGISLATION

Bushmen Relics Protection Act, No. 22 of 1911.

Constitution of the Republic of South Africa, No. 108 of 1996.

Cultural Institutions Act, No. 119 of 1998.

Cultural Laws Amendment Act, No. 36 of 2001.

Dongola Wildlife Sanctuary Act, No. 9 of 1947.

Dongola Wildlife Sanctuary Repeal Act, No. 29 of 1949.

Higher Education Act, No. 101 of 1997.

Natural and Historical Monuments Act, No. 6 of 1923.

Natural and Historical Monuments, Relics and Antiques Act, No. 4 of 1934.

National Monuments Act, No. 28 of 1969.

National Archives of South Africa Act, No. 43 of 1996.

National Heritage Council Act, No. 11 of 1999.

National Heritage Resources Act, No. 25 of 1999.

National Environmental Management Protected Areas Act, No. 57 of 2003.

Native Services Contracts Act of 1932.

Promotion of Access to Information Act, No. 2 of 2000.

Representation of Blacks Act of 1936.

Representation of Natives Act of 1936.

Revised Draft White Paper on Arts, Culture and Heritage, 2013.

Riotous Assemblies (Amendment) Act of 1930.

Slums (demolition of Slums) Act of 1934.

South African Government Gazette Notice No. 1936, 9 September 1983.

South African Government Gazette Notice No. 1756, 17 August 1985.

South African Government Gazette Notice No. 14048, 19 June 1992.

South African Government Gazette Notice No. 19974, 28 April 1999.

South African Government Gazette Notice No. 1306, 10 October 1997.

South African Government Gazette Notice No. 1512, 6 December 2002.

South African World Heritage Convention Act, No. 49 of 1999.

Transvaal Precious and Base Metals Act, No. 35 of 1908.

Transvaal Asiatic Land Tenure Act of 1930.

UNESCO Convention on World Heritage Property, 1972.

White Paper on Arts and Culture, 1996.

World Heritage Convention Act, No. 49 of 1999.

9. MAPS

Baines, T., "Map to the gold fields of south eastern Africa". 1877.

Jeppe, F., "Map of the South-African Republic (Transvaal) and surrounding territories". 1877.

Jeppe, F., "Jeppe's map of the Transvaal or S.A Republic". London: Edward Stanford, 1898.

Jeppe, F., "Map of the southern gold fields of the Transvaal". Johannesburg: Argus Coy Ltd, 1896.

Merensky, A., "Original map of the Transvaal or South-African republic, including the gold anddiamond fields. Berlin, 1875.

Wagner, P.A., "Map showing some of the more important pre-European mine workings of Southern Africa". 1929.